A SEASON IN HELL

A SEASON IN HELL

My 130 Days in the Sahara with Al Qaeda

ROBERT R. FOWLER

HarperCollins*Publishers*Ltd

Published by HarperCollins Publishers Ltd

First Edition

HarperCollins Publishers Ltd
2 Bloor Street East, 20th Floor
Toronto, Ontario, Canada
M4W 1A8

www.harpercollins.ca

Library and Archives Canada Cataloguing in Publication
Fowler, Robert R., 1944–
A season in hell : my 130 days in the Sahara with Al Qaeda / Robert R. Fowler.

ISBN 978-1-44340-204-0

1. Fowler, Robert R., 1944– —Captivity, 2008–2009. 2. Hostages—Niger—
Biography. 3. Hostages—Canada—Biography. 4. Diplomats—Canada—
Biography. I. Title.
DT547.853.F68A3 2011   966.2605092   C2011-903636-3

Printed and bound in the United States
RRD 9 8 7 6 5 4 3 2 1

For Mary, whose love, drive, and spirit brought me back

*For my wonderful girls, Linton, Ruth, Antonia, and Justine,
and their families, who made coming home so important*

For Louis, without whom I would likely not have come through

*For Presidents Touré and Compaoré, their brave negotiators,
and all those in the Canadian government who worked tirelessly
and effectively to make it possible*

For all those who can't go home

It is an ancient Mariner,
And he stoppeth one of three.
"By thy long grey beard and glittering eye,
Now wherefore stopp'st thou me?

The Bridegroom's doors are open'd wide,
And I am next of kin;
The guests are met, the feast is set:
May'st hear the merry din."

He holds him with his skinny hand,
"There was a ship," quoth he.
"Hold off! Unhand me, grey-beard loon!"
Eftsoons his hand dropt he.

He holds him with his glittering eye—
The Wedding-Guest stood still,
And listens like a three years' child:
The Mariner hath his will.

The Wedding-Guest sat on a stone:
He cannot choose but hear;
And thus spake on that ancient man,
The bright-eyed Mariner.

Samuel Taylor Coleridge, "The Rime of the Ancient Mariner"

CONTENTS

Part Four: End Game

Aftermath

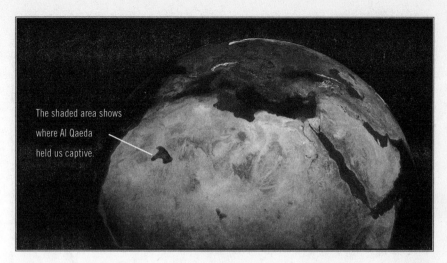

The shaded area shows where Al Qaeda held us captive.

The Sahara desert stretches across northern Africa, from the Atlantic coast to the Nile and from the Mediterranean coast to what remains of Lake Chad. At 8,600,000 square kilometres, the Sahara is larger than the continental United States.

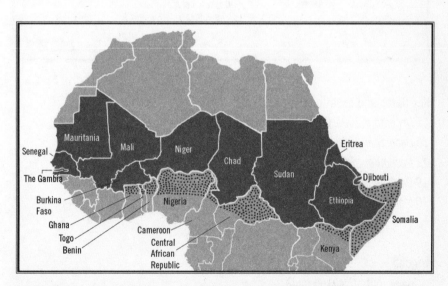

The Sahel (shown in dark grey) is a 7,000-kilometre band of instability that Al Qaeda considers fertile ground for further expansion. It stretches across the widest part of Africa, from Mauritania on the Atlantic to Djibouti on the Indian Ocean. A number of surrounding countries (such as Somalia and Nigeria) have been similarly beset by climate change, desertification, and ethnic or religious confrontation. The dotted areas denote those regions most affected.

Our Descent into Hell

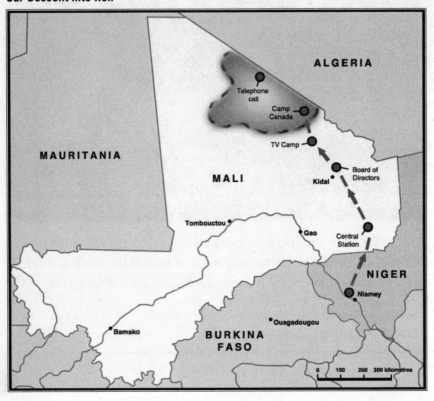

Key Dates and Locations

15 December 2008: Central Station

16 December 2008: Board of Directors

17 December 2008: TV Camp

19 December 2008 to 14 February 2009: Camp Canada

10 March 2009: Presumed site of telephone call

Legend

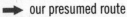 our presumed route

approximate area of confinement

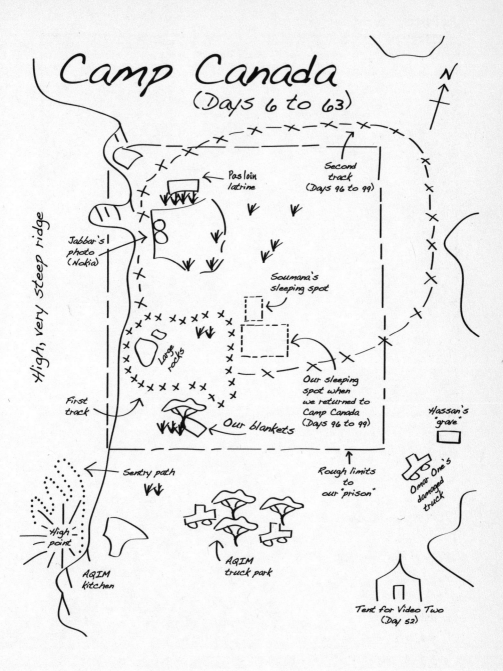

Camp Canada
(Days 6 to 63)

N

Second track
(Days 96 to 99)

Pas loin latrine

High, very steep ridge

Jabbar's photo (Nokia)

Soumana's sleeping spot

Large rocks

Our sleeping spot when we returned to Camp Canada (Days 96 to 99)

First track

Our blankets

Hassan's "grave"

Sentry path

Rough limits to our "prison"

Omar One's damaged truck

High point

AGIM kitchen

AGIM truck park

Tent for Video Two (Day 52)

PREFACE

This is a personal story of a dramatic 130-day period in my life and despite my persistent use of the first person plural, I trust the reader will understand that at no point am I purporting to speak for my friend and fellow hostage, Louis Guay.

Louis decided not to play a role in producing this account. As I submitted this manuscript, he was still a public servant in the Canadian Department of Foreign Affairs and International Trade (DFAIT), and he continued to be governed by the obligations that bound him in that capacity. I must make clear, therefore, that all the reflections and opinions in this memoir, indeed all the recollections, are mine alone. I have sought to limit the extent to which my narrative encroaches on Louis' privacy and that of his warm and supportive family. I apologize to all the Guays for any transgressions in this regard. They will understand that half of this story is necessarily Louis' and, therefore, telling it without regular and repeated reference to him, his steadfastness, stalwart support, and fine friendship would simply be impossible.

This account of extreme camping in the desert in dramatically life-threatening circumstances will describe what it was like and perhaps allow readers to come to their own conclusions regarding the issue that often seems to be on their minds: how would I fare in such circumstances? Most people, I suspect, would do a lot better than they assume.

This book is not, though, an academic treatise on Al Qaeda or Islamic fundamentalism and their catalytic role in causing what is ever more clearly a clash of civilizations. Nor will it be a primer on how Al Qaeda in the Islamic Maghreb (AQIM) can become better kidnappers. As a result I will refrain from offering detailed comments on what the *jihadists* did or did not do well, on how they might have done better or, more generally, provide information that could permit them to prosecute their *jihad* (holy war) more effectively. Some aspects of this narrative may indeed seem to offer such guidance but have been included only where I know that they already possess such understanding. In the same vein, I have sought to avoid writing anything that might cause a future hostage to spend a moment longer in captivity than would otherwise be the case.

With these caveats, and while it is still reasonably fresh in my mind, I hope the reader will find this an informative account of a very particular though by no means unique experience. Many hostages have endured far longer and tougher trials than our four and a half months as Al Qaeda captives. Indeed, as we lay day after day under the unrelenting Sahara sun I recalled—trepidation quickly becoming naked terror—the long, harsh ordeals of Terry Anderson, Terry Waite, Marc Gonsalves and his colleagues, Ingrid Betancourt, the staff of the American Embassy in Iran, and so very many others. And, of course, I was well aware that many had been killed or died in captivity.

A couple of months before our capture, Louis and I discussed with Isabelle Roy (then Canada's Ambassador to Mali) the eight-month long nightmare that Andrea Kloiber and Wolfgang Ebner, two Austrian tourists captured in Tunisia, lived as prisoners of AQIM. They were released just before our abduction by the same *jihadi* organization in late 2008. As we wondered whether there could be a happy ending to our saga, we were also well aware that other Canadians held hostage in other parts of the world were suffering a similar or worse fate.

We knew that the BBC's Alan Johnston had been held for 114 days in Gaza, two years previously, by the Army of Islam, but we did not yet know of the wrenching tale of David Rohde, the *New York Times* reporter who escaped from the clutches of the Taliban just after our release and made his way to freedom after more than seven months in the mountains of Afghanistan and Pakistan's tribal areas, a story he and his wife tell so compellingly in their book *A Rope and a Prayer*. Ever-present in my mind, however, was the execution of Daniel Pearl, another brave reporter, held in similar circumstances by Al Qaeda in Pakistan.

A word on language: the languages spoken by the thirty-one members of the AQIM group that held us were predominantly Arabic and Berber, in what we took to be a variety of dialects, including Tamasheq, the language of the Sahara and of the Tuareg. Neither Louis nor I speak Arabic beyond a few stock phrases and words, and our captors had, for obvious reasons, no interest in having us learn their languages. Thus we spoke with our kidnappers in French. In this account, I have translated almost everything into English, using words and expressions that best convey both the meaning and what I took to be the intent of the speaker.

With regard to the English spelling of Arabic words, names, and phrases, pragmatism, common usage, and, I hope, consistency have been my guides; thus, Qur'an rather than Quran or Koran; Abou over Abu; Mohammed rather than Muhammad or the many other variations of the spelling of the name of the Prophet. I have used *mujahideen,* rather than *mujahadeen* or *mujahedin,* and Al Qaeda as opposed to al-Qaida or al-Qa'ida. The English spelling is that arbitrary amalgam of British and American we like to believe is Canadian. In this account, I have used the French spelling of place names—Tombouctou, not Timbuktu—in deference to the fact that this story takes place entirely in the former French West Africa. When quoting others, I have used their spelling.

Time after time as I stewed in the sand, I thought of Samuel Coleridge's marvellous poem "The Rime of the Ancient Mariner" and was surprised by how much I could recall of this epic work. I was also struck by how startlingly those passages seemed to reflect our horrendous situation and speak to my inner turmoil. I took strength from and found succour in those stirring words, written two centuries ago, and in my head I began to sketch this account around them.

I have never been accused of being taciturn and when the excellent Survival, Evasion, Resistance and Escape (SERE) doctors at the Landstuhl Regional Medical Centre in Germany urged me to share the story rather than keeping it bottled up inside, I had all the encouragement I needed. So, in keeping with my Ancient Mariner–like fixation with telling my tale, this book has already helped to exorcize my remaining Al Qaeda demons.

The epigraph sets the scene and you, my wedding guests, have generously elected to subject yourselves to the account of this grey-beard loon and thereby helped to leave me free. The stanzas at the opening of each chapter are not always in Coleridge's sequence but, as I am confident he would understand, have been selected for their relevance to the progression of my tale.

As will be blindingly obvious, *A Season in Hell* is not intended to be any kind of scholarly work. The bibliography is simply a list of works I consulted, in some part—often in all too cursory a fashion—and I am indebted to their authors, whether or not I agreed with or was influenced by their analyses, conclusions, or objectives.

At the moment of our release, Prime Minister Stephen Harper said very clearly that Canada paid no ransom and released no prisoners, and I have no reason to doubt his assertion. It does seem obvious though, at least to me, that Al Qaeda did not release me *pour mes beaux yeux bleus*. Canada has many wonderful friends in this troubled world, and perhaps some of them were also my friends. They certainly are now. To the extent that such friends may have facilitated our release I cannot be anything but deeply in their debt. Had this not occurred, Louis and I would be dead. It is that simple. The executions by AQIM of Edwin Dyer on 31 May 2009 and Michel Germaneau on 24 July 2010 offer appalling testimony to that reality.

I agreed to take on the job of the UN Secretary-General's Special Envoy for Niger because I am a deep believer in the promise of an effective and engaged United Nations. My ordeal as a captive of Al Qaeda has in no way diminished that belief. Indeed, it has significantly reinforced it.

In writing this book I received no help or advice from the Canadian government—of which I am no longer an employee—and nothing in it has been vetted or approved by, or in any way represents the views of, that government. Of course I have been debriefed by various organizations, but at no point has anybody told me what really went on from the perspective of any government department or agency or asked me to refrain from discussing any aspect of Louis' and my ordeal.

A SEASON IN HELL

PART ONE

The Descent into Hell

CHAPTER 1

THE GRAB

═══

Forthwith this frame of mine was wrench'd
With a woful agony,
Which forced me to begin my tale;
And then it left me free.

═══

A s we waited for the ferry our driver, Soumana Moukaila, over-saw a gaggle of nearly naked young boys as they competed for the privilege—and a few coins—of washing his care-fully tended white Land Cruiser, which proudly sported a United Nations Development Programme (UNDP) logo in pale blue on each front door.

We were surrounded by makeshift stalls that sold small items: tiny bars of soap, a few razor blades, shoelaces, packets of Kleenex, and thin plastic bags of purportedly potable water. With loud voices and good humour, hawkers proclaimed the virtues of a variety of dishes to attract hungry travellers before they crossed the great river. The whole scene was suffused with that wonderful concoc-tion of smells—wood smoke, sweat, rich earth, spices, animals, and just a hint of latrine—so redolent of the essential Africa, a scent that had become embedded in my soul almost half a century earlier when I first set foot on the continent as a nineteen-year-old teacher.

Much of the business of this short trip to Niger had, after only a day of meetings in Niamey, been accomplished. The rest was largely ceremony and making nice. I was relaxed and musing about joining my wife, Mary, in Florida for Christmas.

My colleague, Louis Guay, and I were taking advantage of a quiet Sunday to do a little research into how resource revenues might be used to grease the wheels of a possible peace accord to end the two-year-old Tuareg rebellion in Niger that was further crippling this, the third-poorest country in the world. For such was my mission as the UN Secretary-General's Special Envoy for Niger: get the government and the rebels to the negotiating table.

We had not learned a great deal during our visit to the Canadian-owned gold mine near the border with Burkina Faso. Our visit, on a previous trip, to the vast uranium operation around Arlit, 1,250 kilometres to the north, which the French nuclear energy giant Areva had been exploiting for more than forty years, had been far more instructive. Nevertheless, we left the Samira Hill mine site somewhat later than we had intended, at around four o'clock. Following a pleasant forty-minute drive, we joined the large and relaxed pedestrian crowd and handful of vehicles at the ferry terminal on the southwest side of the Niger River.

The people around us joked and teased, flirted, laughed, and shouted as children darted through the throng, staring with unabashed curiosity at the two old white guys standing out so incongruously among them. It was a friendly crowd, bursting with life.

The inhabitants of Niger have not been dealt a generous hand by fate, but all around us they were getting by with energy and enthusiasm—a far cry from the dour doggedness with which we tend to claw through life in the West. Indeed, as I chronicled the bustle, I recalled a letter our youngest daughter, Justine, had written a couple of years previously when she spent a summer mapping the prevalence of hunger among young children in southern Rwanda. She had observed that she spent her days surrounded by nearly starving people who had nothing at all, yet they always smiled as they extended to her a pleasant, courteous greeting. How that contrasted, she ruefully noted, with people back home who so studiously avoided eye contact as they brushed past each other in the street wearing cold, preoccupied expressions.

The massively overloaded and ancient ferry slowly manoeuvred its way across to our side, crabbing against the strong and tricky current. Once it let down its ramp, there was a good-natured jostling of people, vehicles, and animals vying to get off and on simultaneously. As we set off, Louis, an ardent sailor, chatted with the captain as I continued to indulge my passion for photography in this target-rich environment. We reached the northeast side as the fierce heat of the day was dissipating. The glorious African evening light had allowed me to take some decent people shots on the ferry, and life seemed very much as it ought to be.

Leaving the ferry, we climbed the steep escarpment, and Soumana turned right toward the capital, Niamey, and floored it. The surface was excellent: one of the few paved roads in the country. Soumana was a fine driver and proud of what his nearly new Land Cruiser could do. The traffic was light and there were few pedestrians and domestic animals along the sides of the road. We passed half a dozen cars and trucks that had been ahead of us on the ferry. A van surmounted by a large, fence-like rack holding a number of understandably forlorn sheep was leading the pack. I had seen the van on the ferry and taken a picture of the hapless sheep. After zipping by them all, we found the road clear ahead.

Ten minutes later we crested a hill, and a long empty valley stretched into the far distance. The view was lovely and peaceful. I was looking forward to a pleasant dinner in Niamey with Guy Villeneuve, the head of the Canadian Office, a dependency of the embassy located in faraway Abidjan, Côte d'Ivoire. Louis was on his BlackBerry, arranging the details with Guy. I heard him say, "Okay, we are about thirty-five kilometres from town, so let's meet at 7:30 at the Gallery Restaurant."

I interrupted, a little impatiently, "Louis, we'll never make it. It's 6:30 now and we've at least thirty minutes before we reach the hotel. It will take us more than half an hour to shower, change, and get to the restaurant." Waving his wrist, he gently suggested I consult my watch, and sure enough I'd misread the time. It was 5:30, not 6:30. In fact it was 5:35, on 14 December, and we had no need to hurry.

At this point a pick-up truck appeared out of nowhere and was quickly overtaking us. Its speed seemed out of place, as we were doing about 120 kilometres per hour. As soon as it passed us, it slewed across our front, forcing Soumana to brake. "What the hell!" I exclaimed, woken out of my reverie with some surprise and annoyance, but by then Soumana was swinging out to pass the truck that had just cut us off. As soon as we moved left, so too did the truck, right off our front bumper, again blocking our progress and still slowing hard, forcing Soumana to brake to avoid plowing into it. As we pulled back into the right lane, so too did the truck, which now occupied the centre of the road, clearly positioning itself to block the possibility we might still try to pass either to the right or left.

With gut-wrenching dread, I understood that this was no crazy driver or road rage incident but rather the overture to a hideous nightmare.

Both vehicles were in emergency stopping mode. Soumana was standing on the brakes and it was all he could do to control our SUV. Before we came to a complete stop, I saw two African figures in the bed of the truck in front leap into action. One knelt, raising a Kalashnikov assault rifle, or AK-47, and aimed from about four metres away through the windshield into our driver's face. The other, one hand on the tailgate, vaulted onto the road with his AK in the other hand. They were shouting. Soumana was frozen. I hadn't yet looked at Louis, seated in the back to my left, but I was overcome with the hackneyed yet inescapable thought, "This cannot be happening to me!"

Time does slow in such circumstances, and I thought, "No—not here, not now. I know Africa. I have survived over forty-five years on many of Africa's meanest streets: the three Darfuri states, eastern Chad, the Inturi and Kivu provinces in eastern Congo, the anarchy of Mogadishu, northern Uganda ravaged by the Lord's Resistance Army, central Angola during the civil war, and two widely separated episodes of genocide in Rwanda. Now here it comes, in the 8 percent of Niger that everyone agrees is completely safe, where Guy's staff picnics on the weekends. Not this appalling cliché!"

By then, Soumana's door had been wrenched open and hands were dragging him out by the scruff of his neck toward the truck in front. I don't recall exchanging a word with Louis. Few friends will be surprised that my first instinct was to protect my dearest possession, an expensive camera and valuable lens. I was placing it gently at my feet in the right rear seat-well when Louis' door on the left was torn open and he too was being hauled out.

Through the windshield I saw Louis being frogmarched toward the back of the truck in front as Soumana was boosted, none too gently, over the tailgate. I looked out my window to the right, assessing the possibility of escape. There was a wide, cleared strip on my side of the highway—a line of scrubby bushes, down a slight slope, perhaps forty metres distant. Could I get the door open and run for and hide in that scrub? Would they shoot—how well? Would they linger long enough to come after me? Could I abandon Louis and Soumana to whatever fate awaited them? How much use could I be to them, anyway?

But before I had even fully exited my side, still undecided, the taller of the AK-waving young men had me by the upper arm. He shoved me toward the truck, shouting, "Dépêchez-vous," then pushed and lifted me into the arms of his colleague. Once in the truck bed, I saw that he was standing on Louis and Soumana, who were lying prostrate with horrified looks on their faces. I was thrown on top of them.

The truck then performed a squealing, 180-degree turn and began to speed back in the direction from which we had just come.

As my head was being forced below the side, I caught a glimpse of our vehicle across the highway, doors open and deserted. I was certain, however, that a fourth man, whom we had not yet seen (perhaps a passenger in the cab or in a following blocking vehicle) was about to drive it away. I knew that such a high-performance vehicle was probably the single most desirable commodity in Africa. It made sense that our kidnappers would take it straight into the inventory of one or other of the bands of smugglers, bandits, or rebels that frequent the largely lawless northern Sahel region, or at least to a chop shop.

I therefore assumed that my camera bag was now in the hands of my captors. Inside it was a USB key containing many of the documents relevant to my mission, something I had not trusted to the safe in my room. Some of these reports were sensitive, particularly those relating to my views on the bona fides of the government of President Mamadou Tandja. Also in that bag, I thought, was my Amazon Kindle—an electronic book containing about fifty titles, among them *Kill Bin Laden: A Delta Force Commander's Account of the Hunt for the World's Most Wanted Man*; *The Dark Side: The Inside Story of How the War on Terror Turned into a War on American Ideals*; and *Sniper One: On Scope and under Siege with a Sniper Team in Iraq*. There was also a series of books by Daniel Silva, whose protagonist is a Mossad agent in the business of eliminating the enemies of Israel. I didn't know who had taken us, but I didn't relish the prospect of any kidnappers in that part of the world discovering my reading preferences.

From my what-the-hell realization that something was seriously amiss to our being slung aboard our kidnappers' truck and driven off in the opposite direction, no more than forty seconds had elapsed. It had been, I regretted to conclude, a slick, violent, well-coordinated, and impeccably executed grab.

Much later it occurred to me that it was odd there had been no traffic moving in that long valley in either direction over this admittedly short period. While not impossible, the odds of that occurring so conveniently were low. It seemed likely, therefore, that our kidnappers had had collaborators blocking the traffic. I suspected the sheep-laden van might have had that assignment, but of course that was mere speculation.

As soon as I had been flung down on top of Soumana and Louis, our abductors shouted at us in French to remain absolutely silent and still, while speaking to each other in a language I couldn't recognize. They threw a foul, stinking, oily blanket on top of us, on which they then sat. My face, in the suffocating darkness, was a couple of centimetres from Soumana's. In a whisper, I asked him if he could recognize the language they were speaking. When I received no answer, I asked again and again in an ever-louder whisper, which earned me a haphazard but forceful thump from above and a further admonition to remain quiet. I thought that the language might provide a clue to who had grabbed us, so I persisted. Soumana was almost literally petrified. Eventually I received a whimpered "I don't know, I don't know." I took this to mean either he really didn't know or he didn't want to risk the further ire of our captors. I decided to shut up, and listened for sounds from Louis below and behind me. Hearing nothing, I whispered his name and heard a grunt to signify he was at least still with us.

After ten or fifteen minutes of smooth, fast driving on blacktop, we braked sharply and, though I could see nothing, it seemed as if we had turned right, northeast, off the highway. Now we were clearly running off-road as the bumps and smacks were horrendous, the three of us rising, it seemed, nearly a metre before being slammed back onto the metal truck bed. This merciless pounding continued for maybe another thirty minutes. As we continued to be smashed about in this manner, I heard groans from both Louis and Soumana—and from a third person, whom I eventually recognized as myself.

Suddenly, we stopped in an area of thick brush and the three of us were hauled over the tailgate to join our abductors behind the vehicle. There were three of them: the two twenty-something

Africans who had grabbed us and an older, light brown, Arab-featured man of medium stature in his mid-forties, who subsequently identified himself as Omar. He was clearly in charge.

Omar demanded our papers, and Louis produced his UN *laissez-passer* (a travel document that looks like a passport and contains essentially the same information, in addition to a description of the bearer's UN mission). I had a fair quantity of cash in U.S. dollars and local currency but no identity documents, a fact that irritated our kidnappers no end. First they couldn't understand how I could be so irresponsible as to go forth into the African hinterland without papers, and then they began to believe that I had somehow disposed of my documents in the course of the kidnapping. They asked, again and again, who I was and what was I doing in Niger. While my answers were congruent with the information in Louis' UN *laissez-passer,* my captors were frustrated that they couldn't objectively confirm whom they had taken, or as I was soon to surmise, that they had indeed lifted the guy they had been sent to grab.

We then had to empty our pockets. Aside from our cash, which they pocketed, there wasn't really much to take. They took Louis' watch (an anniversary gift from his wife, Mai) and his *laissez-passer* along with his late edition, government-issue BlackBerry, which attracted a lot of interest. They demanded that he immediately turn it off and remove the battery. Still perplexed by my lack of documentation, they withdrew into a huddle some metres away. I used these moments to say to Louis, "No matter what happens, tell the truth; even if it's not the whole truth. If you don't, you will inevitably be caught in a web of lies, which, at best, will lose their confidence and can only cause problems for us, whatever awaits us." This was also, of course, advice to myself and I hoped that such a guideline might marginally ease Louis' stress level, just as it had eased my own.

I don't recall where Soumana was at the time; perhaps they were questioning him. As Louis and I stood alone together, sore and terrified, I noticed a gash across Louis' left eyebrow, eyelid, and upper cheekbone, which had bled onto his shirt collar. It didn't look deep, but nor did it bode well. He insisted that it wasn't serious and did not hurt much. He said that the son of a bitch we subsequently came to know as Hassan had raked him, quite gratuitously, across the face with the foresight of his assault rifle while Louis was being loaded into the back of the truck. We spoke briefly about who our captors might be but had drawn no conclusions by the time they returned.

When they did return, Hassan, the shorter and stockier of the two Africans, was tightly masked, ninja like: very different from the turbans worn by virtually every male in the region and different again from the Tuareg-type turbans, which hid everything save a narrow slit for the eyes in carefully prepared folds of material covering the head, face, and neck. Hassan's covering was tightly wound around his head and across his face, so that the outline of his skull, cheekbones, nose, and lips was visible through the material. From that point onward, we never saw him unmasked and, given the stresses and strains of the previous forty minutes, neither Louis nor I retained the least idea of what "Ninja Boy" actually looked like.

As soon as they returned from their caucus, I urged them to let Louis and Soumana go free, insisting that to keep all three of us was a burden they didn't need to assume. I explained that I was the prize (something for which they would clearly have liked to have had documentary evidence) and that by the time the other two found their way back to the highway, the rest of us could be long gone in any direction. When this was dismissively rejected, Louis tried to get them to agree at least to release Soumana, who had nothing to offer them. But that too got no useful response.

Louis and I were then instructed to stand face to face about a metre apart, with our forearms stretched out toward each other. They used packing tape to bind (happily, over our long-sleeved shirts) my right wrist to his left, and his right to my left. With words that I did not understand and gestures that I did, Omar instructed Hassan and the tall, thin African, referred to as "le Sénégalais," to load us into the back of the truck with Soumana, who had not been bound but seemed utterly traumatized.

As the two young, pumped-up kidnappers moved to carry out this instruction, I pointed out rather matter-of-factly to Omar that we would not survive long being bounced around in the back of the truck. Surely, I continued, dead hostages were not in his interest, and on the basis of the pounding we had received since leaving the highway only thirty minutes earlier, there was no way we could take much more—particularly if we could not use our arms and hands to mitigate the punishment we would be receiving over any additional cross-country travel.

Omar gave me a long, appraising look. Unlike me, he knew the full extent and nature of the journey we would be undertaking. He could see that we were old (I am about twenty-five years older than the life expectancy of the average Sahel resident) and—compared to them—relatively frail. His eyes told me that he realized that indeed these ancient, soft, Western white guys would be terribly damaged in such circumstances. Soumana was clearly suffering the effects of being repeatedly smashed hard onto the metal truck bed. He was cradling his left arm and seemed to be experiencing some kind of stomach pain. Louis' bloodstained shirt added force to my argument. Further, I had lost my regular glasses as well as my prescription sunglasses in the initial grab and was staring myopically at anyone who spoke.

So, rather pompously noting that his instructions had been specific regarding the fact that we were to be bound as well as blindfolded and placed in the back of the truck, Omar allowed that, as "mission commander," he could modify such instructions to meet operational requirements. After a moment's further reflection, he told his boys to cut the tape binding my left wrist to Louis' right, leave the other binding in place, and get us into the cab. I went first, hoisting myself into the relatively high cab with my free left hand, and then half dragging Louis in after me with our bound wrists. Once inside, we tried to settle, one cheek each, into the single passenger bucket seat. As "le Sénégalais" slammed the cab door, he noted casually through the window, "If the government helicopters find us before dark, we are all dead." I was rather encouraged by the prospect that there might be even a chance of government helicopters looking for us, but I considered this a very remote possibility.

Their truck was the pick-up version of our Toyota Land Cruiser, and was the ubiquitous vehicle of choice for all those who roamed the Sahel. This band of desert and semi-desert stretches from Mauritania's Atlantic coast across Mali, Niger, Chad, and Sudan to the Red Sea, and, effectively, on through the Horn of Africa to the Indian Ocean.

Because our wrists had been bound while we were facing each other, rather than side by side, it was extremely difficult for either of us to protect ourselves in the cab against the brutal buffeting we suffered over the next three days. The way we tried to brace against the dramatic bumps and twists was for Louis, with his window wide open, to hold tightly to the roof with his free right hand, as I reached behind the driver and grabbed the far side of his seat back with my free left hand. We would then twist our bound hands into an X to allow his left and my right to grasp the handle mounted above the glove compartment. Doing this tightened the tape around our wrists, however, and every three or four minutes we had to let go, point our hands in the direction they were in when they were bound, and flex our fingers until circulation had been restored. All in all, it was not a perfect solution to the challenges of the fifty-six hours of hard driving between the moment we were taken and our arrival within the Al Qaeda area of operations in the far north of Mali. Nevertheless, it was an awful lot better than being slammed around in the truck bed, as was Soumana's fate, albeit unbound.

While we crossed two or three open, relatively smooth stretches of desert, in the main the going was rough. In the beginning, we crashed across hand-plowed fields, along *wadis* (dry, boulder-strewn, seasonal stream or river beds, which could be anything from slight indentations in the desert floor to deep canyons), and up and down the sides of impossibly steep ravines, weaving among mesa-like outcroppings. When we reached the Sahara proper, we forced our way over and through massive, vehicle-gobbling sand dunes.

A measure of what this journey was like would be to calculate that about every ten seconds we would bounce in such a manner that, when we had not been able to brace properly, we smashed our heads on the roof of the cab or slammed our faces into the dashboard. This tended to occur when we let go of the handle above the glove compartment in order to restore circulation to our fingers. As a result I suffered a damaged coccyx and a significant compression fracture of my L5 vertebra. In the weeks following this descent into hell, sitting upright was impossible, lying down and getting up were painful, and turning over at night was excruciating.

Omar was a traditionalist. He navigated by the sun and stars. Even I can find Polaris, so I was able to watch him follow the North Star hour after hour, sometimes stopping and walking around to get his bearings but always finding the track or direction he was seeking. Sometimes that meant doubling back for twenty minutes to find an obscure turn-off on a route he had obviously travelled before but that I could not make out.

We bumped across maize fields, the dead stalks whipping against the windshield, and crashed straight through collections of huts but generally avoided inhabited areas—something that became ever easier as we proceeded north. Omar used the headlights rarely and we travelled on a road on just one occasion that first night, and even then for only twenty minutes. From time to time we would see a light from a cooking fire or hut far in the distance and I would try to mark its position and then calculate the distance from that point in the ever more forlorn hope that somewhere ahead we could escape and then make our way back to that beacon of freedom. My calculations were far from scientific and certainly inaccurate. The one constant was our heading: due north.

In addition to the fifty-six hours in the trucks were four or five periods of rest, lasting one to three hours each—perhaps ten hours of rest in total.

These were psychologically tough times as we blasted into what promised to be a bleak future. When would we be missed, and when we were, what would happen? We took some comfort in the fact that Guy Villeneuve would be waiting for us to join him for dinner at 7:30. How long, then, before he knew something was amiss, an hour—two at most? How long after that before he sought police and government assistance?

No matter how we framed it, things didn't look good. I didn't think the Niger armed forces were capable of flying search and rescue missions at night, if indeed they could get their helicopters into the air at all. Our captors were obviously avoiding any chance of running into a police roadblock by the simple expedient of avoiding all roads. Further, every passing minute extended the radius of the search area. Despite the fact that Niger is one of the larger countries in the world, the region from which we were taken in the extreme southwestern part of the country was only 100 kilometres from Burkina Faso to the west (although that would entail re-crossing the river, something they were unlikely to risk), about 160 kilometres from Benin to the south, and about the same distance from the border of Mali, due north. I knew, of course, that we were heading north, but anybody who might be looking for us could not be sure. Every hour, even as we crunched along off-road at only twenty to thirty kilometres per hour, would add thousands of square kilometres to the search area. Dredging up high school math, I applied πr^2 to our laborious progress and determined that at the end of six hours, as we approached the Mali border to the north, the search area would be over 70,000 square kilometres. I did not expect to be rescued soon.

So, when would our families learn what had happened?

This was a particularly acute issue in my case. It was Sunday evening in Niger, Sunday noon in Ottawa. Mary was leaving, unless her plans had changed, very early on Monday morning for Florida, where I was to meet her in six days' time. Would she get the news before she left?

How would she and our girls handle the news? In short—would they be okay? Would the Canadian government apparatus be as supportive as I hoped? Would friends immediately rally round? How would Canada and the United Nations work out responsibility for any negotiations with our abductors and for getting us home? Would Mary and the girls forgive me for putting them through such torment? All these hugely important, very fraught issues and the attendant uncertainty gnawed at my fragile composure. I was terrified, sad, and desperate, and in no little discomfort. What further unpleasant surprises did the immediate future hold? I am sure that similar thoughts were also churning through Louis' mind.

Mostly just to break the tension, we tried to make desultory conversation with Omar. I asked him to teach us his language, which turned out to be Tamasheq, the language spoken by the Tuareg, although none of our captors seemed to me to be Tuareg. We started with numbers, but I was so discombobulated that I could not remember the word for four by the time he got to six.

From time to time, Louis would say something softly to me in English, something he clearly did not want Omar, seated maybe seventy centimetres from him, to hear. The trouble, of course, was that this sounded sneaky and secretive, like my parents whispering to each other *pas devant les enfants* over Sunday lunch, and I tried to discourage him from doing so.

At one point, though, Louis asked, "Do you think we're going to Geneva?" which even in my state of confused dread I could figure out meant did I believe we had been taken by rebels from the Mouvement des Nigériens pour la justice (the MNJ, or Movement of Nigeriens for Justice). The reference to Geneva related to the fact that we had arranged to return to that city in early January to hold a second series of meetings with the MNJ rebels, likely including their leader, Aghali Alambo. Thus, if our kidnappers were from the MNJ, not only would we be saved a trip to see them in Switzerland but we might also be on a roundabout way to freedom relatively soon.

Since conversation proved difficult and possibly dangerous, we gave our dark thoughts far too much rein as we defended ourselves as best we could against the torturous ride. Sometime near midnight, we approached an isolated collection of ramshackle buildings beside a roaring open fire. Omar stopped the truck a good distance away and left us in the hands of le Sénégalais and Hassan. As he approached the shadowy figures around the fire, one detached himself from the rest and he and Omar paced back and forth, silhouettes in front of the fire, deep in conversation. It wasn't long before the dark figure briskly turned back to his colleagues and Omar returned to the truck. Without a word or glance in our direction, he threw it into gear and we were off again. I wondered if a death sentence had been pronounced and whether we would live another ten minutes.

A couple of hours later we stopped by a small, dark collection of low mud huts and a furtive figure materialized out of one of them. Omar consulted him briefly and we were off again. Some hours later we drove through another group of dark huts, which this time was not a way station of sympathizers but rather some kind of family compound. Once we had blundered among those huts, there seemed no way out. Omar turned on the headlights. Figures appeared, first two or three, then many more. African men, women, and children in various stages of undress flitted through the shifting, dusty glare of the truck's headlights. Omar—clearly unsettled—charged about, cranking through the gears, looking for an escape route. He shouted something to the boys in the back, which I assumed to be an admonition to remain calm and keep their weapons out of sight.

The growing crowd was not overtly hostile but they were evidently curious about who we might be and, by their facial expressions, seemed to resent the abrupt and aggressive intrusion. These people did not seem to be aligned with our captors, and I yearned to call to them for help as we flashed past just a few metres away. Perhaps, I briefly considered, Louis could open his door so we could hurl ourselves at the feet of these simple villagers. I was certain, though, that our abductors would never allow such a ploy to succeed. The villagers were unarmed and I cringed to imagine what a couple of AKs, or "Kalashes" as our captors invariably called them, would do to this small crowd of innocent and defenceless onlookers so close at hand.

Omar spun the truck in a new direction and we smashed through a little shed made of sticks and thatch and out into a maize field. I wondered if the people we left in our wake, whose peace and sleep we had so rudely interrupted, would find a way to report the event to some authority as they certainly would have seen Louis' startled, very white face in the truck window. Or maybe they would connect this event with news of our abduction. I doubted, though, that either would occur.

Around three in the morning, by my very rough calculation, we stopped for a tea break and brief rest. My back was in spasm and I was not sure I could even exit the vehicle, however much I needed to pee. But I also needed to see Soumana. I had barely been able to discern through the small back window of the cab what I thought were three dark figures in the truck bed but could not tell if one of them was Soumana. Unmindful of whether Omar heard or not, I repeatedly asked Louis whether Soumana was still with us and with mounting frustration Louis pointed him out two or three times. I suppose it was my disoriented state that caused me to obsess about him, coupled with the damage to my back, which made it difficult to turn around in my seat; and without my glasses I could see little. When we stopped and I was finally able to recognize him, I was hugely relieved. Soumana was not, though, in great shape either physically or psychologically. I could only imagine what punishment he had been taking as he was bounced about on the steel truck bed. When we had a chance to speak, he was uncommunicative, confused—nearly catatonic.

The moon had set. Everyone was tired. Nobody seemed to be paying much attention to me. Could I just wander off? We hadn't seen any sign of life for a long time. There were a few bushes in the starlit lunar landscape. How easy would it be for them to find me? How far could I get in the heat of the following day in such vast and hostile emptiness without shelter, food, or water? Aside from feeling confident that I should head south, was I likely to find anyone who could or would help? Wracked with indecision and declining confidence, I just leaned against the truck and tried to rest—the inglorious path of least resistance.

On and on we drove until a couple of hours before dawn we skidded to a stop following a particularly difficult stretch. Omar announced, "I must sleep," opened his door, and rolled under the truck. Hassan cut the tape binding our wrists, threw a blanket from the back onto the hard-packed sand and told us to rest. He led Soumana away to some other place. Le Sénégalais took sentry duty.

Louis lay down, exhausted, but my back pain was such that I could not stretch out. I was also very cold, clad only in a thin cotton shirt and trousers. I paced a racetrack pattern, taking care to remain well within the sentry's sight and immediate vicinity.

After some minutes of walking the pain in my lower back subsided and I wandered over to where the sentry was brewing tea. He had a tiny fire going, on which he placed a small metal teapot. I asked him if I should call him le Sénégalais, as had Omar. With a surprisingly good-natured laugh he said, "No, my name is Ibrahim, but I am from Senegal."

I was terribly thirsty but had got it into my addled brain that I must not drink the murky, sludgy brown water from their large ten-litre plastic container. If I did so, I was convinced, I would contract dysentery. My state of denial was such that I calculated I must avoid the trots so that I could take my place in the reviewing stand in just three days' time in Tillabéri—an hour down the road

from where we had been taken—to participate in the celebration of
Niger's fiftieth anniversary of independence. Surely all this unpleasantness would somehow be over by then.

Tea, however, seemed reasonably safe. Ibrahim was dropping
handfuls of tea and sugar into the pot, and I hoped to cadge a glass
or two. It was the Arab version: hot, green, very sweet, and served
in minuscule glasses, which would not greatly alleviate my increasing dehydration. When I was standing above him, he looked up at
me with a sardonic, fire-lit smile and asked, "So, have you figured
out who we are yet?"

I had been dreading this moment for most of the preceding
twelve hours and passively avoiding confronting the inexorably
dawning reality. I asked, without conviction, "Are you not the
MNJ?" When his facial expression suggested confusion and not a
little disdain, I added, unnecessarily, "Le Mouvement des Nigériens
pour la justice?"

Ibrahim snorted with derision. "I told you I was Senegalese.
What would I be doing with a gang of amateurs like that?" I simply
stared at him as the fire danced in his menacing black eyes. Finally,
drawing out the moment with cruel anticipation, he fiercely spat the
words, "We are Al Qaeda!" And the bottom fell out of my world.

As I walked away from the fire, reeling from the palpable
enjoyment Ibrahim had derived from his revelation, I did not look
forward to passing on this news to Louis. When I found a private
moment to tell him, while our kidnappers had stopped to pray,
he took it stoically enough, simply noting, "I'd rather be in the
hands of people who prayed." For my part, however, I estimated
that our chances of emerging whole from this ordeal stood at
about 5 percent, principally because I could not convince myself
to accept a lower number.

CHAPTER 2

CENTRAL STATION

===

My lips were wet, my throat was cold,
My garments all were dank;
Sure I had drunken in my dreams,
And still my body drank.

===

Shortly after Ibrahim confirmed the worst of my fears by telling me that we had been captured by Al Qaeda, it was time to move after what couldn't have been more than a couple of hours of rest. Omar rolled wide awake from under his truck. Once he had been served a tiny glass of tea and Louis and I had again been bound, we were underway.

Louis had slept a bit and was groggy, but my adrenalin-suffused brain was in search of something to take my mind off the Al Qaeda implications. I had again lost track of Soumana, who must have flopped down on the other side of the vehicle to grab some rest under the ever-watchful eyes of Hassan. And so I resumed my obsessive worrying. Where was Soumana? Had he escaped or perhaps been freed, or more likely, I thought, simply been killed? I was unable to quell my rising anxiety.

As we crashed ever northward through the gradually greying dawn, there was no sign of habitation or cultivation. Eventually, the sun rose to our right, and I drifted in and out of some kind of stupor, returning again and again to the wretched realization that this was no dream.

As the day broke, Omar produced two long pieces of thin, beige cotton material and we were instructed, "Turbanisez-vous." Evidently we were supposed to use the material to create turbans but neither of us knew how to accomplish that, let alone with only one free hand. Omar gave us a brief demonstration while driving. As he unwound his turban, he revealed a closely cropped head with about a week's growth of stubble. Suddenly he looked smaller, frailer, and ten years younger—a significantly less fierce and commanding person. Louis and I tried to follow his turban-tying example one at a time, as first one and then the other of us used a bound hand to assist in the process. The result was far from perfect, and Omar found this simultaneously slightly amusing and very annoying.

He then told us sternly and with more menace than he had exhibited to that point, that under no circumstances were we to talk to anybody we might encounter. Were we to attempt to do so the consequences would be cataclysmic for all concerned. Further, we were to avert our (pasty-white) faces without having to be ordered to do so, from any person we saw, no matter how far distant. In such circumstances Louis, by the window, was to bring his bracing arm inside the truck, again so that his telltale white hand would not reveal our identity.

For some hours Omar's instructions about how we had to behave when people were sighted seemed rather abstract. But gradually, as we continued to claw our way north, we began to see the odd long, low black tent, usually tucked in against some brush and meagre trees, scenes right out of desert nomad central casting. Omar tended to give these tents and any sign of habitation a wide berth, but now and then we would see a young boy herding goats or sheep fairly close by in that vast emptiness. Sometimes camels dotted the landscape in widely dispersed ones and twos.

On a few occasions we saw, close at hand, shepherds in loose, dark, almost iridescent indigo robes and big grey or blue turbans, their arms draped over long, thin staves balanced across their shoulders. As we approached them we received a sharp glare from Omar to reinforce the no-speak, no-look directive. He would halt the vehicle thirty or forty metres away, exit and saunter over to speak with these fellows, often embracing them. They might then walk a bit with Omar's arm slung about their shoulders, or they would squat together in the sand for a short chat.

All this was of course difficult to follow with our faces supposedly averted. But as it was happening, a brief glance through the small window in the back of the cab (often obscured by the immense clutter of junk—ammunition, bits of clothing, tins of motor oil, tools, bags, small backpacks, jackets, dates—between the backs of the bucket seats and the rear wall of the cab) revealed that Hassan, Ibrahim, and Soumana were rigidly quiet and watchful, but no weapons were in evidence.

These meet-and-greet interludes were obviously exercises in community relations, something our captors knew was important and were unfailingly good at. I suspect that the nomads saw far more of and received more support—however rudimentary—from Al Qaeda warriors than they ever got from government representatives.

We were told that we were headed to some sort of camp, and I convinced myself that such a place would include buildings and possibly a bed, on which I desperately hoped I might find some relief for my screaming back. I also hoped for potable water and food. I realized that it could mean a lot of less salubrious things, but in the main managed to keep such worries from becoming a preoccupation. Above all, I was desperate to see the journey end and the relentless pounding stop. I was convinced that my back was suffering possibly irreparable damage. Like a small child accompanying uncommunicative parents on a long drive, I was hard put not to whine, "How far now, Omar?"

As we crossed a particularly appalling stretch of rough country, one of the front wheels dropped into a deep hole, forcing us to an instantaneous stop. My face smacked into the dashboard with sufficient force that I partially lost consciousness, seat belt laws being improperly observed in the Sahara. For the first of many times, I contemplated the irony of being captured by Al Qaeda only to die in a car accident.

We climbed a long, scrubby hill and without warning rocketed onto a wide, well-maintained, evidently much-travelled dirt road. Omar, very nervous, grew serious and again threatening. He reminded us that whatever happened and whatever the conditions that might cause us to stop, under no circumstances were we to say anything to anyone, or to look at anybody we might encounter.

As he swung the truck to the left, which the sun indicated was to the west, Omar reached across both of us to open the glove compartment and extract a fat, letter-sized manila envelope. It was not sealed, and while driving fast, he checked the contents, which seemed to be a thick wad of unidentifiable currency. He then tucked the cash-stuffed envelope behind his driver's sun visor and jacked up the speed. Clearly this would be the first response to any roadblock or military search. The AKs of the thugs in the back would be the second. When Omar had retrieved the envelope, I thought I had glimpsed the butt of a well-worn automatic pistol partially concealed under a dirty rag in addition to a lot of other junk in the evidently unlocked glove compartment. This gave me something to think about.

We passed a couple of heavy commercial trucks travelling fast in the opposite direction. It was clearly a main highway and was marked by ill-maintained but recognizable *bornes kilométriques,* similar to those that adorn roadways in France. These were small, gravestone-like cement markers with rounded red caps showing the number of the highway. Below the red cap, the distances to the next and to the last town were marked against a background that once upon a time had been painted white. The stones visible along that road no longer occurred every kilometre, but they did indicate a name, and I simply cannot remember what it was. I know, though, that it started with "M," so I assume we might have been travelling along the main east–west highway in the far eastern part of Mali, just north of the Niger–Mali border, toward Ménaka. I don't know that this was the case, but it would make sense.

After about forty minutes Omar suddenly slowed hard and turned right, off the road to the north, and bumped into the scrub. Within a couple of kilometres we came to a fairly large Tuareg encampment, almost within sight of the road. Omar did some extensive schmoozing and then we seemed to head northwest. For the first time, we followed a very circuitous and seemingly random route. Omar announced that he was looking for a shady place to rest and after a long search we stopped under a stand of acacia trees and were instructed to sit on a blanket in incomplete shade, and offered water from their large, filthy jug.

The tape binding Louis' and my wrists together was cut by Hassan's vicious-looking blade, which could have been from the Rambo property drawer: a cross between a bowie knife and bayonet, with holes cut into the body of the blade and a heavily serrated spine. We were told we could relieve ourselves behind some nearby bushes, but there was nothing in my bladder.

I was in bad mental and physical shape. As the afternoon wore on under the merciless sun, the temperature rose to a point I had experienced only in southern Darfur, so I knew it was in the high forties. Still I refused to drink what I had determined was water straight from the polluted Niger River. I was hallucinating, drifting in and out of consciousness. I had a headache and felt nauseated. My mouth was so dry I could not swallow. I was short of breath, gasping shallowly through my mouth. My back was excruciating and I could not contemplate lying down, so I was allowed to stay in the cab with the door open and I let my mind drift off to some better place.

Our captors seemed nervous and vigilant. They made a couple of short calls on their Thuraya satellite-phone, exchanged nervous looks at the slightest sound, and hunkered down on their blanket. Nobody slept, even though Omar must have been exhausted after such a driving tour de force. They explained to us that "the army" was looking for us and that "army patrols" were nearby, but was it the Niger Army or the Malian Army? I think they said it was the second, but don't really remember. Louis and I could not decide whether this was a happy or unhappy development. Our abductors didn't give the impression that they would easily be separated from their prey.

We were offered a can of sardines and a handful of hard and dry dates. The dates were delicious, but, without water, hard to swallow. I was not hungry and left the oily sardines to Louis.

It was stiflingly hot. I hadn't slept for thirty-three hours. My brain could not get its survival priorities straight. Louis urged me to drink but I firmly resisted his advice, asking instead for as many of the small glasses of extremely sweet tea he could extract from our kidnappers. I think I managed four or five over the next couple of hours, during which we were clearly waiting for something. I dreaded whatever it was.

After drifting in and out of sleep, or perhaps consciousness, for an hour or so, in order to escape the still, stifling air of the cab, I finally eased myself from the truck. Slowly, I began, very stiffly at first, to walk around the vehicle and the blankets spread in the shade—one for Louis and me, the other, some distance away, for them.

At one point, Ibrahim motioned me to approach and offered me more dry dates (he apologized for their quality), which I gratefully accepted, stashing a couple in my pocket. He then began a series of malicious games. First, he contrived to leave his AK-47 within my reach but, while pretending otherwise, watched carefully to see what I would do. Had a round been chambered? Was the magazine empty? Which were the relevant positions of the fire selector lever? Could I possibly get all three of them, who were not grouped together, before these battle-hardened warriors got me? While tempted, I didn't touch it, but I suspect that my laborious thought processes must have been transparent. Ibrahim, staring intently at me, eventually scooped up his weapon from in front of me and laughed in my face.

Then he told a series of preposterous tales. As our whole situation was otherworldly, these fables did not seem as outlandish then, even if we knew he was having us on. We were, he insisted, heading to a vast, established, and very well-protected camp. Tuareg leaders will welcome you. There will be a feast in your honour; the chief will offer you his fairest daughter. You will be a hero. Soon you will be released and back in your hotel in Niamey.

Out of the blue and suddenly seeming serious, Ibrahim switched tacks and asked me whether, if the army attacked and escape were impossible, I would speak on their behalf to prevent them from being executed on the spot. I was certain that this was yet another of his silly games, but he seemed genuinely nervous, even afraid— the only time I ever saw one of our captors in that state. I had no idea if anybody was looking for us or if they were close at hand, but rather pretentiously, I informed him we would do what we could to ensure that, in such a (happy) event, they would be treated no worse than we had been.

As the heat began finally to relent, perhaps around five in the afternoon, Omar ordered us to mount up. Louis and I were bundled aboard, but our wrists were not retaped, and we resumed what seemed to be even more random movements across the top of a long ridge. First, we drove two or three kilometres through hilly country, fairly well grassed and with large clumps of dense bushes and trees in the valleys below. Then, after a short wait and a brief satellite-phone call, we headed a similar distance in something like the opposite direction. We repeated this procedure a number of times, keeping to the high ground.

Finally, as the dusk was deepening, we stopped yet again. Omar was about fifteen metres from the vehicle off the driver's side, his door left open. Louis and I had been told to remain in our shared bucket seat. All three of our kidnappers were scanning the countryside around the vehicle, Omar with the phone to his ear and Ibrahim and Hassan standing in the truck bed. Through the small open back window I could see them from thighs to upper chests. Then I remembered that glimpse of what might have been a partially covered pistol butt in the glove compartment thirty centimetres in front of Louis.

My pulse started to race. While I was pretty familiar with rifles and shotguns, I had fired a pistol only once in my life, a U.S. Army–issue Colt .45 over forty years earlier, and I had not been very handy with that weapon. I didn't know what make the gun in the glove compartment might be, if in fact it was even a pistol. I wasn't sure I would be able to operate it, let alone in time and effectively. I assumed it to be of Soviet manufacture like the rest of their weapons—a 9 mm Makarov seemed likely—but I didn't know where the safety would be, and without my glasses I knew it would be impossible to see any markings on the gun. Thus, I would simply have to haul it out of the glove compartment (assuming it was still unlocked), taking care to shield the manoeuvre as best I could with my body and not make noise or spill other junk as I removed it. Then I would have to check that at least there was a magazine in the butt (I knew I'd never have time to extract the magazine to ensure it was full), work the slide—which would make a very distinctive and alarming noise to any of our captors who heard it—hope that the safety was off, and determine where it was so that, if the gun would not fire, I'd be able to move the safety lever and try again.

I thought I could probably twist in my seat and shoot through the back window into the trunks of both Hassan and Ibrahim before they could react—if, of course, I could make the pistol work before they realized what I was up to. As I couldn't see their heads, they weren't likely to see me fiddling around with it until I fired. As they were both between two and three metres away, I thought that even I could hit such a target. I'd fire upward into the centre-of-body mass, but should I attempt to fire one shot into each of them or try the supposedly classic double-tap? That would be more likely to put one down permanently but it would give the second one more time to react, probably by diving over the side of the vehicle. Indeed, I thought it likely that any shot hitting them from such a range would knock them out of the truck and thus out of my very limited field of fire. Therefore, there was a possibility they would be down but not out, and conceivably still in possession of their AKs.

Then there was the question of what Omar would be doing while this was occurring. What was the likelihood of hitting Soumana, whom I couldn't see but thought was still sitting in the truck bed? The immediate threat was clearly the two guys with AKs, and both would have to be put out of action. By the time they were down—and if we had not already been sprayed with automatic fire—Omar would be on the move. He was, as far as I knew, unarmed, but he would be approaching the scrub. I knew I'd be useless with a pistol at fifteen metres in the gathering gloom.

I was confident that either Soumana (if he were in any shape to function effectively) or Louis could operate the four-by-four, but I had no idea where we would head other than south or, indeed, in which direction lay the road we had travelled earlier in the afternoon, but I knew it was not far. I expected that the area was alive with our abductors' Al Qaeda colleagues, the approach to whom, I supposed, was what all the manoeuvres over the past hour had been about. It seemed likely that any shots would be heard and the headlights of our vehicle might be seen as we tried to escape, but travelling in such country without at least intermittent use of lights would be folly. Finally, though, I was not at all sure that their colleagues would rush toward the sound of gunfire.

This seemed to be the best opportunity we had had and perhaps would ever have, but it would be loud, messy, and very risky. I asked Louis to press himself back against the seat and against his door. "Why?" he asked suspiciously. I briefly outlined my plan. Louis stared at me aghast.

"As soon as you open that glove compartment—if, indeed, you

can open it, and whether or not there's a gun inside—we stand a strong risk of being killed. It is," he insisted, "simply not worth that risk."

"Move!" I ordered.

"No!" he growled, moving his body closer to the glove compartment and seeking to stare me down.

We were still glaring at each other when Omar slid back behind the wheel. He must have started to return to the truck just as I asked Louis to give me access to the glove compartment. Looking back, I doubt that even if everything had worked as I hoped it might, I would have had the time to pull it off. But I'll never know. There is no doubt that Louis was right: it would have been a high-risk ploy. I never learned whether, in fact, there had been a handgun in that glove compartment.

Once we were again underway, Omar executed a few more of his travel-ten-minutes-and-wait-five operations, clearly designed to ensure that as we approached their base we were not being followed. After my breathing had settled and some of the adrenalin had leached out of my system following the aborted glove compartment gambit, I was depressed and dejected. I had still had nothing more than some thimbles of tea to drink since our harrowing misadventure began twenty-four hours earlier, and there is no doubt I was severely dehydrated.

In full darkness, during one of these waiting periods and after considerable internal wrestling with the pros and cons of doing so, I croaked out a question to Omar, "Is it your intention to execute us?"

Omar replied with what I took to be gratifying vehemence. "That would make no sense at all," he shot back. "My mission was to capture you and bring you back to my emir, where you could not be found." He then continued with some pride, "If my mission had been to assassinate you, you would now be dead." His unassailable logic was comforting, at least superficially.

He then launched into the first of many sessions of colourful, if not necessarily consistent, coherent, or accurate religious instruction. "We are good, faithful, and dedicated slaves of Allah," he continued a little primly. "The Qur'an contains a specific prohibition against murder, so we could not do that even if we wanted to." This did not seem entirely in keeping with what I knew of Al Qaeda. I was much less familiar with the norms and behaviour of the North African franchise but all too aware of the predations of its predecessors, the Groupe Islamique Armée (GIA, or Armed Islamic Group)—which I did not recall as being particularly squeamish about killing vast numbers of innocents—and the Groupe Salafiste pour la Prédication et le Combat (GSPC, or Salafist Group for Call and Combat). Nevertheless, I was happy with his answer and forcefully suspended any lurking disbelief as I clung to whatever straws he was prepared to offer.

While I was glad to hear assurances that we were not to be immediately executed, it was almost as satisfying to hear his crystal-clear rejection of any possibility that our kidnapping might have been simply a case of our being in the wrong place at the wrong time. We now knew for certain that the UN Special Envoy had not fallen into the hands of Al Qaeda simply as a result of an unhappy coincidence.

Of course, I already knew that any such hypothesis was close to absurd. Clearly they had known precisely where we would be, but even then our capture had been an extremely risky venture. We had been grabbed in a region deemed safe by all, and it would be along that road that the entire government would travel in a few days to celebrate Niger's fiftieth birthday in Tillabéri. In fact, the area from which we had been taken, about thirty-five kilometres from Niamey, was but a couple of kilometres from the large Koutoukaté prison (in which former Prime Minister Hama Amadou, President Tandja's principal rival, was being held), and it was close to a major military base. We took bizarre comfort in the fact that our abduction was not the result of appallingly bad luck.

A little later Omar must have felt we needed more reassurance for, without prompting, he informed us that it was all about ransom; about, that is, raising money for the cause, for *jihad*. It was simple, he proclaimed. They would make demands, the United Nations and/or Canada would negotiate a suitable number, and we would be freed. "It might take a few days, but," he explained, "you could be back in Niamey by the weekend." Indeed, if a deal could be expeditiously concluded, he confidently proclaimed, he would drive us back himself, "right to your hotel."

Louis and I told him that we did not think it would be so simple: that, as far as we knew—and we stressed that neither of us had had any direct experience of such things—neither Canada nor the United Nations would pay a ransom to kidnappers. Omar brushed such observations off as mere posturing on our part. He proudly noted that he had been involved in the negotiations to free the two Austrian tourists who had been taken from their desert camping expedition in southern Tunisia in February 2008 and released in October.

Not wishing to return to the bleak subject of why Omar's optimism was ill founded, I asked him how these things were done. Did someone, I wondered, "deliver a sack of cash to some kind of intermediary?"

"Oh, no!" laughed this desert warrior, who lived comfortably within the confines of a seventh-century belief system. "Things are much more efficient these days. It's all done with a few computer keystrokes—a simple bank transfer into the account of people in whom we have confidence. It's finished in thirty seconds."

How tidy, I thought, and how unrealistic—at least as far as we were concerned. We knew it wasn't going to go down like that, but I don't know what Omar really believed.

Now in complete darkness, there was a last satellite-phone call and, with a new determination and focus, we headed down into a valley and bulled our way into a particularly dense and extensive area of heavy bush. The boys in the back whooped with excitement as they sought, not always successfully, to dodge the vicious, thorn-studded branches that swept along the top and sides of our vehicle as we crashed our way through. In a fairly large clearing, we stopped and waited a few minutes with the motor running and the lights on until we heard a vehicle approaching. Omar extinguished his lights. The other vehicle stopped and through the trees flashed its lights twice. Omar replied in like manner, and with lights now blazing the two vehicles approached each other with much screaming of "Allahu Akbar!" (God is great) echoing around the clearing from all sides.

The other vehicle turned and took off at speed, without lights, through the trees as we followed. There seemed to be several Kalash-waving figures leaping about in the back calling out something to Hassan and Ibrahim, who responded with maniacal excitement. Omar, sporting a happy grin, concentrated on keeping the other vehicle in sight as it twisted and turned through the bush without benefit of lights and at a breakneck pace. Eventually things settled down somewhat as the lead vehicle lost, searched, and then found its way any number of times, with much backtracking, punctuated by near hysterical laughter. Then, in a more orderly convoy with each truck periodically turning its lights on and off to navigate difficult patches, we proceeded through the bushes and trees in an ever more disciplined fashion.

Perhaps forty minutes later we saw human shapes ahead and the two trucks stopped among what seemed to be numerous animated, shouting, largely black-faced figures. Hands reached in through the driver's window to hug Omar or slap him on the back. Louis' window framed half a dozen curious, gleeful faces seeking a glimpse of the prizes illuminated by a number of randomly directed hand-held flashlights. These were very excited, not very aggressive young men who seemed drunk with success and happiness. As they milled about, Ibrahim, having leapt into the crowd from the back of our truck like a rock star, strutted his stuff in all directions, basking in the glory that his mission had won him.

He then spotted a tall, thin black figure in the crowd, gave him a long and excited hug, and ushered him toward Louis' window, proudly introducing him to us as his brother. We understood this to mean his real brother, as opposed to the term they all used to designate each other, *frère*. Unsure of the appropriate greeting to a new captive, Ibrahim's brother simply thrust his large, military-style metal canteen through the window and offered us water.

Suddenly—finally—my all too dormant survival instinct snapped into place. I tore the canteen from his grasp and began to drink, water pouring from the sides of my mouth as I gulped it down. The water tasted muddy, gritty, warm, and delicious. Suddenly, I knew with certainty that this would not be over soon and that I would die if I were not a lot more careful about looking after myself, the trots clearly being the least of my worries. I emptied the entire canteen—perhaps a litre—and asked for more. Surprised but willing, the brother disappeared and some minutes later returned to offer me another full canteen. This time I let Louis have a little as I paused for breath, but, with Louis' encouragement, polished off much of it myself.

Eventually, Louis and I were dragged out of the cab. A couple of slightly older, stern Arab faces had appeared and started issuing orders. Angry comments seemed to be directed at the fact that we were unbound, and suddenly hands were all over us as the packing tape was again wrapped around our wrists (individually, inside wrist to inside wrist, in front), and for the first time, our ankles. We were then dragged a short distance to a blanket on the ground. I asked for help to lie down, and many hands, including Soumana's, rather gently assisted in this excruciating process. But I was down, bound hand and foot, exhausted and freezing cold, staring up into a glorious mass of stars. Louis, Soumana, and I lay rigidly, side by side on the thin single blanket. After some time, maybe twenty minutes, someone knelt at our feet and, without explanation, sliced the tape binding Louis' and my ankles. I don't believe Soumana was bound.

We were being closely watched. There was quiet bustle all around us. Figures and voices would emerge, then fade into the stygian darkness. People cruised by for a look, their faces starless black patches against the night sky. Discussions ensued about a possible, then an expected air strike. Was this to scare us or was it genuine? I think the latter but don't really know. I didn't even know if I wanted an air strike.

There seemed to be many people, certainly a couple of dozen, milling about us in the pitch darkness—thus the name we subsequently gave to this camp: Central Station. The moon had yet to rise. Snippets of conversation registered in my semi-conscious mind, one in particular. As the hubbub settled down and I drifted further toward sleep, I heard what I took to be a young, female, Parisian-accented voice, close at hand, say matter-of-factly, "But surely we did not get into this just to murder old men?" I might, I suppose, have already been dreaming, but I don't think so. I did not hear that memorable voice again.

CHAPTER 3

THE BOARD OF DIRECTORS

===

I look'd to Heaven, and tried to pray;
But or ever a prayer had gusht,
A wicked whisper came, and made
My heart as dry as dust.

===

Tuesday, 16 December, Day 3, started early. Sounds of stirring all around us brought me slowly awake, as confused memories of our parlous situation flooded into my mind. It was still pitch dark. We were ordered to our feet but I could not move. Louis asked Soumana and some others to lift me into a standing position as I strove to keep my back straight during the process. The cold had not helped. We'd had perhaps two or three hours of rest.

As they hustled us toward a couple of trucks there seemed to be fewer, if still a significant number, of people about. Some must have slipped away before we woke. Louis and I were assigned to separate vehicles and each of us bleakly considered the possibility that we would never see each other again.

Louis was put in the middle position in Omar's truck, with Ibrahim by the passenger window. I was envious. I had spent time with them and thought I understood what they would and would not do. They were very much the devils I knew, and now I would have to start all over again with another crew.

Once Louis was settled, Hassan and a couple of additional *frères* we had not seen before climbed onto the haphazardly loaded supplies in Omar's truck bed, and off they went, roaring adroitly down a steep, ragged, boulder-strewn slope that was slowly emerging from the dawn mists.

I was then thrust beside the driver of another vehicle, someone who was introduced as Ahmed, a shifty-looking individual in his late twenties with a face deeply scarred by smallpox. Despite an ever-present grin (we quickly assigned him the name "Smiley Face"), he had the coldest eyes imaginable and exhibited an unrelentingly hostile attitude toward us. His hate for us and all we stood for was palpable.

Ahmed and I were joined by a rather nattily clad, stolid, taciturn, turbaned figure in a knee-length maroon tunic and matching trousers. He did not introduce himself and hardly acknowledged my presence, which was tough to pull off when he was sharing a bucket seat with me. As he swung aboard, he wedged his AK-47 between his body and the door, further adding to our intimacy and to his distress at rubbing shoulders and hips with an infidel. The others called him Abdul Rahman and we subsequently, and unimaginatively, dubbed him "AR." All deferred to his authority.

AR appeared to be in his mid-thirties and often wore a stern, hard, and impenetrable expression. He sported a long, dense, black beard and not much of his closely turbaned face was visible. AR was among the most deeply committed and ardently faithful *mujahideen* we encountered, tirelessly assiduous in his duties. His answer to my unwanted proximity was to try—without great success—to ignore it.

Off we drove in Omar's wake. Ahmed was no Omar when it came to driving skills, however, and within less than ten minutes we were hung up on a large boulder. There followed a Keystone Kops episode with everyone working at cross-purposes. Big egos and fierce pride got in the way at every turn, and everyone seemed anxious to take offence at any suggestion of a deemed slight or disparaging remark. Some pushed while others pulled. Bits and pieces of metal and random tools that had been strewn about the passenger floor-well rarely accomplished what was required and, when cast aside, all too often simply disappeared into the desert sand. It took us about an hour to get free of that rock, during which time Omar's crew, having realized we were not following, returned to wait at the foot of the hill, very careful to offer neither advice nor criticism. Nevertheless, by the time we were on our way, Ahmed had lost a great deal of face and was in a foul mood.

As the sun rose and the day wore on, the topography began to change again as we relentlessly pushed northward. The terrain became less hilly, less rocky; the *wadis* were shallower, and there was ever less vegetation. The horizon seemed to stretch farther and farther before us as the soil became sandier and whiter and harder packed. The temperature, even with the breeze created by our increasing speed over the flattening landscape, climbed high into what I judged to be the forties as we sat crammed together, stewing in the sweltering heat.

By noon we were deep into the Malian desert and the drivers pumped up the pace to well over a hundred kilometres an hour. Soon, exhilarated by the freedom to be reckless and foolish, they raced the two trucks against each other across this flat, featureless white pan. The trucks vied for line and position, sometimes almost touching as the boys in the back screamed insults at each other and encouragement to their respective drivers. The speedometer reached 120, then 130. Everybody was whooping it up and having a whale of a time. Surely, I thought, at these speeds an animal burrow or sizable rock would send a truck and its human cargo cartwheeling over the desert wastes.

After an hour of this craziness, we reached a line of hills lying across our path. The drivers headed, straight as an arrow, for a particular spot and there, under some trees, was an uncamouflaged cache of fuel and water in barrels, one of which proudly wore pale-blue UN livery. Each truck carried a steel drum (forty-five imperial gallons/fifty-four U.S. gallons) of diesel fuel and another of water. After the drums already on board were emptied—the first into the vehicles and the second into individual water bottles, jugs, and canteens—the spent barrels were switched out with the full, with no attempt to disguise or hide the empties left behind. Louis and I had a chance to chat and compare notes. More sardines were on offer, but again I could not stomach the thought, and satisfied myself with the few dry dates I had pocketed the previous day. But at least now I was drinking water, in copious quantities, whenever I could and was finally able to pee a little.

On another occasion, Louis asked Omar if they were not afraid that someone would steal fuel and water from these undis-guised caches. He was shocked by the question. First, Omar explained, there is a strictly enforced desert code: nobody, ever, took anybody's water, tires, or fuel unless it was a question of life or death. Even in such circumstances, only the minimum needed to survive would be taken and then replaced precisely where it was taken as quickly as humanly possible. In the course of our movements we would see many such caches, including stacks of tires, and our drivers would note as we drove by, "That's ours" or "That is someone else's." We could never see any difference in outward appearance. Further, Omar noted, his usual hubris bub-bling to the surface, "Nobody in these parts is willing to incur the wrath of Al Qaeda."

When Ahmed was ready to leave after taking on water and fuel, he ordered his crew to mount up and we were off, unmindful that Omar's crew was not at all ready. Ahmed obviously did not like meekly following in old Omar's wake (Omar's vast age—forty-seven—was always a magnet for sly, derogatory comments along the lines of "You know, he used to be one of the great drivers, but now his eyesight is failing—such a pity"), and Ahmed relished this opportunity for independence, which Abdul Rahman seemed to encourage. Given the dramatic difference in their driving and navigational skills, however, I was not happy with this development.

As we launched across another vast desert plain on the other side of the ridge, there was great debate between Ahmed and AR over the right course, each of them vigorously pointing in directions about thirty degrees apart. The ensuing decisions seemed to me arbitrary in the extreme, except that we continued to head more or less north. Finally, AR concluded that Ahmed had no idea where he was and ordered him to find and link up with Omar. Ahmed, with ill grace, tried to convince AR that with the bright new GPS he brought from beneath his tunic, all would be well. They fired it up, fiddled with it for a few minutes, held it upside down, and punched buttons at random, regularly smacking it against the dashboard to encourage better performance. When that produced no useful results, Ahmed was ordered up a small mesa and once on the flat upper surface, he switched on his lights and proceeded to turn in a tight, slow circle. At the completion of 360 degrees, he stopped and scanned the horizon to the south, southeast, and southwest for about ten minutes, and then repeated the whole procedure.

On the third or fourth try, we all spotted a barely perceptible flash of light on the far horizon. Ahmed pointed the truck in that direction. He then flashed his lights every few minutes and would receive an answering flash from the approaching Omar. I couldn't help thinking that we had wasted an hour exclusively because one driver wanted to avoid having to follow the other.

Together again, probably around two in the afternoon, the two vehicles set off over a final stretch of flatness that gradually gave way to rougher, bumpier terrain: more scrub, deeper *wadis*, more rocks, and more back torture. After another hour or so we mounted the fairly steep slope of a ravine and at the top we were waved to a stop by the other vehicle.

There was an excited conference, some very serious expressions, and macho posturing. None of which boded well—or perhaps it did?

Eventually, Louis came over and said that Ibrahim had told him that it seemed we were being followed by three trucks in the far distance. They were apparently generating a large dust plume, as no doubt we had been as well. I could not see them, but he assured me they were there. But who were they? Why were they following us? And what were their intentions?

The boys prepared for war, strapping on ammunition vests holding ten AK magazines each, in addition to those already mounted on their rifles. They quickly set up a DShK 12.7 mm heavy machine gun on a rapidly assembled mount in the back of Ahmed's truck, and loaded what looked like a twenty-five-round belt of the heavy-calibre ammunition. In addition, two 7.62 mm general-purpose machine guns were unlimbered as our captors prepared to take on whoever seemed to be in pursuit.

The speculation was that these were the forces of Ibrahim Ag Bahanga, a rogue Tuareg rebel leader in Mali's eastern desert area. We had, of course, studied the who's who of distantly related Tuareg insurgencies in Mali and Niger and knew that Bahanga had refused to participate in any of the many Algerian-brokered peace deals between the government of Mali and its various Tuareg rebel groupings. He was known to be fiercely jealous of his territory, attacking anybody who dared enter his desert domain without prior permission, very much including the Malian army and police. And while I hardly knew our captors at this point, I did not think that they were likely to ask anybody's permission to do anything.

Bahanga was also the sometime ally of the Niger rebel leader Aghali Alambo, the Tuareg head of the Mouvement des Nigériens pour la justice (which held sway just across the nearby border to the east), the very guys we had been trying to get the government of President Tandja to talk to about a peace deal in Niger. Louis and I briefly discussed whether our fortunes would be improved were we to fall into the hands of Bahanga's gang, but such speculation was clearly moot as our AQIM kidnappers had no intention of letting that happen.

The first plan was to leave Ahmed's truck and most of the *muja-hideen* and fire power to block Bahanga's advance while Omar's truck escaped northward with Louis and me aboard. But for reasons that were not explained, they then decided to try to outrun them and fight only if the pursuers got close. Thus, kitted out for battle, and with Louis and me once again in the forward truck with Omar at the wheel and Soumana and our two original captors in the back, we set off—very fast. It was all too evident from the outset that nobody was going to worry about the comfort of the hostages. At least this time I had two free hands to mitigate the damage.

My impression was that we were travelling significantly faster than we had before and Omar was doing everything he could to elude our pursuers. Aside from hoping that they would not be prepared to assume the same risks such speed entailed, Omar looked for tracks that he could follow and then suddenly, when some topographical feature obscured us for a moment from our pursuers, veer off over a nearby rise, ideally over a hard-baked surface, in such a manner that Bahanga's trucks might not realize we had left the more evident track. For three hours we tried a variety of these ploys and eventually, at a high point, the truck behind signalled a halt and after a meticulous scan of the area to the south, we were deemed safe. Whether we had lost our pursuers or they had simply given up or, indeed, we had left their territory was never clear.

Late in the afternoon we had another brief rest stop, a glass of tea, a long drink of water, and a couple more dates. I was then reassigned back to the Ahmed/AR vehicle and we were off again, or such was the plan. When we were all loaded up and set to leave, Ahmed's truck would not start, would not even turn over. However, the surface was hard and four of the *mujahideen* simply pushed the vehicle a short distance, Ahmed popped the clutch, and we were on our way. But the generator needle would not register. Nobody seemed the least concerned that we were setting out across one of the most inhospitable regions in the world in a vehicle with a failed electrical system.

This was my introduction to the extreme fatalism of these *jihadi* warriors, where everything comes down to *Insha'Allah* (God willing, or If it is God's will) which flows from the Qur'anic admonition that Allah decides everything: all that occurs is exclusively according to God's will.

The trucks now regularly changed lead so the machismo would not get out of hand. Meanwhile, AR was intent on understanding the new GPS gizmo. After he learned to hold it the right way up and stopped beating it up when it did not do what he wanted, he began to get the hang of it. He had Ahmed veer significantly off course, around hills, and take different lines from Omar's straight-ahead celestial navigation approach so that AR could let the GPS lead him back to Omar's course. AR was clearly fascinated by that marvellous instrument. (Omar never touched a GPS receiver, and, as far as I know, never got lost.) Each time we veered away from Omar and Louis, however, I would recall that the vehicle batteries (that model has two) were not charging. If we got stuck in sand we were going nowhere and would be incapable of performing even that high-ground, light-circle, come-and-get-me manoeuvre to attract Omar's help.

Sure enough, as dusk deepened and the two vehicles were more or less travelling in tandem, Ahmed again sought the lead. He swung out of the track, or *piste,* to pass Omar and drove straight into a patch of soft sand, where, revving the engine, he dug the truck deep and stalled. When he turned the key, absolutely nothing happened, not even a click. Just as when the day began some fourteen hours ago, there was a total muddle about what to do. Louis and I stood to the side and watched. At first, following what I came to understand was their strict code of self-help, Omar's crew also stood aside to let Ahmed's crew solve the problem and extract the vehicle. Indeed, on later occasions when four or five trucks were crossing a particularly challenging passage of dunes, if one became *ensablé* (stuck in the sand) the others would generally charge ahead, leaving the crew of the stuck vehicle to free themselves. I assume this strategy was designed to avoid endangering the whole group in the event of ambush or attack in circumstances in which they would all be particularly vulnerable.

Ahmed's crew dug sand from beneath the wheels, placed long strips of perforated steel matting underneath them, cut from the sheets used to create remote runways, and pushed, pulled, and shoved. Finally they asked Omar if he would offer them a tow, but the thin rope available quickly snapped. As all this was going on I was again, desperately, contemplating escape. I thought I had seen lights flashing on the horizon to the west, and began to convince myself that there was some kind of road nearby. If anything I was in worse physical shape than the day before but was at least putting the dehydration to rest and drinking whenever I could. I was significantly broken physically, however, and my mental state was not much better.

Ibrahim passed by and I asked him about those lights. "Oh," he said, barely suppressing a malicious grin, "that's a main road," and he slunk off into the dark, no doubt to watch what I would do. Knowing full well I was being set up, I still had difficulty preventing myself from simply wandering off westward across the desert. After all, I mused, how much worse could it be? I didn't fall for it in the end and as I stared further at the western horizon I realized that the winking lights were merely the effect of stars setting below.

Finally, without a word, Omar removed the second battery from his truck, shouldered aside the boys gathered around Ahmed's engine compartment, swapped it for one of the dead ones, hooked it up and we were off again. On and on we pressed through the night, over every kind of terrain, across every obstacle. Our tight cones of light slicing through the darkness ahead were mesmerizing. It seemed as if we were enclosed in a tunnel and I had the impression we were heading steadily down a long, sloping hill. Clearly, Abdul Rahman was bored, so he jacked up the volume of some sort of MP3 feature on his cellphone so that we might all enjoy loud, inspirational speeches by Osama Bin Laden, Abou Musab Al Zarqawi, and other Al Qaeda luminaries. I imagined they were about the imperative of tearing out the eyes of the infidels, and AR punctuated these tirades by a braying throat clearing every few seconds, which drove me to distraction.

Many hours later, we reached an extremely difficult passage—almost like descending a dry waterfall—and saw furtive lights far in the distance below. The crew in the back became jubilant. It must have been well past midnight when we rounded a rocky promontory and the vehicles were suddenly surrounded by shouting, leaping, AK-waving *mujahideen*. Ibrahim began to scream "Allahu Akbar!" again and again as he stood in the back of Omar's truck, his Kalash held in a Ché stance, at the end of a straight right arm above his head. A mass of brothers pressed around our vehicles to greet our three original abductors as conquering heroes. Louis and I were much scrutinized at the outset, faces again staring fixedly at us from twenty centimetres away, but soon we were forgotten in the celebration of the victorious warriors. We left our trucks and stood together at the side of the mêlée, each taking some comfort in the simple presence of the other after a long, impossibly tiring, and angst-ridden day. We were largely ignored for a time as the celebration seethed around us. New, mostly young faces of every hue appeared and stared. Others hung back, afraid, as if we might contaminate them with our godlessness. My disorientation seemed about as complete as I thought it could get.

Eventually, we were escorted to yet another blanket on the ground in the lee of a truck, as a fierce, sand-laden wind was getting up and beginning to howl.

Louis and I were too tired, cold, and numb to speak, but soon we were joined by two new faces. None of those we already knew was present. The central figure was an older beturbaned Arab of about sixty, clad in a Saudi-style brown, gold-edged, semi-transparent garment like an academic gown, worn over a spotless white tunic and light trousers reaching to mid-calf, and he wore sandals. He had dark, piercing eyes set fairly close together and a long, straggly, grey, henna-streaked beard. He sat cross-legged before us, accompanied by a portly, short-haired, round-faced acolyte who seemed to be in his early thirties, wearing dark, more operational clothing and round, steel-rimmed glasses.

The older man, whom we saw by the flickering light of a nearby fire, was positively courtly in his manners and gestures. He spoke excellent French and after observing my crabbed position on the blanket (the only one my damaged back would accommodate), asked if there were anything they could do to make me more comfortable. I replied that there was not. He then turned his attention to Louis and immediately expressed surprise and evident anger when he saw the gash across his eyebrow and the blood on his shirt, issuing a stream of invective in Arabic to someone behind him. He asked Louis how he had received the wound but Louis, to avoid exacerbating relations with the sullen Hassan, refused to be drawn and simply allowed that the injury was not serious.

Tea in those little glasses was served and I was asked who I was and what—precisely—I had been doing in Africa before I was taken. I repeated the whole story, essentially reciting my letter of appointment from UN Secretary-General Ban Ki-moon, which had explained that I was to serve as his Special Envoy with a view to arriving at a negotiated settlement of the Second Tuareg Rebellion by bringing the government of Niger and the MNJ to the negotiating table. I said that my initial task had been to explore opportunities for dialogue with both sides and to lay the groundwork for them to enter into concrete talks. To that end, I had been instructed to approach the MNJ rebels to secure their commitment to a peaceful resolution of the crisis, and I acknowledged that this had already been achieved. I explained that my mission, at least during the initial stages, was to be carried out discreetly, with no public announcement, in order to avoid embarrassing the government of

Niger. Our AQIM inquisitors did not seem much interested in the specifics once they had satisfied themselves that I was indeed the UN wallah they had intended to grab.

As I neared the end of my response, the political commissar type with the steel-rimmed spectacles demanded—in near-perfect English—to know what had become of my documents. When I again explained that I had been on a day's outing and had left all my identity papers in my hotel room in Niamey, he delivered a harsh lecture on the irresponsibility of this kind of behaviour. Documents, he insisted, had to be carried at all times. Indeed, it was "illegal" to do otherwise. But the senior man soon tired of this tirade and waved his aide into silence with the back of his hand.

I then asked for their names, and with a small, fleeting smile, henna-beard said that while we might get to such things at some point in the future, now was not that time. Clearly, he noted, we needed rest, and without further ceremony he rose and left, trailing the others in his wake.

That was the first and last we ever saw of either of those two. My impression was that they were high-placed AQIM figures—perhaps the older one was some kind of mullah, or spiritual leader, high up in the food chain, perhaps a member of the Council of Worthies, or Notables—but of course I do not know. I assumed that they had been sent to put eyes on their big catch in order to better inform future decisions, but I have no idea what they got out of our meeting. In any case, Louis and I decided that these were senior players in AQIM and therefore named that camp Board of Directors.

I slept fitfully, flat on my back, incapable of moving much except for my involuntary, violent shivering from the cold, and was beset by horrible dreams for what remained of that night. The essence of this series of semi-waking nightmarish vignettes was a catalogue of horrors that had or would be faced by me and various members of my family: accidents, illnesses, failures, embarrassment, ruination. Whenever I struggled, short of breath, into wakefulness, I contemplated my circumstances and judged the dreams preferable. I desperately wanted to escape my current reality and sought eagerly to return to any dreamland that would have me.

CHAPTER 4

TV CAMP

O Wedding-Guest! this soul hath been
Alone on a wide, wide sea:
So lonely 'twas, that God Himself
Scarce seemèd there to be.

Our fourth day of captivity began well before dawn. And again, while many people—perhaps twenty—had been around when we arrived the previous evening, the only ones present when we woke were the crews of the two trucks that had carried us from Central Station. After a glass of tea and a rather tasty piece of fresh-baked bread we were on our way again. The wind, which had built throughout the night, now was a moderate gale, our first sandstorm. Visibility was down to ten or fifteen metres and, at least at first, our drivers proceeded with some caution.

The two trucks left in convoy, Louis and I again assigned to separate vehicles. But after a couple of hours, Ahmed could no longer stand to follow Omar, so he set off on his own and quickly got lost. We made more light-circles atop a rise, and eventually Omar found us. Fed up with screwing up in front of the prisoners and, I think, because he'd had enough hip rubbing with this weak and damaged infidel, AR had me transferred into Omar's truck while

Louis went with him and the ill-disciplined Ahmed, and we again set off at a reduced pace into the howling wind and hazy dawn.

After a few hours of bumping across undulating and relatively soft sand, we crested a small rise and there before us in a wide desert valley, through the rust-hued gloom, was a magically bizarre sight: a vast and widespread herd of thousands of camels plodding slowly across our path through the veil of wind-blown sand. The animals were led by a trio of Tuaregs swathed in blue, sitting atop their majestic light-coloured beasts and seemingly oblivious to, or at least unmindful of, our intrusion into this timeless tableau.

By mid-morning the wind had begun to abate and visibility had improved, but it was still cold, windy, and overcast. We were driven to the base of a small yet fairly steep, rounded hill and found it was already occupied. A couple of trucks, just like the ones we were in, were stationed at its base, heavy machine guns mounted and manned. Without a word, our vehicles took up positions so that the small hill was boxed with armed vehicles protecting each of its quadrants. We were instructed to leave the cab, mount the slope and, halfway up, to sit on yet another blanket thrown on the drifting sand.

It was now bitterly cold. As we left the vehicles we grabbed a couple of old coverings in which the now-deployed heavy weapons had been wrapped, in order to protect ourselves against the biting wind. One was a light, plastic fibre–filled yellow bedspread decorated with blue roses and numerous burn holes, and the other was a dirty, crusty orange-and-green blanket of synthetic material.

When we reached the designated spot, wearing our newly purloined shawls, I walked in circles around the blanket because I continued to have trouble maintaining any kind of sitting position. Not much was said until we were approached by a figure clothed entirely in black from turban (wrapped Tuareg-like, with only a very narrow slit open around the eyes), through long, tunic-like *jelabiyah,* to pants and high-top running shoes.

This was Mokhtar Belmokhtar, and given the authority with which he moved and the deference everyone paid him, he was clearly the man—their revered leader. He exuded a palpably commanding presence and, we were to learn, seemed to exercise his leadership with skill and subtlety.

He sat down opposite Louis, loosened his turban to reveal more of his face, and motioned to me to join them on the blanket. I knelt instead, seeking to keep my back straight. Omar and Ibrahim sat beside us in their status-enhancing role as hostage takers and interpreters. In response to a quiet question from the man in black, I had the impression that Omar had explained my back problem.

Despite the voluminous black robes and turban, he was relatively slight, with a heavily weathered and deeply lined face and curly black hair. He looked older than what we were told were his thirty-seven years. His eyes were dark and deep set below prominent brows. He had thin lips set in a straight line, and his mouth twisted from time to time into a ghost of a cold, almost wry smile. He wore the mandatory beard and moustache, which—unlike most of the others—seemed to be lightly trimmed. His most distinguishing feature was a deep almost vertical scar that began above the middle of his right eyebrow, crossed his right eyelid, and continued across his right cheek, disappearing into his moustache. He was alleged to have a glass eye, but all I could discern was that the deep scar had distorted his right eyelid and somewhat closed that eye.

His troops called him Khaled. Of course we named him "Jack"—as in one-eyed jacks—which suited him so well that later, during an intense discussion about our fate, I waved a finger at him and burst out, "Come on, Jack!" which confused the interpreter (Omar, at the time) and stopped the conversation cold because nobody knew whom I was talking to or about.

At this, our first encounter, Jack passively and not particularly aggressively scrutinized us for a while in silence. After a time Ibrahim rather excitedly asked me, "Do you recognize anyone here?" While there were a few new faces about, he clearly wanted to know if I recognized Jack.

Truthfully, I replied, "No," to nobody's surprise but perhaps a little disappointment.

Jack was all business and chose to speak through Ibrahim rather than Omar (he was careful to spread his favours about), asking for our names. Then he wanted to know what we had been doing in Niger, and he too focused on my lack of identification papers. The interrogation was superficial, even cursory. Twenty minutes later we were bundled back into the trucks. The weapons were dismounted and we drove for another hour or so to a dry desert valley scattered with some sparse tufts of sharp grass and a few dense bushes and low acacia thorn trees.

These, we soon learned, were the essential attributes of a camp. The vehicles were nestled into the vegetation in a rather casual attempt at camouflage, and everybody rested as the temperature rose at the approach of midday. Louis and I were assigned a position that was, in effect, our designated prison or living space. It was situated between the high bushes and the large left front wheel of Omar's truck, which together offered a fair amount of shade. There seemed to be a lot of coming and going around us but only a few people settled in our immediate vicinity. Omar was nowhere in sight but both Ibrahim and Hassan very much were. We were their captives. To some degree they viewed us as their trophies and they reacted jealously when any other brother, for whatever reason, sought our attention.

As the afternoon came and went, Louis and I considered attempting to play *pétanque* (boules, or bocce) with the small, hard desert melons growing nearby, if only to get our minds off our predicament for a moment. But in the end we couldn't summon either the energy or the will. There is no doubt that I was approaching a state of severe depression, very fragile and afraid. As an experienced geopolitical analyst it was well nigh impossible not to conclude that we were in deep shit. There was no obvious solution to our predicament and none of the usual options seemed likely to pertain.

As we wandered about examining those melons, which we were told were poisonous, we were careful to remain well within the sight and easy reach of our jailers, and we continued walking long after the *pétanque* idea had been abandoned. The walking felt great. It eased the pain in my back and seemed to work off some of the built-up anxiety. Further, it struck us as likely to contribute to a less fitful sleep, so we started to do laps or circuits at a steady pace, not fast but purposeful, more than a stroll.

By the time we returned to our blankets near the truck, a major discussion group had formed around Jack, thirty or forty metres away. About twenty people had gathered in a semicircle in front of him, most of whom we had not seen previously. The discussion seemed very intense. We knew that we had to be the subject, and I began (not for the last time) to fear the worst. Were we being tried in some kind of desert kangaroo court? How would the verdict be carried out? Soon we started walking again.

In the evening we were brought a single bowl of rice containing a few bits of mutton and, at our insistence, we were each given a spoon. Our captors ate out of a common pot using only their right hands, so the spoon was a concession to Western fastidiousness, and clearly our request had not surprised them. We were also given a four-litre plastic jug that had recently contained motor oil and was now filled with what I considered to be pretty iffy water, but by then I was drinking anything.

We were told that while water in the desert was always scarce and needed to be rationed and managed responsibly, we would not be deprived of water to drink. We should, Omar said, approach any of *les frères* with our four-litre container to seek a refill when we needed more.

❖

After our brief and first more or less full meal since our capture, it had already begun to grow dark and we started to prepare for sleep, using the coverings from our morning meeting with Jack to make a bed beside the left front wheel of Omar's truck. Just as we were about to doze off, we heard a great commotion around the front of the truck, a metre from our heads. The hood was opened and three large, heavy tires were thrown into a pile. By the time we had sat up to figure out what was going on, somebody had placed a laptop computer on the stack of spares and was plugging it into the cigarette lighter socket in the engine compartment.

We were at a loss but feared this had something to do with the big palaver that had gone on throughout the afternoon. Had a judgment been rendered? Were we about to star in a new YouTube horror?

With some ceremony, a DVD was produced and inserted into the laptop drive and we were chivvied around to have pride of place in front of the screen. The others pressed about us, the younger ones in front. Three or four prepubescent boys among them, their screen-lit faces rapt with anticipation, excitedly tried to watch us and the laptop simultaneously.

Soon we heard a loudly pulsing, urgent, musical beat and the screen was filled with a black flag, the lower half of which was covered with white Arabic script; in the upper portion was a globe surmounted by an AK-47 assault rifle—the Al Qaeda banner. Using the traditional and mandatory Islamic opening, a voice intoned in Arabic, "In the name of Allah the most merciful," and the centre of the screen began to fill with vignettes of all kinds of horrors: those aircraft slamming into the twin towers, U.S. and allied vehicles being destroyed in Iraq and Afghanistan by IEDs, video cameras slaved to the sights of Dragunov sniper rifles blasting the heads off GIs and then murdering those who came to their assistance, suicide bombers driving explosive-laden trucks through fences and into buildings or crowds, immediately followed by massive explosions. Some scenes carried subtitles giving the date and location of the horror. Others showed the happy, excited suicide bomber explaining his joy at the prospect of martyring himself for such a noble purpose.

There were also clips of their now happily defunct "great emir," Bin Laden, uttering in his quiet and reasonable-sounding voice his latest threats to tear the heart out of the degenerate West. A stocky, heavily bearded, white-robed and turbaned American, whom we were told was Adam Gadahn, a Jewish Californian convert to Islam and Al Qaeda, made his first of many appearances. Gadahn was ridiculing the American president—in English with Arabic subtitles—and issuing dire warnings aimed at U.S. audiences of the disasters that would befall America if the United States and its allies did not quit "Muslim lands."

While Bin Laden was lionized by the young men around us, the star of each show was the brash, in-our-face (and also happily defunct) Al Zarqawi, a Jordanian who was the former leader of the Iraqi franchise of Al Qaeda. Al Zarqawi had walked their talk on cleansing "Muslim lands" of the presence of infidels with passion and utter ruthlessness, and without compromise. He was their man of action. He did, in their view, what others merely talked and fantasized about. The scene the young ones loved best on what we came to call TV Night was Al Zarqawi standing, legs planted wide, with a vicious, open-mouthed grin on his face, firing the entire hundred-round magazine of a Belgian light machine gun just past the camera with the sound jacked way up. We could almost hear his scream of whatever the Arabic equivalent is of "Get some!"

Each time an episode of mayhem and destruction occurred on the screen, the crowd pressing around Louis and me shouted, "Allahu Akbar!" and immediately swivelled their eyes to watch how we were enjoying the show. Without my glasses, I could read none of the signs or subtitles, so Louis read them out loud until I quietly asked him to stop. The DVD did not need a great deal of interpretation.

Obviously, these propaganda videos were intended to pump up the boys, to remind them that they were part of a large global cause in which sacrifice was a major element. And it was having the desired impact particularly on the younger *mujahideen,* whose eyes glistened with excitement as they watched the Western infidels being butchered and humiliated over and over again. The senior members of the group were less caught up in the show, and the laptop operator seemed to be choosing the clips to be displayed with some care. I could only imagine what he was skipping and I did not for a moment presume that anything was being avoided out of generosity but rather cold, hard pragmatism. They did not want to break their hostages, at least not yet.

In many ways, both for the assembled Belmokhtar group of AQIM and for me, the scenes that elicited the strongest emotion were the all too familiar images of black-hooded, orange-clad figures, chained hand and foot, shuffling around those tiny cages in Guantanamo. These were indignities perpetrated by my side—the "good guys." Those images, and the scenes of German shepherds, fangs bared, straining to get at broken men cowering in corners, and the piles of naked bodies forced into obscene intimacy and, always, the iconic black-hooded figure, mutely perched barefoot on a box in a short black poncho with wires dangling from his outstretched fingers in the disgraceful Abu Ghraib prison in Baghdad made me, in the midst of my own mental anguish, feel deep shame.

The leaden and menacing stares of our Al Qaeda captors eloquently made a mockery of our aggressive Western claims to harbour superior values. The looks on their faces declared that any such moral high ground had been well and truly abandoned by the West.

It is therefore at least paradoxical that those wretched videos and photos of Guantanamo and Abu Ghraib may have resulted in Louis' and my captivity being less violent than it otherwise might have been, for it seemed to me that we were spared worse treatment because our abductors were anxious to demonstrate that they didn't stoop to such stuff, which, of course, we know is not generally the case. That particular myth, however, with that particular group of AQIM hostage takers, probably served us well.

Thus, I found that the most appalling of those TV Night video images were not the mass murders and individual assassinations perpetrated by Al Qaeda and their allies against our soldiers and civilians, which were never easy to behold but were less difficult to understand. That was simply Al Qaeda being Al Qaeda. Rather, it was the intimate and almost palpable proof of our side's methodically applied, officially sanctioned, and so casually administered barbarity, parsed into the bureaucratic banalities and legal niceties of officially sanctioned abuse and torture, that was hard to absorb. Viewing such scenes, I could not help but believe that if we were capable of such outrages and carelessly willing to resort to torture-as-entertainment, then we had indeed strayed into truly dangerous ethical territory.

The ease with which faux-legal language was coined in Washington and unopposed throughout the West in a cursory attempt to legitimize the illegitimate, the arbitrary manner in which long-standing international conventions were set aside, and the glibness with which word games were employed to condone such practices should have stunned us all. The methodical development of "black sites" and concepts like "extraordinary rendition" (subcontracting torture) and "enhanced interrogation," the invention of ersatz juridical explanations of why water-boarding was not torture, and other such despicable behaviour indeed made a mockery of our Western pretensions to be champions of human rights, dignity, and international justice. Further, without a shred of doubt, they have massively increased recruitment to the Islamist cause and markedly amplified the threat against Western interests and the security of individual Americans and their friends and allies.

If the dreadful events of 11 September 2001 could so easily dismantle the bulwarks of free, just, and open societies that had taken us centuries to build, then yes, our claims to a higher moral standard were in fact a sham, and surely there were no effective limits to what we were prepared to visit upon our enemies.

No, these were not made-in-Canada practices, justifications, and facilities, but how easily we in our country and our friends throughout Europe abandoned our much-vaunted principles and meekly, often enthusiastically, went along. The bulk of our usually vocal human rights advocates and politicians were muted or stunned into silence when the need to avenge the insult and atrocity of 9/11 was allowed to pervert the law and sully the reputation of our friends and neighbours—perversions that have done and continue to do the West incalculable harm throughout the world. We are clearly guilty by such association. And Louis and I were reaping the consequences.

When the passionate screams from the pumped-up junior *mujahideen* had faded, they disconnected the laptop and left us to try to sleep, snuggled against the wheel of Omar's truck. I managed, with help from Louis, to lie flat on my back on our thin blanket and, for the first time since our capture, I managed four or five hours of nightmare-punctuated sleep. As I drifted off, I was comforted by the fact that it simply didn't make sense for our kidnappers to have gone to such trouble just to execute us. I knew we were unlikely to be quitting those dunes very soon, but we did seem to have an immediate future. The longer term could await the morrow.

CHAPTER 5

VIDEO ONE

===

"I fear thee and thy glittering eye,
And thy skinny hand so brown."—
"Fear not, fear not, thou Wedding-Guest!
This body dropt not down."

===

We awoke on Thursday, Day 5, about a thousand kilometres north of the reviewing stand in Tillabéri. For the first time since that horrible moment the previous Sunday afternoon, we were not being hustled into a vehicle to smash our way cross-country. Looking around us we implicitly understood why.

Quite evidently, we had arrived. We were there, deep in the Sahara desert, impossibly far from any kind of familiar frame of reference. I recalled that when we had visited the far northern mining community of Arlit, in Niger, only three months previously (perhaps seven hundred kilometres east-southeast from where we were), I had been intimidated by the desert's immediate vastness. There had been no transition. Step beyond that runway and there was pitiless nothing—forever, a nothing that would kill you very quickly. Walking on the outskirts of Arlit had been like touching the inner skin of the protective, atmosphere-preserving bubble of some science-fiction mining operation on a far-flung asteroid. But here in the far north of Mali there were no outskirts, no human or geophysical link—however tenuous—with anything I had known beyond, of course, Louis. I had never before felt so isolated and forsaken.

It was chilly but the sun was bright and the air clear. All around us people were stirring. Clad still in the clothes in which we had been captured, we combed what hair we had with our fingers and, in what was to become a morning ritual, shook the sand from our blankets and draped them over nearby bushes to air. Once we had begun to move about, one of the young lads approached with our initial desert breakfast. We then set off on our first self-programmed walk, following in the footprints we had made around our tiny track among the desert melons and between our sleeping position and those of some of our jailers. The younger ones were still asleep, with blankets pulled over their heads to block out the sun, while the older ones were busy with camp chores. Memories of getting teenaged daughters out of bed flooded my mind, along with the manifold ironies.

They let us pace, somewhat bemused as we went round and round. As soon as we began to walk the wrenching pain in my back again began to subside. We probably put in a couple of kilometres before returning to our sleeping position as the heat of the sun began to bite in earnest.

Omar approached and explained what were effectively the camp rules. He told us that we could ask to go *loin* (far) when one of us needed to defecate. We would be unobtrusively accompanied and we had to find a spot far enough but not too far away. However, as it would require revealing our nakedness (anathema to these prudish zealots), that place had to be well out of sight. And only one of us could go at a time, while the other remained in plain sight.

The rules for going *pas loin* (not far) were less complicated. We still had to ask for and receive permission to disappear behind a bush for a pee and we were admonished to do it modestly, prefer-ably from a kneeling position, which was not a bad idea given the usually windy conditions. After a while we stopped asking permission to go *pas loin* and nobody objected.

When I asked for a toothbrush Omar said unconvincingly that he would see what could be done. In the meantime he taught us how to break off branches from a particular kind of thorn tree growing nearby, and then peel off the bark around the break so that the fibres expanded, like a straw broom, and explained how this could be used to clean teeth. The thorns of the same tree, he pointed out, made excellent toothpicks. He also told us of the arak tree, the horseradish-flavoured roots of which made the best toothbrushes. He reverently explained the merits of the arak root, called *miswak,* which was extolled in the Qur'an and had nineteen magical, medicinal, and even strategic properties.

With no arak trees nearby, I borrowed Hassan's great bloody caricature of a commando knife and proceeded to hack branches from the designated substitute tree. Hassan was horrified that his cherished killing tool was being defiled by such a mundane task, but his *frères,* who clearly had little time for his macho posturing, were wryly amused. Louis and I were surprised at how effectively these brushes did the trick.

As soon as Omar had finished explaining the rules of our imprisonment we were joined by Jack and what we came to think of as his senior staff. This time the interrogation was a little more formal and aggressive, but not markedly so. He explained that we were his prisoners, that he led one of many groups of AQIM *mujahideen* and, speaking through Omar, outlined the organization's objectives. He also asserted that he and his *frères* were strict and devout Muslims who unreservedly followed God's word as revealed to the Prophet in the Qur'an without deviation or interpretation and to the letter.

He then, in quiet and measured tones, launched into a tirade against the hypocrisy of the Western-toady "apostate governments" (atheist or, more accurately, those who renounce belief) of the North African states (the near enemy) and the debauchery of the Jew-crusader, American-led Western governments (the far enemy) that had sent vast armies to ravage and occupy "Muslim lands." This was, of course, a theme to which he and almost every one of our AQIM interlocutors returned again and again.

Having got such an opening salvo off his chest and moving fairly smartly to the business of the moment, Jack then explained that we would be making a video to let the United Nations and the Canadian government know that we were in the hands of Al Qaeda so that a negotiating process could begin. I expected them to require us to read some prepared confessional screed, full of strutting rhetoric. I feared that they would also require us to acknowledge blame for all manner of horrors and spout lies and calumny against most of what we Canadians and the United Nations stood for—but there were no such demands. "Just say who you are," Jack outlined, "why you were in Niger, that we now hold you hostage, and ask your leaders to work to resolve your situation as expeditiously as possible, without," he firmly insisted, "resorting to violence, for that would go very badly for you."

That seemed straightforward enough and even in my still addled state I thought I could manage such a script. But I had a question. "If you want me to explain that we are your hostages, you had better tell me precisely who I am to say you are." That resulted in a fair amount of discussion in Arabic without benefit of interpretation. It seems they were trying to decide whether they were Al Qaeda in the Lands of the Islamic Maghreb or Al Qaeda in the Maghreb, or, and as they finally agreed, Al Qaeda in the Islamic Maghreb. It seemed to us that this whole routine was still a little novel for them and they were anxious to get it right. They had taken tourists before, but this was the first time they had grabbed people with international standing and they wanted to maximize the publicity impact of their coup.

Omar instructed us to follow them over a slight rise and down the reverse slope for little more than a hundred metres to a very large dark-green tent, which I had not known was there, nestled among a few sparse acacia trees. At the sight of the tent, my heart lurched, and I became for some moments quite terrified. Working away in the back of my mind over the past days had been the prospect that Louis and I would suffer the same fate as *Wall Street Journal* reporter Daniel Pearl at the hands of Khalid Sheikh Mohammed in Karachi in February 2002. Unlike nearly 300,000 YouTube viewers, I had not seen the dreadful video clip of his beheading but—perhaps worse—I had heard it described in excruciating detail and my imagination re-created the scene again and again, adding a seemingly infinite number of appalling variations.

At the sight of that damned great dark tent, surrounded by heavily armed, turban-wearing Arabs, my re-creation of that horror was given free rein.

Perhaps Omar sensed or even understood the cause of my disquiet, for as he walked between Louis and me he began very methodically to rehearse what we had just agreed would be the script. I was grateful for the diversion. He explained that I was to lead off and then Louis would get his say. I asked when Soumana, whom we had not seen for twenty-four hours, would speak, but this was quickly brushed off as "unnecessary." As I looked around for further clues to what might be about to happen, I noticed no particular excitement in the faces around us: no ghoulish anticipation that something messy and important was about to occur. I began to settle down a little.

As we got near the tent we were held back because they were not ready for us. I grabbed a moment to ask Louis to be sure to add anything I failed to include and to correct any stupidities I might utter, particularly as I had been instructed to speak in French. He nervously agreed to do so. We were both acutely aware that our captors' agenda was not congruent with our own. For them it was all about launching what they hoped would be expeditious negotiations. While that did seem like a useful objective, Louis and I were most immediately focused on the message, both visual and verbal, we would be sending to our families, who we knew would have been suffering terribly since they learned of our kidnapping—whenever that was.

Finally, we were ushered inside and there was a version of the tableau we have all seen in too many newscasts and movies. A black flag covered with white Arabic script was pinned to the wall of the tent opposite the side that had been opened to allow sunlight to illuminate the set. Standing immediately in front of that flag were four heavily armed men, a couple carrying AKs across their chests and the others holding the heavier, belt-fed machine guns. Two or three of them also had belts of ammunition criss-crossing their chests, Pancho Villa–like, and their faces were almost entirely obscured by their black turbans.

Louis and I were instructed to sit in front and at the feet of the armed tableau, and facing us with their backs to the open side, the audience for the impending show, were all the remaining members of the group. As if for a class photo, the youngest and smallest sat cross-legged in front with the bigger ones kneeling or standing behind them. In the centre of the front row was the laptop operator from the previous evening. Later we learned that his name was Julabib.

He was clearly in charge of the proceedings and held in his right hand a small, family-type video camera. My back would not allow me to sit cross-legged like Louis, so I sort of perched sideways on my left hip, my legs bent at the knee out to my right and most of my weight supported by my straight left arm. The entire floor of the tent was covered by a multitude of carpets, which I took to be a good sign. I considered it unlikely that in such a water-starved environment they would purposely soak them in blood.

Once we were all in place the cameraman looked squarely at me until he knew he had my attention, and I got a very clear impression that this was going to be a one-take production. Camera held out before him as he watched the small, flip-out LCD viewing screen, he held up three fingers of his left hand, then two, and one. He pointed and I began to speak.

I tried to speak slowly and articulate carefully. I gave my name and then noted that I was the "Special Envoy of the Secretary-General of the United States [sic] for Niger." I heard the error but was not to be deterred. I then explained that my mission had been to attempt to get the government of Niger to sit down with the Tuareg rebels with a view to forging a peace agreement and that in the course of my third visit to Niger my colleague, Louis Guay, and I had been captured in the late afternoon of Sunday, 14 December— five days previously—thirty-five kilometres from Niamey, Niger's capital, and that we were now the captives of Al Qaeda in the Islamic Maghreb. I urged "those responsible at the UN and in Canada" to engage in negotiations that would lead to our early release and indicated that the conditions in which we were being held were rudimentary in the extreme. I volunteered the fact that we were being treated "honourably" by our abductors (to suggest to our families that we were not being abused) and, as instructed, I cautioned against any kind of military action to secure our freedom.

Then, getting to the bit I cared most immediately about, I sent my love to my wife, Mary, "and my five [sic] children." I stressed how much I missed them, and said how much I regretted the pain, worry, and suffering these circumstances would be causing them. Just before I lost it I turned to Louis to allow him to take his turn.

Louis began slowly. He'd had more time to think—not always a good thing—and had watched and felt me waver as I got into the family bit. I tried to give him as much moral support as I could without interrupting and soon he was filling in the blanks I had left wide open. It was for each of us a wrenching, emotional experience but it was also cathartic.

We considered it a necessary step toward seeing this thing through and getting home. Thus, the dance had begun. We understood that the negotiations had been opened, and we assumed that our families would shortly know that we were alive and relatively well. Yes, they would be devastated by the Al Qaeda part but heartened by this invitation to the government and the United Nations to engage, and they would know that once engaged, the Canadian government could be a formidable force.

Following Louis' segment, we were led out of the tent but told to remain nearby in case they needed to do it again. As we waited near that great dark monster of a tent we could hear angry, shouted words that sounded very like threats and taunts from within, similar to the defiant screaming of slogans and brave posturing we had heard on TV Night.

Apparently the boys were again pumping themselves up, waving weapons and screaming insults at the video camera, decrying all the ills and evils perpetrated by the West and the United Nations against the innocent Muslim *ummah*—the worldwide Islamic community. We knew that such a conclusion to our taped messages would be unlikely to give our families the peace of mind we had so wished to impart. The slogan shouting went on for some time until they thought they had got their messages of hate and retribution just right. Then the cast trickled from the tent, glaring at us as they passed, with wild and adrenalin-suffused expressions. Sometime later we were told we could go, but where?

Suddenly, though, for the first time in five days, I did have somewhere to go and recalling Omar's instructions on hostage toiletry etiquette, I sought out a sentry in order to get permission to "go far." The only person in our immediate vicinity was someone who had evidently been assigned to watch us but I had not noticed him before, which was surprising because he cut an impressive figure. I approached him and asked where I should go and if I might bring a small quantity of water with me. He spoke reasonably good French that he seemed to be dredging up from a long unused part of his memory, and indicated a rather steep skree slope about 150 metres distant. He suggested the other side of that hill would be fine.

As for the water, he sternly pointed out that it was too precious to be wasted on such things. Instead, I should, on my walk to the suitably discreet spot, search for small, flat and smooth stones that would serve the purpose. I was skeptical but in no position to argue from any number of perspectives. The operation was successful and the stones smooth enough, but unsettling was the fact that hand washing, even left-hand washing, seemed out of the question. When I got back to our position, a little surreptitiously used drinking water was the best I could manage.

The new guard was speaking to Louis when I returned. He was atypically tall, perhaps six-two (188 cm), and had a slim but solid physique. His rich, curly black hair escaped around the fringes of his turban and was echoed in his full, curly black beard. He had high, wide-set, and prominent cheekbones over which his lightly pockmarked olive skin was tightly stretched. His large and bright deep-set, dark brown eyes were his most striking feature. They were so startling that it took me a moment before I realized that their impact had been enhanced by the application of kohl, an ancient form of black eyeliner.

He introduced himself as Omar, so, for Louis and me he inevitably became Omar Two. He was one of the more enigmatic and interesting of our kidnappers—deeply, fanatically, religious, very much a Salafist mystic and the closest thing to an Islamic scholar among them. Omar Two seemed to be a warrior-monk, a loner who saw himself as an avenging angel of Islam. He was in his mid-thirties, one of the older members of the group and had, he said, been raised in the crucible of the Islamic Brotherhood. He proudly allowed that he had been engaged in the Algerian *jihad* since he was a teenager. We were fairly sure he was Algerian but even that was not certain, and for these people nationalism—allegiance to or even identification with an apostate state—was something to be despised, but he was certainly North African.

Omar Two was interested in us, perhaps even intrigued, but he never, not for a moment, liked, admired, or befriended us, and that pretty much sums up how I felt about him. At this first meeting he forbade us to use the classic Arabic greeting *Salaam Aleikum* (Peace be upon you, or God be with you), because, as infidels, we were disqualified from invoking Allah in any context. He was both fascinated and appalled by what we represented. We were in his eyes inherently evil, literally godforsaken, and thus his implacable enemy. His only objective was to get us to convert, going to any length or using any tactic to achieve that end.

Only if we became brothers in faith could we have, in his clearly stated view, anything other than a steadfastly adversarial relationship, informed by mistrust and enmity. While Omar One would usually speak of "when you return home," Omar Two would invariably say something much more highly qualified: "Should you be allowed to return to your families" or "If it turns out that you do return to Canada."

We were left alone that afternoon. We walked some more and discussed at great length how long our video message would take to get to New York and Ottawa and how it was likely to be transmitted. Having seen the laptop, the GPS navigation devices, and the ubiquitous Thuraya satellite-phones, we were confident that our families and senior UN and Canadian government officials would be viewing it within hours—two or three days at the most. Immediately following the end of the recording session a truck had left the camp, and we assumed it had taken the video to a place from which it could be transmitted, probably directly to North America but possibly to a Canadian embassy in the region, or perhaps to Al Jazeera and eventual broadcast, a prospect we did not relish but considered a distinct possibility.

That night we were directed to sleep in the tent, on those thick, soft rugs. We had not realized, though, that it would be in close proximity to a dozen of our captors, principally the younger ones. It was an experience I think it is fair to say that nobody relished, and it was never again repeated. Once the tent flaps had been dropped it was absolutely pitch dark. The intimacy of our guards tossing and turning closely packed around us in that airless tent was distinctly unpleasant and, if truth be told, both Louis and I are accomplished snorers and I could feel the distaste of those around us at the sounds and smells emitted by these ancient barbarian infidels.

The atmosphere in the camp the next morning was relaxed and the contrast made it seem like a Sunday morning back home. The weather was cold at dawn and visibility was limited by sand in the air, which gave everything a brown-yellow hue. Our captors were going about their tasks in a rather desultory manner, no rush, no urgency, no excitement. Omar One was almost affable. Business was unfolding as it should. The video had been made and was on its way west. We asked where: to the United Nations or Canada? In response, Omar asked which would be preferable in our view. Without dissimulation we replied we had no idea. He merely shrugged, eloquently letting us know that it was our fate that was at issue and if we chose not to engage it would be at our own peril. Of course, his beliefs held that it was all predetermined anyway: all God's will, and His will would be done whatever our attitude.

As gear was being assembled I noticed that there seemed to be fewer people around and, in particular, that Khaled (Jack) and his staff seemed to have departed. We came to learn this was typical of his behaviour. He would simply show up with anywhere from one to three trucks (usually two) and stay for an hour or a few days. Sometimes he would meet with us but not always. If he wanted to talk to us, he would appear at our sleeping position with, in order of preference (both ours and his, as it turned out), Omar One, Ibrahim, Omar Two, or Hassan to interpret, as well as such senior staff as were available. We would all sit in a rough circle on our blankets and he would state his business, elicit answers, and be gone; there were very few pleasantries, but oddly it was all a little formal and businesslike and not disrespectful of us or our space.

That morning, Omar One joined us in the tent once some of the side flaps were rolled and tied up. It seemed he wanted to chat or, as we soon found out, preach, for such was his profession prior to committing himself to *jihad*. As an itinerant preacher he had travelled widely. He was full of stories about the hot water he had got into and how the purity of his mission and Allah's beneficence had always extricated him from dicey situations. Omar was one of the most natural and entrancing storytellers I have ever encountered. I felt as if I had been transported back in time and was listening to a troubadour from the Middle Ages.

The younger *mujahideen* couldn't get enough of his tales, which all had a religious theme: either his animation of Qur'anic stories, his account of his missionary activities and religious conquests, or his vivid re-creations of numerous *hadith*. (These last were the divine sayings of the Prophet, attributable directly to him as the original transmitter from God, or accounts of something Moham-med did, transmitted through the centuries along an unbroken chain of "learned and knowing" sages.)

Soon we were joined by the half-dozen teenaged cadets or recruits whom we—very privately—dubbed "the children." They sat around as Omar recounted what Christians would call Sunday school stories. As he spoke of Adam and Eve (who were thirty metres tall), Abraham and, everybody's favourite, Noah, I was transported back to my own rather brief exposure to essentially the same stories in church basements in Montreal. I was particularly intrigued by the differences in the Islamic interpretation and by Omar's perform-ance. It was the first quiet, contemplative, non-threatening moment I had had in nearly a week and I found it soothing.

My knowledge of Islam—the world's fastest growing reli-gion—prior to this misadventure had been appallingly cursory, but I did know enough to avoid presenting myself as an atheist. In the eyes of the strict Muslim, there is no greater sin than that of the apostate, one who rejects God. Thus, as their captive, I was the Christian of my youth. In the eyes of our Islamic kidnappers I was therefore at least a follower of an Abrahamic religion—a person of The Book—and as such, less disfavoured among infidels, even by fundamentalist Muslims.

After an hour or so, they began to break camp and load three vehicles. The large dark-green tent was left standing, presumably for some rearguard element to deal with. In addition to the two forty-five-gallon barrels, each truck was piled rather haphazardly with everything else required for the crew of that truck to live and fight: blankets, clothing, a pot and a few steel bowls, the heavy machine gun and its substantial mount, a few linked twenty-five-round belts of ammunition, personal possessions, blankets, and a few bags of rice, pasta, and powdered milk.

In addition to the AK-47s, carried at all times by everyone from Jack down to the smallest of the children, were small arms that normally consisted of a light PK belt-fed machine gun, a few twenty-five-round belts of 7.62 ammunition for that weapon, and at least one RPG-7 rocket-propelled grenade launcher and three or four reloads. Each *mujahid* possessed his own ammunition vest containing eight to ten spare magazines for his Kalash. These were worn on sentry duty or whenever they expected action, and they had to be kept close to hand at all times.

Eventually, we were ordered aboard the trucks now that everything had been elaborately tied down and four or five of the brothers were perched on blankets, folded and strapped atop everything else, giving the vehicles a very high centre of gravity. Normally two would face outward on each side, one hand for their weapon and the other grasping some rope or strap to keep them aboard. The final addition to the load would be firewood, always a scarcity in the desert. Thus, whenever they passed one or more standing dead trees, whose water source had long deserted them, they would halt for a minute or two as the boys broke off such branches as they could for the cooking fire at the next camp.

As the trucks were being manoeuvred in front of the tent where Louis, the children, and I had spent the night, I saw that Omar One, in the vehicle that had grabbed us almost a week ago, was about to back over a black and white soccer ball. I shouted for him to stop. Whether or not he heard, he continued and the ball burst with a loud pop. He got out, inspected the crushed ball, and smiled happily to himself. He seemed glad that the frivolous plaything— the only entertainment available to the half-dozen teenagers among them—had been eliminated.

❖

As we set off from TV Camp, I attempted to put what was happening to us into perspective. I'm not suggesting that I was in any way reconciled to my fate or that I had found some inner peace. Rather, it was just that the feeling of abject, pervasive terror that had characterized the four-day trek north had dissipated a little. Above all, we were alive, and not gravely damaged. My back felt better after two relatively sedentary days at TV Camp. We had recorded what I took to be the classic proof-of-life video message. Things therefore seemed to be taking their natural course in terms of how I thought kidnappings worked, and all my instincts told me that we were not about to be killed, at least not in the near future. Freed, therefore, from the imminent prospect of our own demise, we transferred more of our capacity for worry to the plight of our families.

Our abductors reflected the same sense that the opening phase had been successfully completed and the establishment of contact with whomever they considered to be our principals seemed to be underway. The negotiating gavotte had begun. It seemed reasonable to think that there would now be a pause of some duration. It was clear from their behaviour, however, that they fully expected that a significant effort would be mounted to find and rescue us, despite my scripted "no violence" plea, and their primary focus as we entered the next phase would be to ensure that this did not happen—or at least not successfully.

PART TWO

PRISONERS
OF AL QAEDA
IN THE SAHARA

CHAPTER 6

CAMP CANADA

===

'Twas sad as sad could be;
And we did speak only to break
The silence of the sea!

. . .

Day after day, day after day,
We stuck, nor breath nor motion;
As idle as a painted ship
Upon a painted ocean.

===

I occupied the centre position in the cab of Omar One's truck, while Louis travelled in another vehicle. This seemed a reasonable distribution of their high-value assets. Any number of things could go wrong in these cross-country moves in the Sahara and our kidnappers wanted to ensure that at least one of us would survive any mishap.

The sky was now clear of blowing sand and the sun bright, but it was not overly hot. We were heading north in a three-truck convoy, about a hundred metres apart but not necessarily following the tracks of the preceding vehicle. As a result of the much-needed rest over the past two days and the fact that there was less adrenalin pumping through my system, for the first time I began to study the dramatic nature of our surroundings.

After an hour or so of fast driving over a hard, flat, dark-brown surface strewn with fist-sized rocks, we reached an area of lighter sand that progressively changed into soft, undulating dunes, not particularly high and relatively easy to navigate. Suddenly there was a pounding on the roof of the cab and Omar stuck most of his upper body through the driver's window without easing off one bit on the accelerator and twisted back to see what the boys in the back wanted. They were all excited, pointing and screaming, "La biche, la biche!" This was our first encounter with the elusive, fawn-coloured desert antelope, a protected species that our captors revelled in hunting. The Belmokhtar group alone claimed to have killed 2,500 of them over the preceding four years.

The lead vehicle, driven by Abdul Rahman, was already in pursuit—although without my glasses I never saw it. He was seeking to herd the nimble, waist-high gazelle toward the more open part of the desert so that it would not be able to find refuge among the steeper, rocky outcroppings where the vehicles could not follow. Omar instinctively moved to limit its escape in the opposite direction while the third vehicle followed the beast directly, hoping to get alongside in order to give the *mujahideen* in the back a clear flank shot. On this occasion, though, the antelope jinked behind Abdul Rahman's truck and disappeared in higher terrain, and the hunt was over. I had yet to understand the extent to which this was not just, or even primarily, sport but about food and survival. I would soon become a passionate supporter of the hunt or, more accurately, a committed fan of its product.

The brothers were in a good mood. They had enjoyed the excitement of the chase but their deep, religiously grounded fatalism taught them that if they had been unsuccessful it was because Allah had so decided. Thus there was no point—indeed, it would be an insult to God—to even wish it had been otherwise.

We continued through the dunes and across another horizonless flat reach, the only feature being the odd shallow, rock-strewn *wadi*. After about three hours of driving we started to encounter widely separated acacia thorn trees and a few sparse tufts of rough grass. The first trees were dead but as the trucks worked their way around them the vegetation became thicker; there was more grass, the acacias displayed dusty greenery, and then some chest-high bushes appeared. Soon there were multiple tracks in the hard surface and, moving slowly, we went deeper into what I thought of as a pretty underwhelming oasis. This was not Hollywood, and there were no languid pools or swaying, date-laden palms.

To our left what was at first little more than the bank of a substantial *wadi* grew into a sharply rising cliff of rough, crumbling rock. To the right there stretched a wide, flat depression in the surrounding desert. The boundary of this depression, far to the right, was the opposite bank of the *wadi,* some seven or eight hundred metres distant. Rising out of the *wadi* floor in the middle distance, a couple of hundred metres to the east, were three long, thin, flat-topped, mesas. As the deep *wadi* began to narrow we saw another truck and some people moving about near the west wall. All three of the trucks in our group pulled in close to the parked vehicle, each seeking, not very hard, to squeeze under a sheltering and camouflaging acacia tree.

Everybody disembarked and Louis was brought over to where Omar and I were standing. We were told by Abdul Rahman, who we were informed was to be the camp emir, or commander, to collect our blankets and follow Omar to "your position." This was located about fifty metres north of the trucks, about ten metres from what was by that point an almost vertical cliff face, perhaps fifteen metres high, to the west. The most salient feature of our position was a large, healthy acacia tree, which would offer us some semblance of cover as we placed our blankets on the narrowly focused spot of shade beneath its branches.

Omar traced the path of the sun for us, which at noon at that time of the year described an arc just south of straight up, so we threw our blankets on the ground on the north side of the tree, only later that evening learning that we ought first to have removed the myriad thorns that over time had fallen from the tree and embedded themselves, like sharp jacks, in the sand around its base.

He then very economically explained the rules.

"The UN is, along with the U.S.A., Israel, France, and Britain, in the first tier of our enemies," Omar proclaimed. As representatives of the hated United Nations, we were considered prisoners of war, not (I suppose in a veiled reference to his previous Austrian victims) some tourist targets of opportunity. As prisoners, our activities and our freedom of action would be strictly curtailed, and if we abused their trust there would be unpleasant consequences.

Omar designated the rather limited area in which we could roam freely (a rectangle measuring perhaps forty metres east to west and sixty metres from our tree toward the north. He explained that we could find places within the northern reaches of that rectangle in order to go *pas loin* but would have to ask permission to go *loin* well beyond the designated limits. He reiterated that on such occasions we would be accompanied, and again stressed that only one of us could go *loin* at a time, while the other remained in plain sight.

The issue of appropriate toilet practices and etiquette was far more fraught than I had expected. Not only were our abductors a fastidious group, concerned about health and sanitary issues, including smells, but they were also a religiously inspired, dramatically prudish collection of young warriors. Despite living in relatively close proximity with our captors, we never saw even a naked torso—a far cry from the locker rooms and communal showers of my youth. Our kidnappers were very forceful in their demand that we respect their customs and beliefs in this regard and going *loin* meant just that, far and out of sight.

One day Omar Two strode toward us in a rage evident long before he had opened his mouth. "We told you to be discreet in your personal habits and there you go, Louis, shitting in full public view. It is unacceptable!"

"What are you talking about?" Louis asked, equally offended. "I did no such thing."

Omar riposted, "You did, just this morning."

Taken aback, Louis allowed, "I did go *loin* but I asked permission and was directed to go beyond [pointing] that far dune, well out of sight of the entire camp."

"Not so," answered Omar Two, triumphantly. Gesturing to a high, rocky promontory surmounted by a minuscule figure in silhouette some eight or nine hundred metres distant, he declared, "That sentry saw it all and was disgusted!"

Louis and I said, simultaneously, "We didn't know a sentry was up there."

"Well," spat Omar Two, "it's your business to be aware of such things." I could hardly argue with that logic.

"So," I said carefully, "let's be very clear on this point. When we go *loin* we are to be absolutely certain that we are out of the sight of all sentries?"

"Of course!" Omar Two snapped as he stormed off, and immediately I began to revise our escape plans.

They hated any kind of physical contact with infidels. Our abductors were offended by immodesty of any sort and reserved a special place in their hierarchy of disgust for their lurid understanding of the nature of Western nudist beaches. Similarly, while some of the relationships between the older *mujahideen* and the younger boys seemed to me a little ambiguous, they expressed vitriolic contempt for homosexuality, considering the West to be one sprawling Sodom and Gomorrah. As a result, they drew the line at Louis and me washing together, which would have allowed us to be a little more efficient in our water usage. They finally compromised on those all too rare occasions when we were given enough water to wash our hair, allowing one to pour a trickle of water while the other scrubbed the layers of compacted grime from his own head.

So, we plunked ourselves down in that spot of shade—no wider than our blankets—under our newly designated tree and then chased that shady spot around that tree for about 90 percent of our waking hours. Of course we had no idea how long we would be staying at what Al Jabbar, one of our guards, some days later called, with a wry smile, "Camp Canada." It was in every respect a good camp, where we were well protected from both wind and sun. Also, at Camp Canada we were neither too near nor too far from our keepers. For a while we had our own fire and we built our own latrines. Generally, we were largely left alone and were soon able to establish rules and routines, which mitigated the constant stress of our captivity.

But where were we? Until we could at least make a stab at establishing that, any thought of escape would be completely abstract, not to say foolhardy. We had tried to keep some track of where we were headed and how far we had travelled on the way north, but really to no avail. All our observation told us was that, after about fifty-six hours of hard driving, we had arrived at TV Camp and now we were four hours farther north, perhaps a hundred kilometres. Thus we had reached something like a thousand kilometres into the Sahara desert: the distance between Chicago and Atlanta, Paris and Madrid, or Fredericton and Ottawa.

We were not even certain that we were in Mali. Perhaps we had entered southern Algeria? But we didn't think so, more in view of geostrategic considerations than as a result of any real understanding of how far north we had come. We assumed, therefore, that we were held somewhere within a vast area perhaps as much as 250 kilometres wide, stretching parallel to the Algerian border about 500 kilometres southeastward from just east of Taoudenni toward Tessalit, an area about the size of Portugal. It was therefore abundantly clear to us from the outset that we were not going to be able to walk to safety, even if we could get away from our kidnappers.

At Camp Canada we heard on four or five occasions, always during the day, the distinctive beat of heavy turbo-prop engines (Hercules C-130s, perhaps), sounding as though they were not very far off, somewhere to the south. The first time we heard it we were convinced that the cavalry was coming. When we looked about in panic, though, we saw our captors going methodically about their business, unconcerned by this evident and foreign racket. I could only conclude that they were used to it, and that we were located relatively near some irregularly used airstrip (perhaps the tiny community of Tessalit itself). If so, the airstrip orientation was such that, grouped against the *wadi* wall, we could not see the aircraft on either approach or take-off and, more germane, they couldn't see us. But sound propagation across the open desert is limited so we must have been relatively close, perhaps effectively hiding very nearly in plain sight.

A camp was merely a place where we stopped in the depths of the Sahara. But the term had nothing to do with any image that might be conjured up by a Westerner on hearing that word. There were no buildings or tents, no furniture, forks, plates, lights, cots, or anything resembling a toilet. And no women.

We were under neither roofs nor canvas, though for a while we were able to make a shelter out of a tattered bit of plastic tarpaulin. The only tents we saw were for the dreaded filming of videos. Thus we slept in the open, usually under an acacia thorn tree that offered varying degrees of protection from the implacable desert sun during the day and allowed the caterpillars to drop directly onto our faces at night.

Camps were chosen principally for the availability of a modicum of shade. A bonus was a little protection from the wind. On several occasions, though, camp was simply where we stopped along our route on an open stretch of desert where, usually well after dark, everyone threw blankets on the sand and slept by the trucks, before setting off again the next day at first light. The selection of camps seemed to have little to do with the degree to which the location was concealed or concealable.

Although we were ill prepared for the extreme conditions of the Sahara, Louis and I convinced ourselves that we were relatively lucky. Surely high temperatures are easier to suffer outdoors than while imprisoned in a rank, stifling cell with a fetid, overflowing bucket close at hand. We saw the stars at night and watched the moon wax and wane, and we stared at the contrails of high-flying jets carrying free, happy people—well into their second cocktail— to and from Paris, London, Rome, and Berlin. We discreetly waved at satellites and observed the antics of insects, reptiles, and migrating birds. Pretty basic exercise was readily available, and Louis and I were together and could speak candidly—if carefully—to each other. All things considered, the conditions of our imprisonment were preferable to many alternatives.

On arrival at Camp Canada in late December the weather was cold at night, usually, we estimated, in the single digits when we awoke before dawn. It rained eight or ten times in those early weeks, twice fairly heavily.

We had been captured as we were returning from what we had expected would be a relaxed Sunday outing in very warm weather and were dressed the way most Canadian men might be dressed on any Sunday in July or August. Louis, an efficient packer and traveller, was wearing the belted pants of the suit he wore to official meetings and a wash-and-wear, long-sleeved blue shirt, underwear and nylon socks, and his black leather loafers, along with the ball cap he had bought in a rural Niger market the day before. I had on what I wear most weekends (Mary would say most days): a long-sleeved khaki cotton shirt, tan trousers, a sturdy leather belt, light cotton socks, cotton underwear, my ball cap—without which my thinly thatched head would already have been fried to a crisp—and moccasin-type, slip-on brown leather lightweight shoes.

We wore these things twenty-four hours a day as they progressively fell to pieces. Our clothing was manifestly inadequate for the cool temperatures of the desert at night and particularly so when it was both cold and wet. My pants were the first to go, wearing through at the seat. As my posterior became visible, our prudish jailers sent one of the children over with a pair of cast-off, calf-length, clam digger–style trousers with a cloth tie around the waist. I still have a fetching indelible tan from mid-calf to the sock line.

Our shirts began to disintegrate next and were much repaired by Louis, who could see well enough to perform that task, using a needle and thread supplied by our captors. Eventually, my tattered shirt was replaced with a many-holed, hand-me-down *jelabiyah* tunic.

After some weeks the heat was such that the ball caps offered insufficient protection to our ears and necks even when we kept such exposure to an absolute minimum. Further, our kidnappers were concerned that ball caps looked "too Western," so we were given lengths of grey cotton and, eventually, became competent turban tiers and big fans of that headgear for such circumstances. However prosaic, socks and underwear were our most immediate clothing requirement, bearing in mind that we were only rarely allowed to wash. Deteriorating shoes presented the most serious challenge to our health, and Louis' skills as a cobbler were stretched to the limit as he sought, day after day, to keep our footwear in sufficient repair to allow us to maintain our walking regime: something we considered essential to both our physical and mental well-being.

Using thorns, bits of scrounged rubber, strands from twists of plastic rope, and pink, heavy thread provided by our kidnappers for our clothing, with a lot of painstaking work Louis kept the soles of our shoes more or less attached to their uppers. But the holes were inevitably getting larger, a few tearing through, and the leather of the upper parts was becoming ever less able to withstand being worked.

We often wondered whether AQIM was purposely keeping us in inadequate footwear to make any attempt at escape the more improbable. This theory gained credence when we subsequently learned that a big, very full bag they had buried in full view of our position had contained numerous pairs of new boots. We had observed that, a couple of days prior to their caching that sack, almost all our abductors were sporting new and sturdy hiking boots. Despite what must have been our annoying nattering about our need for new shoes, none had been offered to us.

As we settled in to Camp Canada, keeping warm at night and in the morning was our most immediate challenge. Up to this point we had simply crashed, exhausted, onto a blanket for twenty minutes or a few hours of desperately needed rest wherever we were so directed. But now we had to think about how best to proceed over what might be a very long haul. We had survived that horrible initial phase; now the challenge was to organize things so that we could do the distance, whatever that was to be. Instinct, which had served us well, would have to give way at least in some part to planning and calculation.

How should we make our sleeping arrangements? We had a blanket each, well, really one thin blanket and one cheap summer-weight quilt. We could each wrap ourselves in one of those, or we could put one on the ground and the other atop us both and thereby hope to generate additional warmth. We chose the second, deciding that our captors already viewed us as moral degenerates, so why disabuse them? Even this arrangement was far from adequate. We still shivered through the night and we would each wear one of the coverings around our shoulders as a shawl for our pre-dawn walk until the sun warmed things up by about eight in the morning.

Our kidnappers knew we were suffering from the cold and out of a desire, we guessed, to preserve their assets, or to gain points with Allah, or perhaps even out of sympathy, in our first days at Camp Canada we were lent additional items. First, Omar Two brought us a thick, deep-red, very large rug that looked to me as if it were Afghan. This was followed by a large, plastic woven mat from Suleiman, a young man from the Mediterranean coast. Then on 24 December, five days after our arrival at Camp Canada, Belmokhtar and his staff showed up, bearing all kinds of "gifts" and an exciting message, and the two seemed to be closely related.

With smiles and a little formality Ahmed unwittingly played Santa, distributing gifts: first, a blanket and jacket, still in their plastic wrappings, for each of us. Then cookies and candies, and a cherished bar of soap, tiny toothbrush, and minuscule tube of toothpaste each. The two synthetic, hairy blankets were large and welcome. One depicted animals, the other, tulips in various shades of grey. The jackets were windbreakers lined with fleecy material. The zippers of these windbreakers soon gave out, but they were a happy addition to our sparse wardrobes. We wore them every night and into the mid-morning until rising temperatures in the spring made that unnecessary. With the mat against the sand, followed by the rug, then the two blankets on top, we were warm enough and, on all but the coldest nights, we could roll the thin quilt into a pillow. The grubby green blanket was returned by our captors to its use as cover for a heavy machine gun. From Day 11, Christmas Eve, keeping warm at night was no longer a significant problem.

Keeping dry, however, remained an issue until the second or third of January when, in the midst of a heavy rainstorm, Abdul Rahman and Omar One arrived in the middle of the night with an irregular, torn remnant of blue plastic tarp full of holes, which we hastily threw over our sodden blankets. From that point, the rain issue and the more benign sandstorms became manageable.

Sand was in and on everything, and we ate prodigious quantities. We were continually covered in a greasy, smelly slurry of sand and sweat. It was caked onto our scalps, packed into our ears, and seemed to collect in the places where it would be most uncomfortable. We were desperate to wash, but that happened all too rarely. Normally, the sand invasion was manageable but sandstorms were always a challenge, and I was surprised that our eyes did not suffer more. We experienced three major sandstorms and four or five less severe but still difficult ones. They were always dramatic; at worst it was difficult to breathe, and impossible to see or move even a short distance.

The tarp unleashed many of Louis' hidden talents. First, he's a natural scrounger. He would have put James Clavell's King Rat to shame. He picked up and pocketed everything he saw: bits of string, rubber, pieces of cardboard drifting on the wind from their

"kitchen" to our position, Mylar bags that had contained powdered milk, discarded and tangled pieces of plastic rope, glass
jars, plastic bottles, simple tools (needles, a leather punch, a Second World War entrenching tool)—discarded or not, borrowed
and not returned—containers of every kind. This talent served us
well. Second, Louis' Boy Scout training, coupled with his mariner's
instincts, came nicely together in erecting a variety of jury-rigged
shelters with that bit of tarp, held together with a colourful array
of fragments of rope attached with dazzling knots.

A few days after the delivery of the tarp, our captors returned
from a water run and unloaded some forty-five-gallon drums near
our position. We asked Omar One to see if the camp emir, Abdul
Rahman, would allow us to use a couple of them to create a shelter.
After some hesitation they agreed, once we had accepted that any
time the water was needed they could tear apart whatever we had
erected to get to it (and on one occasion they did just that, in the
middle of the night).

We set the two barrels up at the head of the "bed" and stretched
the tarp over the top, weighing it down with rocks and sand at the
base of the drums and more rocks piled on their tops, then pulled
it taut to a little past the foot of our blankets, where we held it in
place with more rocks. There was sufficient tarp remaining to cover
the sides of the sleeping area, and we used short sticks to prop open
the sides, allowing air to circulate at night but bringing the flaps
down in a storm. The clearance—perhaps ten centimetres—above
our faces at the head of the bed and zero clearance at the foot made
it difficult to move, but we solved that by digging long, cocoon-like
trenches side by side into the sand, which made a smoother mat-
tress and afforded a little more head and foot room.

We had been told by Omar One that we had only to ask any of
les frères to refill our plastic drinking water container when it was
nearly empty. Nice in theory, but it rarely worked out that easily.

When we asked about washing, he allowed that this more complicated matter would have to be decided case by case, for us and every
other person in the camp, by the camp commander, Abdul Rahman.
Washing was discretionary; drinking was not. We then received a
long lecture on the value of water, the risks and costs associated
with supplying it, and the discipline this imposed on its use.

Specifically, Omar insisted that water was never to be wasted
(thus not to be used for going *loin*) and that the brothers had been
instructed by the imam to use sand instead of water to perform
symbolic ablutions before each set of daily prayers. The water was
obtained from deep desert wells and collected, stored, and cached in
steel drums. About every three days a truck departed on what Louis
and I termed a water run, usually leaving early in the morning and
returning late at night, and sometimes not until the next day.

The full drums were then unloaded at a central water point
near their trucks; those on kitchen duty that day would fill their
pots, and the individual *mujahideen* would top up their water bottles at will. Drawing water from the drums involved siphoning it
with a three-metre length of plastic hose that (in company with a
roll of packing tape used to bind prisoners) was stored around the
principal stick shift in each truck. Unfortunately, the same tube
was used to siphon diesel fuel into the trucks' dual fuel tanks. We
soon learned to avoid asking for water whenever we heard a truck
returning, as they were immediately refuelled and we were eager to
avoid getting the half litre of fuel remaining in the hose added to
our water jug.

Indeed, the greatest problem with water, particularly for me,
was not quantity but quality. Perhaps one time in five the taste of
the water made it wholly undrinkable. It was often contaminated,
if not by fuel then by whatever chemical had been in the drums
to begin with. Clearly they had not, and would not, "waste" precious water to rinse out their barrels. A number of the drums were
decorated with the large, inverted triangle with skull and cross-
bones inside denoting poison.

When I couldn't drink the water, Louis or I would, Oliver Twist–like, return to the imprecisely designated frontier between our zone and theirs, wait until someone deigned to recognize us, and then, offering that person our newly refilled jug, try to explain that whatever it was contaminated with was so strong that I could not keep it down. This often did not have the desired effect on those who did not agree with the priority I assigned to staying alive, particularly the children. Some were likely to snatch the container from my grasp and return after a long time with the same or sometimes worse water. At that point it would all become vastly more complicated, with face involved, and would take hours before I got something I could drink. Louis' stomach was tougher than mine, but not much.

Often, especially as the water level in the barrels got below a third full, the water was cloudy with sand, sometimes dark brown and opaque. In these situations we would very carefully pour a cup full and allow most of the sand to settle to the bottom for an hour or so before drinking off the upper portion without jiggling the cup. This was a much easier issue to deal with than unpalatability but required management. When the water became really sludgy, we strained it through our (filthy) scarves before allowing it to settle.

After a while we managed to scrounge a cast-off second container for wastewater (the final muddy half cup in our drinking container). We tried to keep this one more or less out of sight and use it surreptitiously for going *loin* and washing our hands afterward, but after a few weeks we got busted and lost the second container. One day, without a word, one of our kidnappers simply picked it up it from behind the rock where it was hidden, without breaking stride, and walked away with it.

We were given water with which to wash on few occasions. Some were what we called "small washes," for which we were given ten litres to share. That allowed us a sort of kitty wash, using our scarves and a little soap to deal with strategic parts of our bodies. Then we would use the filthy water to wash a couple of items of clothing, usually our tattered underwear and socks. The rare but wonderful ones, though, were the "large washes," for which we received thirty litres. That allowed full body, head, and hair washes. And by capturing most of the water by standing in a large tub we were sometimes allowed to use, we were able to wash and minimally rinse our clothes, while still preserving a little dirty water to contribute to our waste water container. The thirty litres would be delivered in a black plastic container. Leaving it in the sun for an hour ensured that the water temperature was pleasant.

Only once did we witness how they did the watering business and it was startlingly "handraulic." In the middle of a flat, featureless expanse of desert, we pulled up at an "improved well." That is development-speak for a well that has been hand dug but equipped with a large, pre-cast cement lip, perhaps two metres in diameter and rising almost a metre from ground level. This serves to protect the well, and water drawers, from cave-ins and makes the task of drawing water a little easier. Two of the trucks drew up to within a couple of metres of the wellhead and their crews unloaded the enormous amount of baggage in order to stand half a dozen water drums upright.

Everyone was a little tense and sentries were sent deep in every direction. From somewhere, an enormous pan (the cut-off bottom third of a forty-five-gallon drum) was placed on the roof of the cab of one of the trucks and the sturdiest of the youths girded himself for the task. Placing one foot on the rim of the well, he lowered a bucket made of some kind of animal skin attached to a rigid circular rim on a long, thin, frayed, yellow nylon rope and proceeded to haul water up from what looked to be about a fifteen-metre depth. When the soft, leaking bucket cleared the well, it would be handed to another of the young *mujahideen,* who, grabbing the rim and hoisting it above his head, walked to the truck. A third, standing in the truck bed by the cab, would reach down, take the bucket, and dump its contents into the pan atop the cab. On and on it went. As the pan filled, water was siphoned down into the standing barrels.

Witnessing this exhausting procedure was, in itself, a lesson in water conservation, and we understood full well how vulnerable they clearly felt when engaged in the long watering process.

We ate badly, and worried about scurvy and other ravages of vitamin deficiency and nutritional insufficiency. The UN Food and Agricultural Organization deems that a daily intake of 1,800 calories is needed to maintain nutritional health, but a fifth of the people in our troubled world do not manage anything like that. I very much doubt that we were receiving even half that amount. When one evening we were served a satisfying lentil soup I tried to encourage more of the same by offering compliments. The answer was fiercely dismissive: "We eat out of necessity, not pleasure." And we saw no more lentils.

They insisted that we all ate the same thing and, although we did not see what they ate except on a couple of occasions when we were fed en route, I never found any reason to disbelieve them. That said, I don't know how they did it. They were fit. Hassan would escort the half-dozen younger ones on training missions at the run and they practised small-unit tactics, slithering among the rocks and dunes for hours in the blistering sun. They ran up and down mountains and did sentry duty at least twice each day, in addition to performing their various chores and going on missions (for water, communications, and so forth) outside the camp. Louis and I, however, were tired out by our daily walks and despite our relative inactivity, we were each losing weight at about a kilo a week.

Our daily regime consisted of a breakfast of a large (shared) cup of powdered milk and a kind of fritter shortly after dawn, and a lunch and usually identical dinner of rice or pasta, delivered in a cracked and dented communal aluminum bowl, with bits of filthy string wedged into the rents in the metal. Sometimes, if we were lucky, there would be trace elements of tomato paste or sardines. Wonderful meals would see gristly bits of goat, sheep, or camel added to the rice or pasta, which guaranteed an hour or so of methodical tooth picking with a thorn snapped from the tree above our heads. Neither a sheep nor a goat nor a can of sardines nor a tin of tomato paste goes far among thirty young, hungry males.

At first our rice-filled bowl was simply dropped, sometimes flung, onto the sand in front of us. It was usually delivered by one of the children, who went to great lengths to avoid the possibility of touching us and to ensure we received a good portion of sand with our meal.

After a week at Camp Canada, a supply truck showed up late one evening and we were given an enormous bowl of fresh lettuce, tomatoes, beets, peppers, and onion for breakfast, all smothered in some kind of store-bought salad dressing, which we wolfed down with enthusiasm and excitement. That happy experience was never to be repeated. The same delivery provided us with, among a few other things, a large bag of raw peanuts, which we roasted over a small fire, and a tiny tin of Nescafé, which we added, a few grains at a time, to our breakfast cup of powdered milk.

Now and then there were surprising acts of generosity. Al Jabbar one day brought us a haunch of a desert antelope, skin and hoof still attached, and indicated, giving us matches, that we could cook it over our own small fire. He understood we had nothing with which to remove the skin and lent us a small penknife for the purpose.

A couple of days later he came by to ask for his *petit couteau* and we reminded him that we had returned his penknife later on the same day he had lent it to us. Shrugging, he wandered away and was seen over the next few days searching the sand throughout the camp. Several of the children strode up to us in the days that followed, gruffly demanding to know where *le petit couteau* was. I indulged my paranoia, frantically searching our plot in case we hadn't returned it as both of us were sure we had. I recalled with a sinking feeling Omar One's recent reading of a *sura* (Qur'anic

verse) recounting a slightly different version of the Sunday school
story of Joseph and his coat of many colours. The key bit about
trumping up a charge by vengefully hiding a golden cup within the
baggage of his evil brother was very much in my mind as I worried
that *le petit couteau* would suddenly be discovered by our guards
among our miserable possessions.

On arrival in Camp Canada I realized I had to find some way of
keeping track of time or my grip on reality might well slip. I worried that if I lost the ability to measure the passage of time, I might
well lose hold of other anchors. Above all, I needed to be confident
that I could keep my wits about me, could track and even perhaps
encourage progress toward a happy conclusion to our misadventure—to the extent that might prove possible from the middle of
the Sahara. I wanted to ensure that if I emerged from this trial it
would not be as a cringing, broken disappointment to my family.

Our watches had been taken. So, borrowing ideas from POW
lore, I determined we needed a routine that included the methodical and accurate registration of the passage of time. Further, it
would have to be reasonably discreet and portable, as I had no idea
of how long we would remain in one place or what we could take
with us if and when we moved. Thus the classic scratching of lines,
Count of Monte Cristo–like, on the prison wall or a rock or tree
was not an option.

After a few days, I decided to try to record the passing days
on the underside of my belt, using the ubiquitous long and very
sharp thorns that adorned the acacia tree under which we sheltered. However, the rough surface of the underside was not suitable for fine markings, so I switched to the polished outer side and
developed symbology that would serve us rather well: short lines
for days of the week, longer lines for Sundays, to distinguish the
passage of weeks, and a line across the full width of the belt to
denote the end of a month.

The only other symbols were slanted finials on the lines marking the days on which we were allowed water with which to wash. These washing marks enabled me to approach the camp emir with a very precise pitch, which clearly had some effect, as in "We haven't been able to wash in seventeen days and we need to do so." Later, I added symbols to denote other significant events such as the recording of video messages and when we moved to a new camp. All of which, in addition to offering us that vital connection to the real world, has also assisted me enormously in creating this account.

In order to keep this record circumspect, if not secret, I could not use the belt to hold up my ever-looser trousers. As it turned out this was not a problem because just as I lost enough weight to make keeping my pants up without a belt problematic, the trousers began to disintegrate from their hard, 24/7 use. So I simply removed the belt and kept it in the plastic bag with my few possessions (soap, toothbrush, and paste). I don't know if they were aware of the belt-calendar but I suspect they were, for two reasons.

First, they were remarkably observant and had us under close scrutiny twenty-four hours a day. We were a curiosity and their principal entertainment, just as they were ours. Early on in Camp Canada, Omar Two, the mystic warrior ("I have my faith and my gun, what more could I possibly require?") approached in a stormy mood and demanded to know what sort of uniform I was wearing (a point my daughters have also raised on more than one occasion). I insisted that it was no kind of uniform, even if the pants and shirt were very similar in colour. Fully appreciating the satisfaction he would get out of establishing that I was part of some uniformed service—and the likely unpleasant consequences—I was at pains to demonstrate that mine were standard Western casual clothes. Not so, he claimed, for they all sported the same distinctive military-looking logo. When I then examined what I was wearing and the devices to which he was pointing, I realized with some dismay that he was quite correct. My trousers, shirt, and even my shoes displayed the Dockers logo, which, with its anchor flanked by impressionistic wings, did look pretty operational. I had not been aware that I was so loyal to the Dockers brand.

Second, they became very used to the fact that I knew the date and day of the week. Occasionally, one or other of our jailers would approach us and ask, "Is it Monday or Tuesday?" or "the twenty-third or the twenty-fifth?" Clearly they had accepted that in some manner or other, I was keeping track of time.

It is difficult to overemphasize the importance, at least for my mental well-being, of the decision to maintain the belt-calendar. Perhaps on two or three occasions we let the marking of the days slip when we couldn't update it sufficiently discreetly and then had to add a couple at a time. Often Louis reminded me to do so before I had thought of it. Having that record and knowing how much time had elapsed between significant events helped keep everything in an orderly perspective and gave us some sense of control over our lives. I wonder if our captors realized that too and simply decided that our mental stability was also in their interests in that sick, suicidal, or dead assets were not much use to them.

Knowing the day, date, and precise length of our imprisonment also nourished what came to be an important morale-building ritual. Each day when we awoke, and before our rudimentary ablutions, we would start with an exchange.

"Good morning, Bob. It's Wednesday, January 7th, and we are still alive."

"Indeed we are, Louis, on this the twenty-fifth day of our captivity."

While our jailers never told us how long we would be staying in any particular location, on arrival in Camp Canada we had the impression that we had reached a final destination: perhaps not *the* final destination but the place to which we had been travelling for six days, and the attitude of our kidnappers seemed to suggest that we'd be here a while. So, just as I had decided that we needed to keep track of the passage of time, so too did we determine that we needed to establish some kind of rhythm and structure to our days.

We were always conscious of the rather self-evident link between the states of our mental and physical health. I remain convinced that had one suffered significant damage, the other would have followed in short order. Neither of us had previously come close to experiencing the intensity of the psychological and emotional stress we were under, nor had we known such austere conditions or extreme climatic challenges. There were dangers we understood implicitly, like sunburn, sunstroke, infection, water-borne diseases, and dehydration, but we had little understanding of the potential ravages of depression, isolation, and extreme fear.

Also, we were unaware of what other challenges to our physical health might lurk in the food, the water, and the sand or be transmitted by the insects that abounded. While we knew that scorpions and poisonous snakes inhabited the desert, we knew little about how to spot and avoid them, and less about how to treat stings and bites from such creatures. In fact, we didn't know whether they were treatable or necessarily fatal in such remote circumstances, so far from any kind of professional medical assistance. We did know, though, that the "I've got a hangnail or a thorn in my foot so you've got to let me go" gambit was not going to get any traction.

So, like Donald Rumsfeld, we didn't know what we didn't know, and that bothered us a lot more than it seems to have him. What else could harm us? An Algerian or American or French or British air strike, certainly, but what about 54°C (129°F) heat, poisonous plants, or the hyenas we often heard yapping and howling at night? Our captors—particularly Omars One and Two—spoke obsessively and with palpable fear about *ces monstres*—that is, of the possibility of hyena attacks. They were full of stories of people walking home across the fringe of the desert and only a bloody belt and shoes being found in their wake the next day. This too seemed to be intended as an inoculation against escape but that realization did not mean it was ineffective.

Finally, there was the largely unspoken yet constant threat of being physically mistreated, beaten, or tortured. There had been a few signs in the early days of their wanting to abuse us but they had not been repeated. What, though, if negotiations did not go their way or a sadist among them (and a few candidates had already identified themselves) simply decided to have a go? Would Jack's discipline prevail?

Without a doubt, my greatest and most debilitating concern was that one day we would be marched into a tent, required to kneel before the AQIM tableau of black flag and heavily armed masked men, and executed, probably beheaded, as the video camera rolled. It was a worry that never left me. Sometimes it was very present, sometimes more abstract, but it was always there. I knew with absolute certainty that their patience and fatalism could work both for and against us.

I thought there was a finite period over which whatever negotiations were ongoing could be stretched, then no further. But I had no idea what that period was. The two Austrians had been held for eight months in 2008, the thirty-two German, Swiss, and Austrian tourists for four months in 2003. In our case, they had thirty people tied up babysitting two feeble old men. I could perceive no capacity for or interest in Hezbollah- or FARC-type long-drawn-out, multi-year sagas, which of course spelled good news and very bad.

The desert was well populated with birds of every description wintering over from Europe. Louis and I lay for hours watching pairs of hawks questing for prey in the sky above Camp Canada and we saw the odd vulture. Two sorts of bird became close companions. The first we named "Ted," a small, black sparrow-like bird with a white patch on his head and white on the underside of his tail. The second was "Sven," about the same size but in the livery of the Swedish flag, a brilliant blue and bright yellow. These birds had no reason to fear humans and either Ted or Sven sometimes perched on the toe of my outstretched shoe. The most interesting bird we saw, we ate: a large, turkey-like Houbara bustard with brown and white plumage that the *mujahideen* had shot on one of their cross-country travels. Big though it was, it did not go far among so many semi-starving people.

We were not bitten by snakes although we saw a few. Indeed, we had a number of close encounters with the Sahara's dark side. One afternoon, I was sitting outside our tent-like shelter, which then consisted of our tarp hung over a collection of ropes tied together between two acacia trees and supported by stolen metal tent poles. I was observing a Ted foraging beneath another tree, about four metres distant. Suddenly the bird seemed to freeze in place, and then there was subtle movement, almost a vibration in the sand around him. I was curious but saw no cause for alarm, so I walked up to less than a metre from where the small black and white bird seemed to be glued in place. Despite my proximity, the bird did not move. I leaned myopically closer and realized that the jaws of a snake encompassed the lower part of the bird, and were rhythmically working to swallow the hapless creature.

Knowing nothing about desert snakes, we called to the guard on the nearby high point. On seeing it, he grabbed the antique entrenching tool we had been using and began hacking into the sand around the snake's head. Soon it was in bits, but the head never let go of the bird. And it was the large, flat, triangular head of a viper. The snake was under a metre long but very thick, about the girth of my wrist. That same evening as we shook out our blankets to make our bed, out popped a light-green, almost translucent scorpion, six or seven centimetres long. I killed it and showed it to our jailers, who assured us that it was extremely dangerous.

Sleep did not come easily that night but finally I dozed off, only to struggle back into consciousness it seemed just moments later with my entire face and neck covered with hundreds of tiny, squirming caterpillars. They were harmless, but not pleasant.

Omar One had been assiduous in teaching us about the need to honour all God's creations, animate and inanimate. However, while all of Allah's creatures were to be protected even if they could be used to sustain life, there were, as we suspected, exceptions, though they delicately omitted infidels from the list. Prominent among the exemptions were poisonous snakes, scorpions, and hyenas, which were to be dispatched on sight. Their fear of these things was contagious and neither their fatalism nor mine was sufficient to overcome it.

One night at Camp Canada, Louis awoke with a shriek, sitting bolt upright and thereby jerking the tarp away from the barrels behind our heads and bringing down the retaining stones on top of us, loudly proclaiming there was a snake in the bed. We extracted ourselves from tarp and blankets in a flourish and the sentries came running with Kalashnikovs ready while Louis breathlessly explained the situation. We then began a methodical and careful disentanglement of the tarp, the rocks, and the bedding, seeking the offending reptile. Suddenly, in the otherworldly glare of a sentry's LED flashlight, a tiny desert mouse scampered into the night.

Often on our cross-country treks the driver or the boys in the back would spot a desert lizard, a somewhat iguana-like creature. They were usually about thirty-five centimetres long and the big, sand-coloured males carried vivid patches of red or yellow on their backs. The *mujahideen* loved to eat them and had a very specific way of hunting them. As soon as one was spotted, the driver, helped by kibitzers in the back shouting conflicting directions, looked for the lizard's burrow and then blocked it by placing a truck wheel over the entrance. That accomplished, the boys would leap off the truck and seek to grab it as it skittered among them. Once captured, it would be dispatched the way all living things were killed: throat slit while the *mujahideen* intoned, "Bismil Allah" (In the name of God). Always, for me, a chilling ritual.

The dung beetle was our constant companion wherever we travelled in the desert. These hard-working little insects left endless tiny tracks in the sand and seemed to like building their burrows close to where we slept, inevitably heading in our direction.

Although they were harmless we did not relish their crawling over us at night and were taught by our guards to blow in their faces to divert them from their invasion of our blankets. If flicked away, they would do an ostrich-like faceplant wherever they landed and remain motionless in this ludicrous position until they summoned the courage to scuttle away, often hours later.

The plant life was sparse and unremarkable. In widely separated locations, or oases, a variety of types of acacia thorn trees and a good mix of scrubby bushes and grasses grew, most of them capable of giving a nasty cut or puncture. Very little in the desert was without defence mechanisms. Aside from the shade-providing acacias, the most valuable vegetation was dead, furnishing the only fuel available.

The nomads are herders of goats and sheep but above all of camels, and some have herds well in excess of a thousand. Often in the most desolate places, we came upon camels spread across a wide area, apparently grazing, but there never seemed much for them to eat or drink. They came in all colours from snow white to almost black. Only very rarely did we encounter a herd on the move with minders in evidence. On those occasions we would be instructed not to show our faces.

A couple of times a *campagnard,* as the *mujahideen* called them, led a string of two or three camels right through the camp or majestically posed, backlit, at the rim of the depression in which the camp lay. Usually Omar One would amble out, unarmed, to chat them up. Our abductors were very careful about maintaining good relations with the local population, sharing what little food and medicines they had and generally treating the nomads with openness and respect, a policy that clearly paid dividends. Our kidnappers claimed that the Algerians offered a $100 reward to anyone calling in with an AQIM location.

I've already discussed how the desert antelope formed an important part of our diet and one Louis and I very much looked forward to. In addition, our captors would—relatively rarely—buy a sheep or goat when they encountered nomads moving through the desert. Sometimes, even when we hadn't seen any protein in a week or two, a truck would return from a water or telecommunications excursion without a trussed, bleating beast in the back and our abductors, armed to the teeth, would explain that the price had been too high.

Louis and I were awoken one night by a loud commotion right beside us. It sounded as if some savage beast were being abused, or, more precisely, like the much-amplified voice of Han Solo's side-kick, Chewbacca (the Wookie). A tethered three-year-old camel, which Omar One had purchased for the kitchen, was reluctantly being unloaded from the back of his vehicle and loudly protesting such an indignity.

We gorged ourselves on fresh meat the next day and almost everyone was involved in the butchering process. Thirty-centimetre-long narrow strips of camel meat were hung from every acacia tree in camp and thoroughly dried in the intense sun within a few hours. We ate that camel for the next seventeen days. The chewing became ever more challenging, claiming one of my teeth, but the meat remained entirely palatable.

On the day after the camel was slaughtered, Omar One offered us a large, odd-shaped flap of skin, which he said was a delicacy, the fatty camel's face. I'm afraid that despite our need of fat we declined. The next day, looking a little green around the gills, Omar allowed we were right to have refused, as he had found it much too rich.

Every now and then we would see a wary desert jackal crossing an open space in the distance, but it was the hyenas, barking and howling singly or in packs, seemingly close by, that got everybody's attention.

I was surprised, given the variety of drinking water sources (and the fact that now and then tiny swimming things could be observed in our cup), that we were not plagued by dysentery. In fact, my problem was quite the opposite, and it threatened my life very directly.

All that worry and the bad back, coupled with poor water quality and a diet bereft of fruit and vegetables, consisting of little more than rice cooked in powdered milk, did not make for regularity.

Almost from the moment of capture, constipation became a worry. Shortly after we reached Camp Canada on Day 6, it had become a concern. I would ask to go *loin* and remain squatting and forlornly hoping for great lengths of time. Then my captors would—to the embarrassment of all concerned—come looking for me. Louis usually asked, as we walked and walked, whether I was receiving any "signals" to suggest, finally, that relief was on the way. And always, always the answer was negative.

I began to limit my intake, but there was still no output. As I grew increasingly concerned, the resolution became the more elusive. By Day 41 (23 January) I had been sixteen days without a bowel movement of even the most modest kind. My belly was distended and I felt nauseated and light headed. I knew water should help but the quality was so iffy that I did not drink as much as I ought to have done. I genuinely believed that there was a real likelihood I would die of peritonitis following a ruptured bowel, and I was at a loss to know what to do about it. I asked Omar One repeatedly if there were any pills in their rudimentary medical kit that might encourage a resolution, and I was swallowing two or three gulps of their olive oil each day from a small bottle that constituted their entire supply. Omar seemed to understand that this was not a trivial issue and he too began to worry, albeit for more mercenary reasons.

Louis was as concerned as I. He kept asking what could be done and I replied that absent appropriate medication, the only solution was an enema, which we did not have. Knowing that some of the sorties were not exclusively for water and phone calls, I urged our guards to seek medication from a pharmacy and to see if an enema of any kind could be procured. But to no avail. By the sixteenth day it was clear that no help would be forthcoming from outside and that I was on my own. I determined we would create the required instrument ourselves. Louis asked me what the component parts of an enema were. When I told him and drew diagrams in the sand, his scrounger/Boy Scout mind began to machinate. He solicited Omar One's assistance as I walked for longer and more desperately in an effort to get things moving.

Omar agreed to furnish one of the Mylar bags that had contained their staple powdered milk. Louis asked for the Bic ballpoint pen we had seen from time to time in the hands of our kidnappers. Sorting through his hoard of foraged stuff he came up with a piece of inner tube. He asked for a knife, and with some reluctance it was produced. Louis then cut a thin strip of rubber from the piece he had saved.

We had been provided with a bar of soap, so we built a small fire and heated water, then stirred in the precious soap in our borrowed tin cup over the flame. We punched a small hole in the bottom of the Mylar bag, removed the nib and plastic ink reservoir tube from the pen, inserted the wide end of the Bic through the hole in the bag and sealed the pen in place with the rubber strip.

Soon we had a concentrated warm soapy mix, which we poured into the bag so we could cook up a second batch, explaining to Omar what we were up to because he was going to have to allow us to go extremely *loin* and together.

I told Louis that I was embarrassed in the extreme that this had to be a two-man job but, thankfully, we were both way past such niceties. We retreated to a spot beyond our habitual latrine in a small cave high among the rocks, and found a suitable and fairly inconspicuous location among another group of boulders below the cliff face to the west. I stretched over a reasonably smooth rock and inserted the business end of the ballpoint pen while Louis squeezed the bag. And the liquid all went where it had to go.

It seemed to be working. I was filling up with warm soapy water. I asked Louis to refill the bag from the second batch in the heated cup. In it went and the pressure deepened and increased. Then we waited. Remembering the experience of previously endured medical tests, I sought to keep that solution inside for as long as possible—then longer. Soon I became very excited by the increasingly urgent signs suggesting that relief was indeed on the way. Within a few minutes I waved Louis away, staggered behind the rock and let go the most satisfying bowel movement of my life.

Louis insists that his subsequent sighting of that long, very compact, glistening turd was one of his life's finer visions. He may have been overly taken with the joy of the moment or, then again, maybe you just had to be there. Be that as it may, my immediate and extremely acute problem was solved. And at least as important, we had proven the technology and if the problem recurred, we had the solution, as it were.

It was a good day. We had rectified (I'm getting carried away) a life-threatening issue, and even our kidnappers were taken with our ingenuity, much as they were with our various structures. Both Omars sometimes asked, "Which of the brothers showed you how to do this?"

When we replied, with ill-disguised pride, "Nobody" (and after they had checked the veracity of that response), they were gratifyingly impressed by our creativity.

We suffered all the usual scrapes, blisters, burns, and bruises that are the stuff of any extended camping expedition. Unique to our particular situation were the constant piercings by thorns: hands, arms, and even faces but, thank heavens, not eyes. At one point Louis' foot was deeply impaled by an eight-centimetre thorn right through the sole of his shoe but, again, we were fortunate that the desert climate is unfriendly to infection. At that point, "the doctor" was in camp, a figure only ever seen in the far distance, but he flatly refused to see Louis. They did, though, provide alcohol to allow us to clean the wound.

We removed small splinters with the sewing needle we had been lent, and were very careful about avoiding serious sunburn. Our teeth took a beating and we were all too evidently losing weight, which worried me more and more as I contemplated how long our ordeal might last. Beyond the ever-present concern about execution, a significant threat throughout our captivity remained the possibility that we would be killed or maimed while travelling across the desert, either in an attack by the various armed forces looking to wipe out AQIM or in some freak accident. We spent hundreds of hours in and on those damned trucks, covering huge distances.

Our kidnappers were, in the main, instinctive, highly skilled drivers but the risks they took were well off the reasonable scale. Often, particularly when driving far too fast across flat, hard desert surfaces, we came close to hitting other trucks at speed. Regularly we skidded to a halt, at night, at the very edge of a steep *wadi*: a near-vertical cliff, perhaps fifteen metres high or more, dropping into blackness almost beneath the front wheels. We would crash over—really through—the tops of knife-edged dunes without knowing anything about what kind of slope was on the other side, and it is fair to add that drivers who did not approach dune passage in this manner but flinched before their trucks reached the top generally became deeply embedded in the sand, which required twenty or thirty minutes of hard labour before they were in a position to back down the dune and try it again.

At one point, Omar One returned to Camp Canada a day and a half overdue with a harrowing tale to tell that says a lot about our kidnappers. They were on a communications run and, he explained, he had stopped at the edge of a steep *wadi* to make a sat-phone call when he felt the rim begin to give way. He stood on the brakes and then attempted to reverse, but his truck began to slide inexorably over the edge. He screamed at the four in the truck bed to abandon ship, which they were already doing, joined in short order by the young *mujahid* in the passenger seat, who rolled out of the door cradling his weapon. Omar decided to ride it down and as the truck, almost vertical, began to gather momentum, he succeeded in preventing it from flipping or rolling with judicious application of the brakes and minor steering corrections.

UN Secretary-General Kofi Annan and I confer during the Canadian presidency of the Security Council in February 1999, in Canada's sixth term (1999–2000).

We left Niamey's Grand Hotel early on Sunday, 14 December 2008, to visit the Samira Hill gold mine. We hoped to learn how resource revenues might be used to grease the skids of an eventual peace deal.

Around five o'clock in the evening on 14 December, we prepared to board this typically overcrowded ferry to cross the Niger River. Thirty minutes later we were prisoners of Al Qaeda in the Islamic Maghreb.

Once aboard the ferry, Louis Guay began chatting up the captain, sailor to sailor. Here he is, fifteen minutes before our capture, in the clothes he would wear twenty-four hours a day until they disintegrated in the course of our captivity.

Omar One, left, was the commander of the AQIM mission whose soldiers kidnapped us from the outskirts of Niamey, the capital of Niger, on the evening of 14 December 2008. He was also the last captor we set eyes on as we left the desert 130 days later.

Mokhtar Belmokhtar, above, was the commander of the AQIM group, or *katiba*, that captured and held us. We named him "Jack," as he was one-eyed. The scar across his right eye and cheek, allegedly acquired in Afghanistan, is visible even in this poor photograph.

Al Jabbar, right, gave Camp Canada its name and was unfailingly decent to us.

Imam Abdallah sought to have as little to do with us as possible.

Abou Isaac, left, was one of two steady sergeant types brought in to replace the unstable "children," who were expelled on Day 95.

Moussa, right, was a bomb maker who'd had a bad day, losing his eyesight and right hand.

Harissa was one of "the children," or young recruits. His gentle disposition and fierce pride at being an AQIM cadet were an unsettling combination.

In 1987, Chadian troops equipped with "technicals" drove the heavily mechanized Libyan army across the Aouzou Strip, which separated the two countries. While this shot is almost twenty-five years old, the method of packing and riding, the weapons, and the style of dress are all very similar to those we witnessed during our hundreds of hours spent traversing the Sahara in AQIM battlewagons.

The deathstalker is one of the more deadly scorpions and among the most common in the Sahara. Along with the venomous Sahara desert viper, they were a constant threat.

Both of these landscapes are fairly similar in appearance to Camp Canada.

We made the second proof-of-life video on Day 52, a full forty-seven days after recording essentially the same message on Day 5, but this time we were joined by our UNDP driver, Soumana Moukaila.

Agence France-Presse reported that I was wearing a *serviette*, which, in Canada, the English-language media translated as "briefcase" (which it is) rather than "scarf" (which it is also). This mistranslation resulted in stories that insisted we—being tenacious bureaucrats—were still in possession of our "briefcases."

He reported that the slope was long and steep and the ride down terrifying, and finally he was unable to avoid a large boulder near the bottom that brought him sharply to a crunching stop, seriously damaging the heavy bumper, collapsing the bodywork around the front, and smashing the radiator. Also, somewhere in the precipitous descent, the muffler and tailpipe had been torn off.

At first look, Omar said he was convinced the vehicle was a write-off, "good only for parts." But then, divinely inspired of course, he summoned his crew down from the lip of what was more a deep, not very long slit in the desert floor than a *wadi*, and began to calculate how he might extract his damaged vehicle. His young colleagues were unanimous that it was an impossible task but Omar, calling for Allah's assistance, instructed the five of them to completely unload the truck and schlep everything up the slope and then to get behind the truck and push as he engaged the four-wheel drive. He set a shallow zigzag pattern, and with straining muscles and engine, they made thirty to forty centimetres before the truck stopped its forward motion, whereupon one of them would hurl a sizable rock behind a rear wheel to stop it from slipping backward. And so they proceeded for seven hours without a break.

Omar recounted that at one point his second-in-command on this mission shouted through his window that the boys needed water and was dispatched up the slope to get some. He returned in a panic to report that the water drum was all but empty; whoever was supposed to have checked it prior to departure had not done so. Omar shushed him into silence to avoid discouraging the crew, who still had to push a heavy truck up a cliff in the middle of the Sahara without water. Omar then demanded that personal water bottles be collected to ensure that all the available water would be used only to refill the broken, steaming radiator. Yes, they had a satellite-phone and knew their GPS-generated coordinates, but to call for help would have been risky and a humiliating defeat.

They reached the top—those few centimetres at a time—and draining the last liquid they could find into the radiator, limped slowly back to camp in the cool of the night. When they showed up, utterly broken, there was quite a commotion as many believed they had been ambushed and killed by some passing patrol. One of the children, who had been talking to us at the time, threw himself at Omar's feet, forehead pressed to the ground and arms stretched forward, shouting "Sheik Omar is safe, *al-hamdu lillah*"—praise be to God.

For weeks afterward they took turns hammering away, hour after hour, attempting to repair that radiator, but eventually a replacement radiator and muffler had to be installed. The body-work and bumper were beaten out. Omar was not criticized—at least not within our hearing—for driving his truck over a cliff, but he was widely praised and admired for his stalwart faith and perseverance in bringing it back in not quite one piece.

In its stark variety, the desert is as stunning as it is daunting. Unlike Louis, though, I had trouble appreciating beauty in such circumstances. Yes, the plethora of stars in clear air so very far from any light pollution was stunning. And it's true that the many faces of the Sahara, from the high ridges of classic, shifting dunes standing across our route to the absolutely flat, almost pure white, horizonless shimmering pans of the Malian desert, or the sharp, rugged, black and red stone mountains rearing out of the desert—some streaked laterally with white salt deposits—were all dramatically different, imposing, and not a little frightening in their harsh and unforgiving primordial vastness. To me, however, that all highlighted our lack of freedom and a terrifyingly uncertain future. Louis enjoyed the glorious sunsets but I had trouble seeing past the circumstances in which we were viewing them.

From time to time, when we remarked on some aspect of our desert surroundings, our AQIM captors—usually Ibrahim or Omar One—would point out how fortunate we were to be touring the Sahara and ask if we were aware of the exorbitant prices European tourists and Saudi princes paid to see such sights. We usually just shrugged and stared them down and they grew tired of that play.

Aside from the tiny salt-mining settlement at Taoudenni, where only a couple of dozen hardy miners remain year round, there are no permanent communities in the vast region of Mali north and west of Tessalit, rather similar in its unforgiving austerity, dramatic weather, and stark emptiness to the Barren Lands of northern Canada. Nor is there an effective police or military presence anywhere in this bleak region. Mali's ill-equipped, underfunded, and poorly trained army ventures warily and rarely into the Sahara, which is the realm of a variety of nomadic peoples, and dominated by rebels, bandits, traffickers of all kinds, and, of course, Al Qaeda in the Islamic Maghreb.

The nomadic population is predominantly Tuareg, a Berber people who have a distinctive language, culture, and rather violent history, and only the vaguest allegiance to any of the half-dozen countries through which they roam. They never accepted French colonial authority and whereas boys of my generation in North America were brought up on tales of cowboys and Indians, in France it was all about Legionnaires defending little white crenellated forts against indigo-garbed Tuareg hoards mounted on pale camels and wielding flashing sabres (the archetype being the 1939 movie *Beau Geste*).

There have been a succession of Tuareg rebellions in both Mali and Niger, and in every negotiated settlement, usually brokered by not necessarily benevolent outside interests—most notably those of Algeria and Libya—hold-out factions have insisted on continuing their struggle against the governments in Bamako and Niamey. Yet Tuareg serve in the armies of Mali and Niger as well as in specially raised militias in northern Mali, and, of course, in AQIM. More recently they have become the core of Muammar Gaddafi's "African mercenaries."

Thus the Sahara houses a complex netherworld of people operating outside and beyond any law. Gun runners bring weapons and ammunition of every description, mostly of Soviet-era origin and mostly from Sudan, Somalia, and Chad, to clients across the western Sahel. Drug traffickers are reportedly paid $40,000 by Colombia's FARC rebels or their West African partners to run a shipment of cocaine from, say, Guinea-Bissau across the Sahara to the eastern Mediterranean littoral, from where it is taken into Europe's soft underbelly or to the Arabian peninsula and the Gulf States.

Such vast sums of drug money are wreaking havoc within the traditional Tuareg leadership structure. The elders find it increasingly difficult to hold sway over, and can exert little discipline on, the flash kids with weapons and pockets full of cash. Absent the traditionally strong Tuareg cultural foundation and clan discipline, the kids are easier pickings for AQIM as the region drifts toward the anarchy of Somalia and the turmoil of Darfur, which, my jailers told me, was very much their objective.

Then there are the people movers—the African equivalents of the Asian snakeheads—who for a substantial fee escort desperate people from West Africa who brave the perilous Sahara and the Mediterranean crossing to attempt illegal immigration to Europe. Their hope is to find employment in those lands of plenty so they can send money home to their all too often starving families. Many of these people had been awaiting their moment to get across the Mediterranean when they were caught up in the piteous suffering, turmoil, and upheaval currently besetting Libya. And finally, there are the ordinary smugglers who have worked these regions for millennia.

Escaping from AQIM into the clutches of any of these shadowy groups would not necessarily have changed our circumstances for the better.

CHAPTER 7

SURVIVAL IN THE DESERT

══

His great bright eye most silently
Up to the Moon is cast—

If he may know which way to go;
For she guides him smooth or grim

══

As we took stock of our surroundings and as the miasma of terror and pain that had been the currency of our first five days of captivity began to dissipate, we girded ourselves for the long haul. But how long was that going to be?

Louis was adamant that we must set our clocks to eight months, for we knew that had been the period the Austrian tourists had spent as hostages of AQIM in northern Mali. This seemed an awfully long time to me but I could not fault his logic, nor did I want to contemplate the implications of other models, most far longer and tougher than the ordeal the Austrians had faced. Still, eight months—240 days—seemed longer than I could bear.

We understood from the outset that our greatest strength was each other. So far, we had remained together. We had been able to help, comfort, support, assist, cajole, challenge, shame, sustain, and encourage one another. We had not been close friends before this nightmare nor had we worked together for very long on this UN mission, but we understood that we were fortunate to be in this mess together. We were also well aware that alone the chance of coming through unscathed would be considerably diminished for each of us.

We decided that we needed a business plan. We would strive at all costs to maintain healthy bodies in the extremely hostile environment in which we found ourselves, with the hope and expectation that physical health would help preserve mental health and maintain morale, which we took to be our greatest challenge.

To achieve this we determined to institutionalize that first walk among the desert melons at TV Camp, so we designed a track, or *piste*, in the immediate vicinity of our designated acacia tree at Camp Canada: one sufficiently modest in its dimensions, we hoped, to avoid arousing the suspicions of our kidnappers that we might be up to something. We paced out a richly contorted route, nineteen circuits to the kilometre, and decided to walk it twice a day—at dawn and dusk—with a view to putting in a total of between four and six kilometres each day.

Usually we managed two and a half or three kilometres by breakfast, and thus had a minimum of one to one and a half to do in the evening. Although four was our minimum, we often managed five or six each day. Our cost–benefit analysis of the physical and psychological advantages to be derived from exercise versus the calories we had to expend, which we knew were not being adequately replaced, capped our ambitions at six, although on rare occasions of extreme stress I would exceed this.

Louis would carefully mark each circuit in the sand with a twisted stick. Six kilometres meant 114 circuits on this track so the markings stretched half way around. Our captors became so used to this ritual that we would see them in the far distance mimicking our gestures, no doubt mockingly, but relatively good naturedly, which we took to be a good sign.

Initially, this regime was quite a challenge: first because this was more exercise than either of us had managed for decades in

Canada; and second because we had not anticipated any of the psychological, climatic, or nutritional challenges we would face in maintaining such an exercise regime. Still, we stuck with the program, and while there were always reasons why one or the other of us should not proceed with what our abductors came to call *votre sport* (as in, "Est-ce que vous avez déjà fait votre sport?"—Have you completed your exercise?), we almost always reached our target.

At first we began with various warming-up exercises—knee bends, body twists, and a variety of stretching exercises—but Louis wasn't very interested in such things. So I resolved to embellish my walking with some of the upper-body moves, switching them every few circuits. Needless to say, these additional antics only added to the amusement of our captors.

We usually began before sunrise and as the rim of the sun appeared above the horizon the flies would begin to gather and I would estimate their numbers on Louis' jacket. Often I counted more than a hundred and, of course, they covered his pants and turban as well. I knew I was also covered with flies but focusing on Louis helped me to ignore mine. Soon, though, our exercise would be augmented by a jerky flailing of arms as we sought to rid ourselves of the gathering swarms. For each of us our exercise regime was very therapeutic. It never failed to reduce anxiety and help us to sleep in the evenings. Not at all incidentally, it also helped to ease the pain in my lower back, which never felt better than when I was walking.

As we walked and thought about if and how we were going to get through all this, being a tidy bureaucrat I developed guidelines, which were effectively rules to govern our behaviour.

First rule—*no what ifs or if onlys*. We agreed, first tacitly and subsequently explicitly, that it would be perilous, counterproductive, and downright self-indulgent to wallow in any musings about what had brought us to this pretty pass. Thus we never—not once—discussed whether or not I should have accepted this assignment from the UN Secretary-General; whether Louis should have agreed to sign on as my assistant; if we really had to make the trip from which we were abducted or whether we ought to have remained by the pool at the hotel in Niamey that Sunday afternoon; or, indeed, to play the blame game of wondering if we would be in this pickle if only the other guy had . . .

Second rule—*no discussing bad stuff after midday.* Very soon we realized that if we shared our worst worries and fears late into the night, we would not be able to sleep with such thoughts chasing each other toward what my brother, Bruce, calls "the hour of the wolf": that period just before dawn when even at the best of times everything looks bleak. Thus, in a ridiculously effective act of self-delusion, we decreed that those dark thoughts could be aired and dissected in the morning, and they regularly were, but not after lunch. Often, though, one of us would start to verbalize a thought only to bring himself up short with, "It will wait until tomorrow," and the other would not press. Sometimes this ritual became blatantly ridiculous as one of us would suggest, "Remind me to ask you about [whatever horrible thought] tomorrow morning."

Third rule—*no discussing anything sensitive after dark.* We could not tell where our kidnappers were and they might be close enough to hear, which they tried to do at least once.

Fourth rule—*absolute avoidance of rabbit holes.* This was the most important and had to be strictly enforced. As soon as one of us started into some spiral of desperate worry, the other was to use every wile or insult to pull him back out. Such dangers were ever present. Sometimes such pits of despair were easily avoidable; on other occasions and with no warning, one of us would begin to slip into such a hole and resist very aggressively the other's rescue attempts. I always knew, though, that Louis was there when I was down and my feelings of responsibility for him meant that I would not let myself, or him, wander too far or for too long underground.

We both understood that we had to be particularly vigilant about diving down separate holes, or the same rabbit hole, simultaneously.

❖

Our daily routine could not have been more rudimentary and it varied very little. We would get up before sunrise, discreetly splash a small handful of cold water over our faces and work at our teeth with the faux-arak-root sticks, rinsing with a small mouthful of water. Then the walk and breakfast as we stood trying to find warmth in the rising sun.

After breakfast we would shake the sand out of the blankets and spread them over rocks and bushes to air in the sun. Sometimes I might fiddle with improving our position in the shade of the acacia by using the purloined entrenching tool with a broken handle to build a long, curving couch around our tree in the sand and Louis might work at improving the imperfect shade offered by the thin canopy of the acacia by collecting armloads of long, sharp grass and spreading it in layers among the thorny branches above our heads.

We were then chased by the growing intensity of the sun onto that couch and would move along and around it as the sun ever so slowly tracked across the sky. Eventually the uninviting, battered aluminum bowl of lunch was dropped nearby and we would dutifully dig in, with little enthusiasm.

Both Louis and I are pretty gregarious guys but even I was surprised by how rarely we ran out of conversation. We spoke of everything, ranging over our upbringing, our families, our children, and our professional lives, to politics, national and international, the state of the world, our friends and colleagues, public service, the private sector, religion, music, even sports, and the physical environment and, inevitably, updating our exhaustive analyses of our captors, individually and collectively. Always, the conversation would turn to our current circumstances, a reading of the latest indications from the behaviour of our kidnappers and speculation about what might be occurring back home vis-à-vis our families and efforts to get us out of there—and what it would take to find freedom.

One or both of us would usually drift off into a fitful sleep in the building heat, but we were mindful that if we did too much of that we would not sleep at night and we knew we needed that sleep to keep our wits about us.

In the late afternoon, as the sun began to set behind the cliff face to our left, we watched the shade line stretch across the space in front of our tree and, when it reached a designated bush, it would be time for the evening portion of our walk, if, that is, Omar One had not shown up for a reading from the Qur'an, or Omar Two did not loom above us to assess our readiness to become his brothers in faith.

Those sessions, or our walk, would eventually be interrupted by their evening prayers. After some discussion Louis and I decided, almost from our arrival at Camp Canada, that we would show respect for their so deeply cherished religion by standing—during the daylight prayers—while they assembled in a single line facing east fifty metres away from us. That practice was fiercely resented by those few who believed it to be cravenly designed to curry their favour but admired by most, who took it to be a freely offered sign of respect. In fact, I found the chanting, rhythmic, soft voice of the imam rather soothing, and those became welcome contemplative moments during which I developed a ritual of my own.

I have, since an early age, found religion faintly ridiculous. I do not write this to cause offence to anybody and hope I have not done so. Indeed, I respect the evident fact that many wise people and some close friends profoundly disagree with me on this rather fundamental point, beginning with Louis. So, while these *jihadi* fundamentalists prayed to their god and Louis spoke to his, I talked to my family.

I imagined we were all gathered before the fireplace in our log cabin in the woods northeast of Ottawa. I saw myself approaching each member of my family, beginning with Mary. Taking her face between my hands, I kissed her eyes and then, lightly, her mouth, and looking into her eyes I told her how much I loved her and how much she had made my life better, fuller, and more enjoyable than ever it could have been without her. I thanked her for her love, her generosity, and for being such a wonderful mother to all our children and their families. And I asked her to forgive me for the pain I was currently causing her.

I then went through essentially the same ritual with each of my daughters, in order of age: first Linton, then Ruth, Antonia, and Justine. Then it was the turn of the grandchildren, Grier, Alice, and Henry. Their men received more macho treatment: a squeeze of the shoulder, a look in their eyes, and my thanks for taking such good care of our girls and grandchildren.

This intimate rite was repeated each evening, beginning on the third night at Camp Canada. I found it both emotionally wrenching and deeply comforting.

Once the sun had dipped well below the high *wadi* wall to the west, darkness would fall fast and we prepared to bed down. I would smooth out our cocoon-shaped side-by-side sleeping positions, removing thorns and stones and checking for scorpions, and then we again shook out our well-toasted blankets, made the bed, and stretched the tarp over the barrels. We'd have a brief conversation—mindful of the relevant rules—and sometimes sleep came quickly, and sometimes it would not.

We really didn't know much about how our captors organized themselves, other than what we saw from our tree. Usually we were woken up by the sounds of their pre-dawn prayer (for which we did not stand) in total darkness. Many of our jailers then returned to their blankets, widely dispersed throughout the camp, for a little more sleep, while the designated kitchen staff lit fires and began to make the rudimentary breakfast.

They shared all the essential tasks. Everyone—including Jack and his staff, when they were in the camp—took his turn at kitchen duty and everyone stood sentry duty on the basis of an established roster. We would often see Omar One wandering around the camp, working out that roster on a scrap of cardboard.

There were always sentries out, one with a belt-fed PK machine gun on the highest point near at hand, which at Camp Canada was on a small peak atop the cliff face to the southwest, from which the sentry had a clear field of fire over our entire designated area. As well, mobile sentries ranged widely to the north, west, and south. At night, Soumana would be brought to sleep near us and at least two sentries watched the three of us—one static, sitting a few metres from us and usually in the company of one of the children, the other mobile, patrolling a radius of about twenty metres from our position.

Aside from the water and telecommunications sorties, our captors would spend the day repairing trucks or tires, sleeping when coming off sentry duty, or praying, chanting, and reading the Qur'an. When on the move they only very reluctantly travelled in the extreme heat of the day, between about 11:00 a.m. and 4:00 p.m. If the journey they had in mind required more travel than could be accomplished before or after that, they found somewhere to wait out the brutal part of the day, but I was never happy when that meant we would be travelling fast across the desert at night.

Extreme worry and fear were enormously debilitating and physically taxing (memory loss, diminished appetite, insomnia). Certainly, they were major contributors to my constipation issues.

But for somebody who has spent most of his professional life analyzing geostrategic challenges, it was also fascinating to be living, talking, and sleeping with Al Qaeda. At one point I said to Louis that if only we knew this nightmare would end well, from a professional point of view this very intimate opportunity to examine militant Islamic fundamentalism—arguably the greatest current threat to international stability—would be a unique and informative experience. I think it was at that point that I decided if I got out in one piece, I would write this book.

Unfortunately, of course, we did not know if it would end well. I admit to a sometimes pessimistic outlook (my wife calls me "Cassandra"—and each time she does, I remind her that although nobody believed her dire prophesies, the youngest daughter of Priam was always right in her predictions), and I just could not convince myself that a happy ending was likely. Therefore, increasingly, I turned my thoughts to the daunting prospect of escape and the unhappy calculations pertaining to rescue scenarios.

Our escape plotting centred on the fundamental issue of establishing our location. Unless we knew where to head and that getting there was feasible, any attempt would be futile and quite possibly fatal. Would we be able to get a reasonable start before we were missed, given 24/7 guards? And, of course, the cost–benefit calculation had to measure the prospect of a successful attempt against the certainty of reprisals which would follow a failed attempt.

We knew we were about a thousand kilometres into the Sahara, north of Gao and at a somewhat greater distance northeast of Tombouctou. I figured that if I could slip away into a moonless night, I could probably walk twenty kilometres before dawn, carrying—if Louis agreed—our communal four-litre plastic jug of water. That would leave only 980 kilometres to go. I knew I would not last long once the sun came up and, unless I left during one of the relatively rare sandstorms, which itself would probably do me in, a child could follow my tracks across the desert. They would accomplish that in a few minutes in one of their trucks.

Then there was the issue of where to head, and the only plan I could come up with was to go south . . . hundreds and hundreds of kilometres across the Sahara desert. Even if I could find a well-travelled track and a passing vehicle were to pick me up, there was a good possibility that anyone transiting those regions would simply hand me back to AQIM or turn out to be worse abductors. As for retribution for any escape attempt, I had to consider the likelihood that it would be visited upon both me and Louis, whether or not he were to join me in the attempt, and likely to be worse for him in the extremely unlikely event that I succeeded.

If we attempted to escape, we understood that we would, in effect, be breaking the rules of the limited, Middle Ages style of "parole" that had been tacitly accorded us and had won us at least the freedom from being blindfolded and bound and the right to walk for health and sanitary reasons. Losing such privileges would have dire consequences for our psychological and perhaps physical well-being, and would have changed our relationship with our captors—and a number of them would have welcomed such a development. Finally, I was well aware that were I to proceed with an escape attempt without Louis' agreement and assistance, that decision would also change the relationship between us, one on which I heavily depended.

I realized that the essential escape parameters were unlikely ever to be satisfied, but I never wrote off the possibility that that could change.

❖

My constant, clearly obsessive, running of rescue scenarios risked driving me crazy, but here too I never stopped gaming out how a successful rescue operation might or should go down in whatever circumstances we found ourselves. Obviously some situations offered better opportunities than others, the night only four of our captors were present being dramatically better than when the full complement of thirty was on hand. I must say, though, that I considered the chances of a totally successful rescue only marginally better than those of a successful escape attempt, less for on-site operational reasons and more because I believed that the policy decision making back home would necessarily be too timid and too late.

For a rescue to stand any chance of success, we would have to be precisely located; moreover, the chances of success stood in direct proportion to the amount of time any potential rescuers would have to observe and understand the conditions of our captivity. But would the political decision making take into account such an operational reality?

Obviously, any rescue mission would depend on our would-be saviours incapacitating anyone with a gun on us before we could be killed as the attack came in. Would our kidnappers shoot us at the first sign of trouble? The answer, I determined, was an unequivocal yes. I am absolutely certain that our guards and sentries had firm orders to dispatch us first—before, that is, they took any measures to defend themselves. Their body language was explicit in this regard.

I often worried that some extraneous event—say, some smuggler blundering into the camp in the middle of the night or one of our captors inadvertently discharging a weapon—would cause us to be shot by some jumpy, hair-triggered sentry.

Some years ago, I'd had something to do with establishing Canada's outstanding special operations and hostage rescue force, Joint Task Force Two (JTF2). I know and admire them and their remarkable capabilities. While I thought a successful rescue was unlikely, as our situation deteriorated I hoped on occasion that they would come, and I was prepared to accept ever-longer odds on success.

So we lay in the sand, gazing up at more stars than I had ever contemplated, trying to keep hope alive, both anticipating and dreading a rescue attempt as we fixed rendezvous points and now and then went to bed wearing our shoes.

CHAPTER 8

OUR AQIM CAPTORS

―――

God save thee, ancient Mariner,
From the fiends, that plague thee thus!

―――

In most cases, the names with which our abductors introduced
themselves were either their *noms de guerre* or some other fabrication, which may or may not have resembled their actual names.
For instance, our masked interrogator (whom we sometimes called
"I" so no one would know whom we were discussing) told us his
name was Hassan, but when we spoke of him to the others they
said they did not know who we were talking about. Despite this,
we heard them referring to him as "Hassam," but we assumed that
too was an alias.

We did not speak Arabic and only three of our captors spoke
French fluently: Omar One, Ibrahim, and Hassan. Omar Two spoke
it reasonably well. He had had a good French secondary education
some twenty years previously and although his French was rusty, it
came back quickly through conversation with us. Of course, we did
have many and, on some occasions, long conversations with others,
including Jack and his principal lieutenants, Omar Three, Ahmed,
Abdul Rahman, and Jaffer, but these "discussions" always took
place through the not necessarily good offices of one or other of the

fluent French speakers, acting as interpreter. In sum, the vast bulk of our interaction with the AQIM group that held us was with Omars One and Two and Hassan. While Ibrahim could have acted as an effective interpreter, and on a few occasions did, he was a member of Jack's staff and, as a result, visited our camps only sporadically.

Four more had a more tenuous grasp of French but it was possible to hold simple conversations with them: Suleiman, young Al Zarqawi, Ahmed, and Adama. To a significantly lesser extent, this was also true with Ali, Al Jabbar, Julabib, and the young "AR2." All the remainder had some familiarity with French, but they tended to understand it better than they spoke it and, we suspected, far better than many let on. The gentle Nigerian, Obeida, spoke some English but he was discouraged from practising it with us.

While our captors refused to teach us Arabic, Louis and I liked to think that we became good at interpreting what was going on within their group and vis-à-vis us, simply by observing gestures and body language and listening to their tones of voice. Even at the best of times, though, their dialect tended to sound angry to our Western ears.

Some of the main characters among our captors have already been introduced, but some additional observations about those most relevant to this story and their relationships with us are in order.

Jack, the commander, or emir, of the AQIM group that held us, was a natural leader. He exuded understated authority and an ever-present degree of menace, which served to maintain a palpable if reasonably relaxed discipline among his disparate gang. I never heard him raise his voice or upbraid one of his crew but regularly saw him managing and advising them. While they called him Khaled, it was with evident deference, and to us they usually referred to him as "our emir." He was correct in his behaviour toward us, never warm or friendly but not gratuitously unpleasant either. Others among our guards were habitually aggressive and threatening toward us, but they did not behave this way in Jack's presence.

There were three Omars in Khaled's *katiba,* or battalion, but Louis and I had more to do with Omar One than with all our other captors combined. Omar was a Malian Arab who had travelled widely as an itinerant Islamic preacher. He spoke of having visited France and all the countries of North Africa, as well as India, Pakistan, Somalia, Sudan, Chad, Niger, Burkina Faso, Senegal, and Mauritania.

From various clues, we deduced that Omar was forty-seven. He was a shortish, wiry type, with brown eyes and the full, well-defined lips and cheekbones of a North African Arab. His beard was light and his hands were hard and rough. He was a tireless, relentless worker—always busy—and a seemingly accomplished mechanic. Despite his extensive travels he had no real understanding of the complex, contradictory reality of life in the West, nor did he have any significant intellectual experience outside his narrow Islamist milieu.

While a deeply committed and charismatic preacher, Omar's extensive knowledge of the fundamental texts of Islam was learned by rote and he seemed to have a superficial, even simplistic, understanding of and little curiosity about the underlying theological issues and historical context. He could quote great swaths of the Qur'an and recite a withering number of *hadith*. In addition, he was an animated and compelling raconteur, but he was incapable of adapting the circumstances and meaning of those divine words spoken and written fifteen centuries ago to encompass any kind of twenty-first century reality. The words in which he had invested his entire life were precisely those that had been dictated over twenty-three years by the Prophet in the seventh century as he received Allah's revelations from the Angel Gabriel. Nothing that had occurred since had any relevance either to those words or to Omar's being, purpose, or direction in life.

Thus, Omar the preacher sought to establish a personal bond with us, as potential recruits to Islam. His preaching was very much oriented to his *jihadi* vocation. He regularly offered proof of Allah's support for their cause by citing instances in which angels, clad in radiant white, accompanied the *mujahideen* in battle, which enabled them to overcome impossible odds. In one case he claimed that nineteen of their brothers had held off a 3,500-strong Algerian mechanized brigade for five days. After killing over 500, they slipped away, leaving behind three fallen martyrs who had ascended to the *mujahideen* house in paradise. The eyes of the young acolytes would grow bright and round as Omar described such battlefields, which, he breathlessly insisted, had been strewn with the dismembered corpses of the apostate enemy, blackened stumps evident where the avenging angels had smitten off limbs with their fiery swords.

There was no one among our kidnappers with whom we spent more time, nobody whom we knew better than Omar, even if he always remained something of an enigma.

We were his project. Our impression was that he was our advocate vis-à-vis his *mujahideen frères,* but not in any sense our friend. He led the team that took us and was a full, committed, and enthusiastic participant in our kidnapping. His exclusive concern was that it serve their *jihadi* purposes. He considered it his Islamic duty to explain and justify their *jihad* to us. Effectively, he was Khaled's hostage liaison officer, a responsibility he took very seriously and jealously protected.

Omar offered us slightly different accounts of the Old Testament favourites: of Adam and the duplicitous Eve; of Abraham being catapulted into the massive fire, which consumed only his bonds; of Moses' miraculous parting of the Red Sea (into twelve channels, though, unlike Cecil B. DeMille's version). He read to us Miriam's story from the Qur'an, which told of the life of her son, the prophet Isa (Jesus). But he aggressively and disdainfully explained why Isa could not be the son of God, that no one could be associated with Allah, and how Isa did not die on any cross.

Joining Louis and me as we watched a meteor shower one evening, Omar explained how thousands of *jinn* (genies), acting for

Satan, would climb upon each other's shoulders until they reached just below heaven so that they could eavesdrop on the angels' plans and how, when the *jinn* were discovered, the angels would hurl bolts of fire, dashing them to the earth, which was what we were seeing in the sky.

Omar spoke rapturously of the delights of paradise. Yes, there were the seventy-two virgins, but I hadn't been aware of the refinement that they were invisible to each other, I guess to avoid uncomfortable comparisons. There were indeed rivers of milk and honey, and the meanest dwelling was ten thousand times more resplendent than the most magnificent palace on earth. Only the most perfect among the faithful would be able to view the face of God, and it would be so beautiful that they would not blink for forty days.

Omar told us with great reverence and detail what would occur leading up to the Day of Judgment and then on that day itself, of Gabriel's questioning, on Allah's behalf, of each part and each organ of the body—none of which, of course, could speak anything but the absolute truth—to determine the individual's worthiness for admission to paradise. He described the tortures of hell in as meticulous and vivid detail, and again and again he urged us to consider our options very carefully. The Day of Judgment was indeed nigh in his view, and he wanted us to be fully aware of how relevant this ought to be to two weak and elderly unbelievers held by Al Qaeda in the Sahara. If we died without having submitted to Allah, the horrors of hell would be immediate and extreme. To that end he detailed the Five Pillars of Islam and regularly explained the simple act that would make us their Muslim brothers.

One day, Omar One stumbled past us looking terrible. Clearly he was going *loin*, and he was away a long time. He stopped by our tree on his way back, ashen faced and worried. "Have you ever known a situation in which you have to vomit while passing bloody stools?" he asked. That afternoon, looking worse, he came by to say he was off to see a traditional healer but expected to be back in a few days. In fact, we did not see him for more than three weeks.

When he returned, looking fit, he explained that three "old women" had managed to suspend him from a frame made of sticks and he had spent hour after hour hanging upside down while they periodically beat the soles of his feet in order to cure his stomach ailment.

Our relationship with Omar One was complex. He was our original abductor, with whom we had descended into our own hell. Yet he was one of the few who ever stopped by just to chat, seemingly to pass the time. Ostensibly, he came to proselytize—and that he did, with passion and zeal—but, uniquely among our abductors, he seemed genuinely interested in our well-being, beyond, that is, the maintenance of valuable assets. He desperately wanted us to convert because he believed it would save us from the fires of hell and, yes, make his own place in paradise a little more secure. But he was never much interested in learning about life outside of the seventh-century bubble in which these soldiers of Allah lived. In military-speak, he was always on "send," never on "receive."

Our biggest concern in seeing Omar One leave us at Camp Canada was less that we would lose our entertaining preacher and conversationalist and more that we would be deprived of what we took to be a reasonably well-intentioned interpreter, thereby abandoning us to the manifestly ill-disposed mercies of either Hassan or Omar Two. Not a happy prospect.

We were to learn just how unhappy during one of our rare meetings with the camp commander, Abdul Rahman. That bizarre discussion among AR, Louis, and me, with Hassan interpreting, was conducted in pitch-black darkness so we were without visible gestures or facial clues. At one point, risking his ire, I asked Abdul Rahman what he could tell us of whatever negotiations might be underway. When this was interpreted by Hassan, to our surprise and excitement, AR replied dispassionately and at great length, perhaps three minutes' worth, following which we turned expectantly toward Hassan, who flatly offered, "They are proceeding." Louis and I sat, holding our breath, desperate for more, but no more was forthcoming.

There followed a short, sharp exchange between AR and Hassan, which we could only assume was about what Hassan had not interpreted. We had the impression that the camp emir was instructing Hassan to tell us what he had said but that the latter refused, insisting we had no right to such information. However tempting, Louis and I decided that there was nothing to be gained by entering this discussion and demanding a fuller or better interpretation. Had we done so, somebody would have lost a lot of face, which would have boded ill for us, and even if AR prevailed, there was still no guarantee that Hassan would say anything he did not want to say. AR seemed to understand this as well and, with evident frustration, let it go. There was no way, though, that we could take any of this as an indication that an early resolution of our situation was in the offing.

Omar Two, the curly-haired, bearded, dark-eyed *jihadi* warrior, was by any definition handsome: a harder, bigger, lankier, more tightly wound, mid-thirties version of Omar Sharif. I once told him that he seemed to me to be from the same mould as the great warrior-prince Saladin, an image he clearly enjoyed, although in painting it I was seeking to remind him of Saladin's well-established reputation for chivalry in battle and toward prisoners, including Christians.

In the middle of the desert, Omar Two used cologne and applied kohl to highlight his large, wide-set, and menacing eyes. Both were sanctioned, even encouraged, he assured us, by the Qur'an. He was the one who decreed that we must not cut our beards and periodically provided us with a shard of mirror and tiny scissors to allow us to trim our moustaches (which was permitted—for sanitary purposes) and, on too rare occasions, nail clippers. He was also the one who would sometimes (and sometimes not) lend Louis needles and thread to repair our shoes, clothing, and much-torn blue plastic tarp.

He was much intrigued by dreams and constantly inquired

about ours in order to exercise his training in interpretation. Strangely, we never seemed to have had any—neither of us wanting to have Omar Two playing around in the dream spaces inside our heads.

On one occasion I was sandwiched between Omar Two, at the wheel, and Abdul Rahman, when the latter was giving driving lessons to the former. Clearly these were early days in this seasoned warrior's driving career and he seemed to possess no aptitude for it and no appreciation of the mechanics involved. Omar Two sat hunched around the wheel staring fixedly ahead as, time after time, he popped the clutch and stalled while three other vehicles waited for him to lead off. The others seemed to enjoy his humiliation. He appeared to be particularly embarrassed that I had been assigned to act as the primary witness and I feared there would be a price to pay for observing this spectacle, which I never saw repeated.

He was an odd creature, very detached and darkly mystical. The others gave him a fairly wide berth. Both he and they spoke to us about his large hoard of religious texts, which he would consult for hours on end. On one occasion, we were speaking with Hassan when Omar Two's name came up and Hassan, not a little dismissively, referred to him as "old school." Hassan then wryly allowed, "They don't make them like that any more." You could almost hear the "thanks be to Allah" he was thinking.

Ibrahim, "le Sénégalais," was, of course, one of our original abductors. Most memorably, he had given me the news that we had been taken by Al Qaeda and then, some hours later, confided in a hushed whisper how much he admired Céline Dion. He was a tall, rangy, good-looking young man, full of barely controlled energy. He was the only one among our captors who seemed to be naturally, irrepressibly gregarious, indeed mischievous, and whenever he was in camp he usually dropped by for a chat. He spent a few days at Camp Canada with us following our arrival but then disappeared with Jack and seemed to be a permanent fixture on Jack's immediate staff.

He never explained what had caused him to take up the path of *jihad*, but at one point I was in a truck with him when out of the blue he told me he had a sister in Montreal who had been continually after him to immigrate to Canada to join her. He then turned to me, guilelessly, and asked, "I guess it's a little late now?" I was hard put to tell him otherwise but then, if we didn't return, maybe it wouldn't be.

Ibrahim had a sense of fun and impish humour, but he had an equally evident mean streak and from our point of view, he was unpredictable and utterly untrustworthy.

Al Jabbar was perhaps the most genuinely sympathetic among our jailers. He said he was thirty-four, but looked older with his rich, long black beard. He too was tall and fit and, demonstrating unique immodesty, pulled open his tunic one day to show us the two bullet wounds (one in the upper chest and the other in the lower back) he had acquired in fifteen years of *jihad*. He had been brought up in a middle-class family in Algiers but, surprisingly, spoke almost no French. He was a machine gunner and never very far from his cherished PK weapon. Eventually, he too was assigned to Jack's staff.

On occasion, when Omar One or Omar Two was chatting with us, Al Jabbar would drop by, plunk himself down and just listen for twenty or thirty minutes before nodding to us all and leaving. From time to time he brought us little things (matches, a candy) on his way to sentry duty.

He took the "proof-of-life" photos of Louis and me together and separately with his Nokia cellphone, explaining, largely with sign language, what he wanted to do and where he wanted us to sit. As for why, he said, "famille, famille" and then mimed the tracks of tears, adding crying sounds, "waah, waah," before he took the pictures.

On the same phone he regularly showed us photos of his nineteen-year-old wife, Miriam, who had died in childbirth in early January just after we were taken. The daughter, their second child, had survived and been named Aisha. On one occasion, as he walked by our position late at night, he awakened Louis, with whom he had a particular bond, and wordlessly showed him the photos and then moved on into the night. Through Omar One—who evidently did not want to transmit such information—Al Jabbar explained the whole story of Miriam's death and told us of his dreams in which she had appeared to him from paradise, where, she said, she was preparing the "*mujahideen* house" for them all.

We knew Omar Three first as "Big Guy" when we saw him in the distance after a few weeks at Camp Canada. He was different from the others. He was rotund, a little older, and clearly not a warrior. It became evident to us that Big Guy, while not in command, was the senior officer in camp and was probably providing Jack with back-channel reports.

One day, I asked Big Guy for his name and to the evident surprise of Omar One, with whom he had been talking, he replied "Omar." It was probably one of his many names but to us he then became Omar Three, or "O3." While he too remained fairly distant (his French was very basic), he invariably sent us positive messages.

Suleiman was twenty or twenty-one, a rather simple boy from the Mediterranean coast to the east of Algiers who went with the wind, blowing hot and cold toward us according to the last person he spoke to. Prior to joining up, he had been a honey catcher; that is, he would follow bees to their nests, grab the honey, and sell it in small local markets. He was slow to the point that Jack clearly found him dangerous and eventually he disappeared, leaving the large plastic mat he had lent to us.

At least as important as the mat was the fact that after a few weeks at Camp Canada, we had mentioned to Omar One and also to Suleiman how much we would welcome something to read. We had been refused their Arabic–French edition of the Qur'an—as infidels we could not be allowed to touch the holy book—but hoped for old newspapers, magazines, in fact anything at all. Suddenly one day, Suleiman showed up bearing a large-format paperback history textbook from what appeared to be the final year of the Belgian *lycée* system. It was about three centimetres thick and was the second in a four-part series on the history of the world and of Belgium (they received about equal treatment), from prehistoric times to the present. The volume Suleiman delivered to us covered the period from the birth of Christ to the year 1000, and the introduction explained that volume three would take students through the Renaissance and Reformation, while the fourth and final volume would cover the seventeenth through twentieth centuries.

The book was well illustrated, with lots of highlighted boxes and seminal quotations. It was precisely what we had hoped for. Immediately Louis began to read it aloud for about forty minutes each afternoon in what came to be a much-anticipated respite from our monotonous daily routine. In addition to being interesting and providing lots of food for thought and discussion, the textbook was well thumbed, with intriguing handwritten marginal notes and carefully highlighted passages, particularly, of course, when we reached the seventh and eighth centuries and the birth and spread of Islam.

As we spent more time with Hassan and became familiar with his manner of thinking and speaking, we were ever more certain that the books were his. We were, though, careful to avoid suggesting to the masked man that we had made that connection, as we suspected that doing so might have caused him to feel less secure in his disguise.

Both Omar One and Hassan aggressively inquired how that book had come into our possession and we saw no reason to prevaricate, allowing that Suleiman had responded to our request for reading material. They were clearly not happy, though not only were we allowed to keep it but when we had finished reading it we were provided with the third volume. We never set eyes on the first or final parts of the series.

At one point Suleiman walked by on one of the rare occasions we were able to wash our clothes. Observing this for a while, and with evident distaste, he asked what in Canada would have been a politically charged question: "At home, do your wives do that?" Even here the truth seemed to make sense and I replied that, yes, that was usually the case, but sometimes we did it ourselves. When he shook his head with a combination of disgust and amazement, we asked in return if his wives (he had said he had two) did his laundry. He reacted with genuine horror. "Of course not!" this honey-hunter spat. "We have slaves for that!" and walked away appalled.

"Socks" was a Tuareg kid of eighteen or nineteen with a big chip on his shoulder. He would sneer at us whenever he deigned to look in our direction, which was not often. He was a loyal disciple of and completely in thrall to Hassan, whom this impressionable kid recognized as the most ruthless and militarily disciplined among them. There is no doubt in my mind that he too would have liked to do us harm. We called him Socks in view of his habit of tucking his pants into whatever fluorescent knee-length green, yellow, or blue socks he was wearing.

There was one other Tuareg in the Belmokhtar group. He was right out of central casting, about seventeen, very surly, tall and thin, neither dark nor light skinned, with classic Tuareg features, nose strong, thin, and straight. We knew him as "the Tuareg Kid." I don't think he ever said anything to us but in the early days at Camp Canada he was often the guard designated to accompany me *loin* and would inevitably come close and forcefully gesture at my wedding ring, and point to himself, signing, "Give it to me." I would sign that I could not get it off, which failed to satisfy him, and then walk faster.

He too was part of Hassan's adoring posse, and eventually Hassan approached Louis and me and demanded our wedding rings. We had the impression that this was more in order to show his entourage that he could deliver than to acquire more booty of war for himself. Each of us made an effort to remove our rings. Hassan produced soap, but they would not budge, even in our increasingly emaciated state. Eventually, Hassan just threw up his hands and stomped off, a rather happy outcome, given the alternatives.

The most prominent among the children was, without a doubt, the infelicitously named Al Zarqawi, a small, very European-looking boy of twelve or thirteen. He was something of a mascot for the group, which loved to encourage his aggressive swagger and preposterous, macho posturing. Initially this mini-*mujahid* seemed to represent a volatile, classic child-soldier package of viciousness and invulnerability, combined with an urge to please his seniors. Al Zarqawi spoke French well but, aside from a high-pitched attempt at a growl, in the first couple of months he rarely spoke to us. But he never failed to walk across our bedding, kick sand at us at night, and otherwise keep us awake as much as possible when he was on sentry duty.

The others made no attempt to stop such conduct. For some reason he was allowed to get away with any sort of behaviour while the others were not. One night Louis got up for a pee in the middle of the night to find Al Zarqawi and Suleiman sitting four metres away, dry-firing into our position as they laughed hysterically. Al Zarqawi was so small that when he trudged by on the way to sentry duty with his Kalash on a sling over his thin shoulder, the butt would leave a shallow trench behind him as it dragged through the sand.

Eventually, Al Zarqawi started to thaw toward us, even dropping by for chats (the only child permitted to do so, and brave enough to want to).

Another prepubescent teenager, young Abdul Rahman, or "AR2," was a more complex case. From around the fire he had picked up that his seniors wanted us to convert, so one day he grabbed the venerated Qur'an, plunked himself down on our blanket, and began to read, in what language we could hardly tell. It was some version of what he thought was French, but we had no idea what he was saying. After a good bit of this, he snapped the holy book closed and asked, "Are you ready now to submit to Allah?" As soon as we began our elaborate and well-practised explanation of why not, he stomped away without a backward glance.

We told Omar One of AR2's efforts, believing he would be pleased by the zeal and initiative the kid had shown, but instead AR2 got in serious trouble. Not only had he sought to assume the role of religious instructor, for which he was dramatically unqualified, but this upstart had also presumed to usurp Omar's privileged position as converter-in-chief. As a result we earned AR2's implacable enmity.

We had limited interaction with most of our captors, either because—like Abdul Rahman, Jaffer, Abou Isaac, Abou Mujahid, or even more markedly, Socks, Ahmed, Abdallah, and "Sideburns"—they simply wanted as little to do with us as possible or because, like Obeida, Ali, Harissa, and AR2, they were actively discouraged from doing so. But even among those who hated us and everything we stood for with an abiding passion, some engagement was unavoidable.

Moussa, "the Veteran," was a bomb maker who'd had a bad day. He was blind and had lost his right hand but he was treated with respect and sensitivity most of the time. He required a great deal of care, however, and the decision to keep him with an active fighting unit in the field was remarkable given the enormous price in operational efficiency they had to pay. They seemed quite prepared to do so, and I can only assume they felt he was owed. His only contact with us was a single attempt to preach the joys of

Islam, which he did as a duty in the hope that it would improve his chances of getting into heaven.

We didn't see much of Imam Abdallah, but we heard his soft, lilting, velvety voice many times each day as he led the brothers in prayer. In truth, it was a soothing and comforting sound. He was a good-looking young man in his mid-twenties. Omar One explained to us that imams were selected on the basis of their superior knowledge of the holy texts. Abdallah spoke little French and was not much interested in us. He was Moussa's prime caregiver, and ensured that this ambulatory charity case received the help and attention he required.

Obeida was a quiet twenty-year-old from Kano, in northern Nigeria. He was shyly friendly toward us and spoke some English, but the brothers discouraged any contact. He would sit for hours in the open sun chanting verses from the Qur'an, but he seemed to us to be lonely, and despite sporadic efforts from Omar One, who incongruously shouted "Go, Nigeria" whenever he saw Obeida, the lad seemed not to belong.

Ali was another PK machine gunner. Like Hassan, Ibrahim, Obeida, and Abou Isaac, he was black, and there was a big gulf between those who were black and those who were not, however much the Omars and Jack insisted otherwise. Louis and I guessed that Ali was from the northern part of Côte d'Ivoire or perhaps Guinea, but in the basic exchanges we had with him in pidgin French we never got a clear answer.

Although he had filmed the proof-of-life videos, our first conversation with Julabib occurred some weeks into our captivity. The moment was memorable. Alone, he approached our relatively isolated position and, standing at the edge of our blanket, introduced himself, saying, "Hi, I'm the media guy"—in English. We soon learned that this was practically the only English he knew but found it interesting that he would take the trouble to present himself that way. In fact, he wanted to learn more English and on three or four subsequent occasions I gave him rudimentary lessons. He was a serious student with an outstanding memory and a good ear.

In the course of such lessons we too learned a great deal. Within the group there was a distinct if informal hierarchy, rather like the distinction between officers and enlisted ranks in most Special Forces units. In this case the officers were almost all Algerian (we called them "the Mafia"), while the "enlisted men" were either from sub-Saharan countries or very young Algerians. Most officers were members of the council, a body that seemed to meet irregularly to consider important issues of policy and, perhaps, theology as it affected operations. It was also convened to confer with Jack whenever he visited. The council included Jack's senior staff (Ahmed, Julabib, and Al Jabbar); his man inside the camp, Omar Three; the camp emir (first AR, later Jaffer); as well as Omar One, Omar Two, and Imam Abdallah. Hassan was particularly bitter about his exclusion from this body.

Julabib was the only member of the council who might have been Mauritanian rather than Algerian, but we were never certain. He was clearly well educated and probably had attended a technical school somewhere in the region. He knew his IT business, and was comfortable surfing deep in the Internet. He also knew the lingo and all the technical terms, and showed me photographs on his cellphone of me from the time I had been Ambassador to the United Nations, pictures I had never seen before. On one occasion we talked Photoshop (he used the old Photoshop 5, while I had progressed to CS2) and he showed me various photo manipulations (George W. Bush turning into a pig and other exciting clips), demonstrating that he knew how to get things off the Web.

Although he was usually smiling and very relaxed, I could tell from his eyes that Julabib was always our enemy. He was the most technically sophisticated among our captors (keeping up to date regarding news coverage in Canada of our kidnapping) and, along with Jack and Hassan, among the most dangerous. I suspect that rather than being a full-time member of Belmokhtar's *katiba,* he belonged to AQIM's media and propaganda arm, Al Andalus.

Hassan, like Julabib, was in his mid-twenties. He was by far the most complicated, intelligent, and scary of our fanatical jailers. He spoke French with an educated, colloquial European accent, and was familiar with western Europe and aware of the principal politico-economic currents of its history, asking me one day, "Which was the better leader, Napoleon, Hitler, or Stalin?" He was well trained militarily and seemed to have good military instincts. He would switch back and forth between a student–teacher relationship with me and that of captor–hostage in the blink of an eye. He was almost invariably menacing and aggressive, and I've never seen anybody sport a larger, heavier chip on his shoulder. He wanted to get even with everybody, but I was never sure for what. At one point he mused, "I thought of joining the Red Brigades or Baader-Meinhof but they were not really serious. Al Qaeda suited me much better."

I strongly suspect that Hassan suffered from some kind of mood disorder. To this medically ignorant observer, he had all the signs but no medication. He had an IQ that was off the charts in terms of his ability to learn and process information. He said to me one day, clearly aware of the degree to which he made us uncomfortable, "I regret imposing myself on you all the time but it's not every day I get to talk to a university professor"—which, of course, I'm not, but he was willing to settle for someone even associated with a university—"and I want to take full advantage of the opportunity," adding darkly, "while I can."

I taught him how to play Twenty Questions, and—paternalistically—decided to choose subjects that I considered would reasonably be within his ken. The first time, he got Winnie Mandela in seven. I failed to get his Al Capone in twenty.

He was starved intellectually. None of the brothers were remotely interested in engaging the issues crowding his mind. The kinds of discussions he had with me ranged across the entire spectrum. What, beyond greed, are the causes of and solutions to the growing wealth disparity gap within capitalist economies? When does the politics of the far right meld with that of the far left? What would have happened if Napoleon—or Hitler—had not invaded Russia? Is the United Nations a failure? While he tended to enter such discussions with a pretty classic leftist-contrarian perspective, once engaged he allowed himself to go where his abundant curiosity and inquiring intellect took him. Sometimes it was exciting to see where that would be.

He was full to the bursting point with pent-up anger and violence. And he scared the hell out of me. He was there at the abduction but I have no recollection of what he looked like during the initial grab. Subsequent to those fleeting and violent moments, he was always tightly masked and obviously that was for our benefit. I dreaded the day he would show himself unmasked.

At one point Hassan ran to us, brandishing his shortwave radio, and demanded that we listen to a Radio France Internationale program on Darwin, and then sought our reaction. It put us in a difficult position, and I retreated into some preposterous diplomatic bafflegab along the lines of "Well Hassan, an awful lot of wise people believe that Darwin's evolutionary theory is proved daily," and then I made the mistake of pointing out to this relatively short individual that people across the world are becoming taller and bigger and living longer as their diet improves.

He bristled and insisted that in fact people were becoming smaller and more compact and living shorter lives (perhaps relative to the 950-year-old giants in the Islamic scriptures or the satanic torturers in his hell). Obviously he was deeply conflicted, and did not report our heretical doubts as, so very clearly, they were also his. But he was disturbed by our gently tendered evidence and by our conviction, as I hummed, quietly to myself, George Gershwin's wonderful "It Ain't Necessarily So."

A week after our arrival at Camp Canada, Hassan provided us with a few sheets of graph paper torn from a spiral exercise book and a single, much-chewed Bic ballpoint pen. Each of us was told to produce a detailed curriculum vitae. Without my glasses I wrote in large block letters and, as I still could not read what I had written, asked Louis to read it back to me to ensure that it was somewhat legible and that I had not written anything that would aggravate our situation.

Louis was summoned to meet with Hassan separately, and I could see them talking in a cave about four metres up the *wadi* wall, perhaps two hundred metres to the south of our tree. Some hours later, Hassan came for me and took me a few hundred metres in the opposite direction, leaving Louis in the cave. When I asked when I would see Louis again, he told me that was not my concern. I would not accept that and he partially relented with "in a few days," which was the most I could get out of him.

First he took me through my public service career and current UN assignment, but he did not seem much interested in what I thought might have been salient details (like, say, the six years I had been Deputy Minister of Defence). Instead, he seemed to be filling in the blanks as if he were completing a form. As issues were raised and discussed in my various "interrogation" sessions, I was required to write short essays on topics such as whether the Israeli action in Gaza, just getting underway, was a war crime, or why Canada chose not to participate in the 2003 Iraq coalition but then agreed to join the one in Afghanistan. The interrogation was, at least as far as I was concerned, never violent. Indeed, I was never threatened with violence although Louis was. The discussions invariably turned into strident and often sophomoric debates on world issues and quickly I came to appreciate the extent to which this was far more about the provision of academic oxygen to the intellectually starved Hassan than anything to do with nourishing Al Qaeda's information banks.

The most distressing aspect of this period, however, was Louis' and my continuing separation. And then, as suddenly as it began, after three days, it ended. We were reunited late at night during a cold, heavy rain when the then commandant, Abdul Rahman, and Omar One escorted a wet and shivering Louis back to where I was occupying our old position. I am almost certain that that was because Hassan—whom they neither liked nor trusted—had been instructed to back off. As far as the group was concerned, his games were over. The others, at least his seniors, were not the least interested in his "product" but did want to ensure our survival in mind and body, if only for their own purposes.

Louis' experience was different: more aggressive and less an intellectual stroll through Contemporary World Politics 301. Hassan threatened him with being stripped naked and staked out in the midday sun. It did not happen but he feared that at any time it might. We were awfully glad to get back together.

In sum, mine was not a serious interrogation. Hassan did not appear to us really to be one of the brothers, remaining essentially an outcast. His military skills and instincts were by far the most well founded but such knowledge, despite a dogged effort by Hassan to share it, did not dent the fatalistic day-to-day practices of the *katiba*.

Hassan particularly had it in for Louis and was constantly fomenting mistrust of his every action. Although his fellow *mujahideen* did not have much time for Hassan, some of his calumny stuck and was the principal factor in building a baseless case for the accusation that Louis had a *mauvais caractère* (roughly, a nasty personality).

When my clothes had finally deteriorated beyond the help of the cast-off pedal-pusher pants, they provided me with a rather formal and incongruous grey-on-grey striped *jelabiyah*, a cassock-like garment reaching well below the knees. It had a high Chinese collar and closed down the front with a score of buttons and came with matching pants. Louis' clothing was doing only marginally better than mine so I gave him the tunic and kept the pants. The next morning as we began our walk on the Camp Canada track,

Louis, decked out in his new long tunic, was greeted from afar by Hassan with a very loud "Good morning, Rabbi." I doubt that any of those rural Salafist fighters, other than the European-educated Hassan perhaps, had ever even seen a rabbi, but the children liked the game and joined in with excitement and exultant menace.

This business of proclaiming Louis to be Jewish first started as a taunt by Hassan, who understood full well how we would interpret such a charade. It all too quickly developed strong legs and soon our guards, particularly the younger ones (who worshipped Hassan and his dark passion), sought to catch Louis in profile to ascertain that his nose was indeed Semitic. The more intrepid among them asked Louis or me to confirm that he was indeed Jewish, so they could confidently observe up close an example of their sworn, most bitter enemies, so regularly and grotesquely demonized by their unsubtle propaganda machine. However absurd, the assertion was chilling stuff coming from people who regularly and matter-of-factly insisted, "Whenever we encounter a Jew, we eliminate him."

In response I would maintain, hating myself all the while for playing into their sordid, racist game, that Louis could not be Jewish; that since leaving La Rochelle in the early eighteenth century, his family had been Canadian for fourteen generations; that Cardinal Richelieu and the all-powerful Catholic Church had refused to allow "unstable elements" (like Jews and Protestants) to travel to the colony of New France—but to no avail. Nobody was interested in such facts, which were irrelevant, suspicious, and obscure to these desert dwellers. They had their story, it worked for them, and it was inexorably becoming received wisdom around their cooking fire.

After a couple of weeks of this, we were sitting on our blanket one soft, languid evening listening to Omar One spin his colourful Qur'anic tales of the derring-do of the Companions of the Prophet when we were joined by a succession of others: first Abdul Rahman, then Al Jabbar and Omar Two, and finally young Al Zarqawi and a couple of others.

At a break in Omar's tale, Al Jabbar, pointing at Louis, said something in Arabic and rather formally asked Omar to interpret for him. Al Jabbar had, Omar said, been struck from the first time he had set eyes on Louis, had in fact been moved almost to tears, by how much Louis looked like Al Jabbar's father—same chin, same nose. Indeed, he noted a little wistfully, were he to see Louis on the street in Algiers he would have taken him for his father, whom he had not seen in nearly two decades. There were a lot of pointed looks around the group and from then on there was little further discussion of Louis' Jewishness.

Once that myth had been so effectively put to rest and references to "the rabbi" had abated, more subtle and baseless suggestions arose to the effect that Louis was insensitive to the attraction of Islam, or irascible, or anti-Arab, or friendly to Western engagement in Iraq and Afghanistan. While I sought to diminish Louis' suspicions that this was all about setting him up for some unpleasant fate, that is precisely what it was, and we both knew it. These zealots needed a politico-religious justification for every act, every thought, every prejudice.

Nor did Al Jabbar's carefully modulated gesture put an end to Hassan's baiting of Louis or to his accusations that Louis was somehow disrespectful of the brothers or engaged in various forms of intelligence gathering. It just drove them underground.

CHAPTER 9

US AND THEM

———

Like one that on a lonesome road
Doth walk in fear and dread,
And having once turn'd round, walks on,
And turns no more his head;
Because he knows a frightful fiend
Doth close behind him tread.

———

Louis and I spoke English to each other in the hope that this would make our own conversations a little more discreet. Louis is perfectly bilingual, speaking accentless English. I am very comfortable in French, even if I regularly hear myself making errors. We were well into our fourth week, however, when I spotted Omar One approaching our position one evening with the Qur'an in one hand (his right, of course) about twenty metres distant. I turned to Louis, who was a short distance away on the other side, and observed, I think fairly neutrally, "Louis, here comes Omar for a reading."

Before Louis could reply, Omar proclaimed casually—in remarkably good English—"Yes, and I hope you will enjoy it today." As the Brits would say, Louis and I were gobsmacked and immediately began to scroll through everything we might have said in English within earshot of Omar over the previous thirty days. We had been pretty careful but was that careful enough? When, a little shaken (which he so enjoyed), we queried him on his language skills, we learned that English was but one of the seven languages in which this itinerant preacher was proficient.

Louis and I worked hard to establish an effective, useful, even respectful working relationship with our captors, without appearing obsequious or submissive. Our obvious purpose was to build a rapport that would make our captivity as painless as possible while forging a connection that, we hoped, might make our execution less likely. We tried to keep our demands and complaints to an absolute minimum so that when we really needed attention, it might be forthcoming.

We sought to win their confidence and respect by demonstrating that we were strong, self-reliant individuals, secure in our belief in the value and importance of our UN mission and the purpose and direction of our work and lives. But we also endeavoured to demonstrate by word and act that we were not hostile to Islam or its practitioners, a religion and people we respected, even if our knowledge of the Muslim world was not what it might have been.

From the beginning of this ordeal, it was crystal clear that their particular fundamentalist take on Islam would affect everything to do with our kidnapping and its resolution. Thus we sought to learn as much as we could about this important world religion, to be seen to be interested in its texts and underlying philosophy and, most challengingly, to be open to its teachings. We therefore welcomed Omar's preaching and were interested in Omar Two's Salafist philosophy, mystical beliefs, and lifestyle, and we sought to keep open the matter of our possible eventual conversion.

Our treatment at the hands of AQIM might usefully be compared with that of Soumana Moukaila, our UN driver. Soumana was a Muslim, a slave or servant of Allah, a brother in faith of our abductors, a member of the *ummah*. From our significantly ill-informed perspective, he also seemed to be a conscientious and observant Muslim. Having met him only thirty-six hours prior to our kidnapping, we knew all too little about him save that he was a pleasant companion, a committed family man, an outstanding driver, and that whenever possible he participated in daily prayers.

Clearly he did not adhere to the extreme philosophy of seventh-century fanatical fundamentalism espoused by our Al Qaeda jailers but as his co-religionists they were obliged at least to go through the motions of treating him differently from the way we *kafirs* (unbelievers), the infidel enemy, were managed: at a long arm's length.

In fact, I believe they treated him considerably worse. He ate with them—which we never did—sat around their fire and dug into their single dish. He prayed with them and was plagued by their incessant preaching, sometimes three or four of them at a time going on and on at him, a few metres away from us, late into the night. They bent every possible effort to bring him into their fundamentalist fold, effectively seeking to brainwash him. I do not think that they succeeded, but how would I know?

We were instructed never to talk to him but we cheated a little whenever we could, if only with a wave and a few discreet, encouraging words. At Camp Canada, I recall Soumana, after being summoned one evening to prayer, stumbling past us muttering to himself, "Je deviens fou, . . . un fou" (I'm going crazy, . . . crazy).

The AQIM *mujahideen* who held us seemed to live an enormously joyless life. They did laugh, but rarely, and when they did I was not always sure why. Now and then Louis and I would chuckle about something but tended to quickly suppress it. Bearing in mind that we had limited control over our demeanour, we disagreed over whether we should appear to our captors as bearing up (staunch, brave, and healthy) or frail and dejected (depressed and vulnerable).

I thought the former would yield better results while Louis tended to believe that the latter would elicit a more sympathetic response.

We agreed not to cut our hair as we thought they would come to believe that sawing off the head of an old, dishevelled, frail-looking person would not make a good propaganda video. They insisted during our religious indoctrination sessions that they venerated age and that Islam required them to be generous to the weak. We hoped that our wild hair and gaunt faces would stimulate that charitable instinct.

We determined as well that we would seek to conduct ourselves with dignity at all times and in all circumstances, and that we would be respectful, open, and correct in our dealings with our guards in the hope of encouraging them to treat us in the same manner.

Jews and Christians are considered by Muslims as believers who follow an older—but, of course, superseded—revelation from God and therefore, in the eyes of our kidnappers, are closer to Islam than any other brand of *kafir*. Beyond that, Omar One wasn't at all interested in the differences between our Biblical parables and their Qur'anic parallels. He couldn't have cared less about the evolution of the Christian Church or the sectarian distinctions and theological and liturgical points on which Louis, the Catholic, and I, the posturing Protestant, differed. His certainty was absolute. No other religion was of any import. His version was right—completely and utterly—on all particulars of faith, and we and most Muslims for that matter were at best dramatically misguided ("Seventy-three of seventy-four sects are wrong," he would intone) and at worst screaming heretics.

I found the lack of intellectual curiosity among the *mujahideen,* evidently including religious curiosity, startling but little different from the fundamentalist Christians and Jews I have encountered. The closest parallel I can conceive of (and one that would have enraged my abductors) is that of the warrior-monks of the Crusades, those good Christian knights who screamed, "Deus lo volt!" (God wills it) as they took Jerusalem in 1099 and allegedly slaughtered every man, woman, and child in the city—wading through blood up to their knees—simply because they were infidels occupying the holy land. Not so different, I'd argue, from *muja-hideen* screaming "Allahu Akbar!" as they shred themselves and those around them in suicide attacks seeking to rid Muslim lands of occupying infidels.

Anything we believed, especially about religion but also about most anything else, they considered to be false, corrupt, and therefore not only unworthy of discussion but also intrinsically evil. Even talking about such differences was likely to incur the wrath of their vengeful and famously jealous god.

The issue of religious conversion dominated our relationships with every one of our captors. It was the only subtext of any relevance to Omar One and the exclusive consideration in all our dealings with Omar Two. The children, despite their limited understanding of French, were mesmerized by Omar One's performances as he acted out his stories, so they could not understand why we were not similarly moved. They hung on his words, and revelled in his enthusiasm and his antics as he reenacted the Prophet's battles. Omar would dance about, swinging his imaginary sabre and—assuming the persona of Khalid, "the sword of Allah" (who, we were told, won 127 consecutive battles in the name of the Prophet)—vanquish multiple enemies, invariably against odds that ought to have been overwhelming. Why was that not enough to convince us?

Our kidnappers believed fervently that Allah was on their side and that His vengeance on their enemies would be terrible, if not necessarily swift. They could therefore not begin to comprehend why, having benefited from so much instruction from such a fervent and truthful preacher, we had not quickly signed on.

They were also at a loss to understand why we always rebuffed such entreaties by insisting that we needed to know more about Islam before we could contemplate such a decision. "What more needs to be said or learned?" they inquired with growing frustration. "It is really simple: accept Allah into your hearts and commit to observing the Five Pillars of Islam, and it will be done. We will be brothers. We will pray together, eat together, and do battle together, and you won't go to hell." Their indefatigable optimism seemed to flag, however, as they contemplated engaging fearful odds when accompanied in battle by these two frail and ancient Westerners. None of them expected to die of old age or even aspired to reach our decrepit state. They dreamed constantly of a glorious death in battle, or in "martyr operations," and often recounted such dreams, radiant smiles splitting their faces.

Louis and I discussed the pros and cons of conversion on any number of occasions. The issues for us were never of conscience. Louis knew that his God would understand, and for me the question was even more one of practicality. Whether or not conversion would help our plight was the only issue.

I never believed that it would, and considered the chance at least as strong that it would make the whole thing worse. I did not relish the prospect of chummily eating and praying with them and thought that any such pantomime would add to my already heavy enough psychological burden. I accepted that it was at least theoretically possible conversion might ease the conditions in which we were held or make the all too unrealistic possibility of a humanitarian gesture more likely. But on balance, I thought that if we were to convert, it was less likely they would let us go. If we became committed *jihadi* fundamentalist Muslims, like them, why would we want to return home? Joining their *jihad*—making it ours—was the option they were presenting.

That said, I kept an open mind and decided that were it likely to yield some specific and significant benefit, I would reconsider. For instance, might conversion permit, say, our choosing the manner of our execution? Might I bargain conversion for a bullet instead of having my head slowly sawn off? Would it prevent a Daniel Pearl–type video appearing on YouTube?

❖

We were never beaten or tortured. It was clear that it would have been all too easy by word or deed to bring it on, but Jack's standing orders were evidently that unless and until we did, we were to be managed rigorously but correctly.

In dealing with these zealots, everything was about Islam, and so was the manner of our treatment. Jack was in charge and his interpretation of what the holy texts had to say about the care of prisoners and hostages set the tone and the detail of how we were to be treated. He determined that we would eat the same food as they did, drink the same unlimited quantities of always-scarce water, and have the same access to their meagre medical and clothing resources. So yes, we were lucky from that perspective.

In their preaching, both Omar One and Omar Two insisted that Islam was a completely ecumenical religion: that although fifteen centuries ago Allah had decided to entrust his revelations to an Arab, it could as easily have been anybody, anywhere. God had no favourites, and all races and individuals were equal in God's eyes. The way the perfumed Omar Two explained it was, well, particular: "No matter how black they are, how ugly, how flat their noses, or how much their sweat smells, God considers them equal." They preached equality, but did not practise it. Sub-Saharan Africans were clearly second class in the eyes of AQIM. Hassan was explicit, saying of AQIM: "It is true that racism is a problem."

Our abductors' belief in the Qur'anic legitimacy of their *jihad* was unshakable, and their life's purpose as soldiers of God was to do His will by prosecuting a holy war to rid Muslim lands of the infidel's defiling presence while also overthrowing the apostate regimes of toadying and venal Arab governments. They were fighting to restore an Islamic caliphate of uncertain—possibly worldwide—dimension, to be strictly administered by Islamic sages exclusively according to holy Islamic *Shari'a* law.

Their steadfast engagement to the death in *jihad* would guarantee their access to paradise: no small thing as, we were repeatedly told, the Prophet said ninety-nine out of a hundred wouldn't make the cut on the Day of Judgment. Our captors would recount the horrors of hell in a way that put to shame the fire-and-brimstone Christian preachers of the Middle Ages. However, they were comforted by the certainty of finding all their brothers in arms and loved ones beside those streams of milk and honey in paradise.

At one point, as we were crossing a particularly challenging accumulation of huge sand dunes, each of the three vehicles had become *ensablé,* mired to their frames in deep, fine sand. Everyone was tense and clearly felt vulnerable. After the truck in which I was travelling had been extracted from the soft sand for the third time, the taciturn and stern-faced driver, Omar Three, backed down and pointed his vehicle at a notch in the high dune before us and gunned it, going full bore toward this opening with absolutely no idea of whether the other side was effectively a cliff. We smashed through and were flying through the air before blasting down the nearly vertical gradient on the other side. Thankfully he knew not to brake as we rocketed down the reverse slope. We came to a stop on a relatively solid patch and contemplated rank upon rank of formidable dunes marching before us toward the far horizon and looked back to see the other two vehicles, about a hundred metres away on the crest of the dune, buried up to their axels.

It was going to be some time before we could all get underway again. The other passenger, "New Guy"—who had first appeared the previous day—and I left the cab and had a sip of water, sitting in the shade of the vehicle while Omar Three and the boys from the back of our truck hurried back with shovels and metal planking to assist the others. That left just me and New Guy, who I was eventually to learn had played a rather crucial role in our saga, acting as my guard.

He had shown up with Jack and was a paunchy, tall, city guy in his mid-thirties, quite unlike the hardened warriors, his *mujahideen* brothers, who were our captors. His French was pretty basic but we had spent a fair amount of time over the previous twenty-four hours chatting mostly—inevitably—about Islam. At this point, though, he was pensive and began pacing back and forth in front of me, muttering all the while. Suddenly, with a focused stare, he grabbed his Kalash, which had been hanging off his shoulder on a sling decorated with Mali's flag, and thrust it in my face, vertically, saying, "Shoot me! Right now! I am ready for paradise!" I did think about it, but not for long. There is no doubt in my mind that he was, literally, deadly serious.

I have never met a more single-minded and committed set of individuals than the AQIM *katiba* that held us. By almost any modern standard their ideas were naïve and unsophisticated in the extreme, to say nothing of dangerous and just a little anti-social. Their version of Islam was simplistic and dramatically dated. But there must be no doubt about the depth of their faith and their absolute commitment to what they perceived to be its fundamental principles, including, of course, *jihad*—to which a growing number of Muslims refer as the "Sixth Pillar of Islam." These self-styled soldiers of God demonstrated over and over again the extent to which they are prepared to use extreme brutality to achieve their ends, but their viciousness appeared to be neither arbitrary nor casual. Their every act was considered and needed to be justifiable in terms of their chosen path of *jihad*.

Almost since 9/11, there has been a loud debate among securocrats over whether Al Qaeda and its franchises, like AQIM, are bandits, opportunists, thugs, psychopaths, and restless, underemployed youths flying a flag of Islamic convenience, or, conversely, deeply committed religious zealots engaging, Robin Hood–like, in banditry, kidnapping, and trafficking to finance the achievement of their Islamic vision. Many, probably most, have opted for some variation of the convenient first option, and many security services still seem to favour this interpretation, mostly, I suspect, because it makes these movements easy to belittle and should make them much easier to defeat. Whatever the reasoning, based on my own experience, I know it to be the wrong answer.

Similarly, some anti-terrorism "experts" express doubt that the *jihadi* warriors of AQIM are "really Al Qaeda." The question strikes me as startlingly moot: if they think like Al Qaeda, are motivated by and want to achieve the same things as Al Qaeda, behave like Al Qaeda, fight, kill, and die like Al Qaeda, and say they are Al Qaeda, then, quite simply, they are.

They told me over and over again how much they despised the United Nations and all its works. Their obliteration of UN headquarters in Algiers on 11 December 2007, which killed thirty-seven, including seventeen UN staff members, makes the point rather forcefully.

They also hated all Western development efforts undertaken both by state actors and by NGOs and were particularly exercised by Christian missionary activities, either overt or what they termed "covert," which of course often included development work. There is no doubt in my mind that they wanted to grab me first and foremost because I was a senior officer of the United Nations, while also wishing to demonstrate that their reach was long and their cause universal. By so doing they hoped to discourage UN and NGO activity throughout the Sahel region. The fact that I was also a detested Western infidel, an invader and defiler of Muslim Afghanistan, only made the proposition more attractive.

Their most immediate operational priority remained the "near enemy": the so-called apostate regimes of the secular, nominally Islamic states of North Africa and the Sahel region, declared *takfir* by these zealots. This meant that our captors rejected the credibility of the Muslim allegiance of all these governments, thereby, in the eyes of AQIM, setting them apart from the *ummah* and effectively excommunicating their members from Islam. As deemed non-believers, the political leaders, and the security forces that kept them in place, became, in the eyes of AQIM's *mujahideen*, legitimate targets.

AQIM's larger, and ever less secondary target, particularly following the acquisition of their Al Qaeda franchise in January 2007, was what they considered to be the decadent and debauched West: the "far enemy."

Many Muslims insist that no more than 1 percent of their number hold radical fundamentalist beliefs and profess a commitment to *jihad*. But 1 percent of 1.4 billion is still 14 million. Such number games are not quite meaningless, even if they don't really get us beyond the stark premise that *jihadism* poses a real and seemingly growing threat to Western interests and values.

I have hung around soldiers a fair bit. At least in the West, the men seem to favour talk of women, sports, and cars (not necessarily in that order or, indeed, separately). My Al Qaeda abductors wouldn't have understood a word of such conversations. We in the West seem to get a big kick out of the seventy-two virgins bit but my captors didn't seem to care much about women. In fact, they were absolutely uninterested in anything other than praising the Lord while passing the ammunition in a fight that they deeply believed to be His fight.

Never have I seen people less interested in material stuff. Most of them were under twenty-five, all under forty-eight. They neither expected nor wanted to grow old and considered me to be extravagantly time expired. They did not covet cool sneakers or sports paraphernalia; they did not ape the latest fashion, or seek to emulate the antics and ethics of rock or film stars, or even dream of nickel-plating their AKs.

Similarly, I have never met a less horny group of young men. There was no skulking out of the desert for a little R&R or even for chaste reunions with family and friends. Admittedly, this would have been risky for them as I suspect that the Algerian intelligence apparatus watches such people very carefully. Normal familial attachments and pleasures of the flesh seemed to hold little attraction. The *mujahideen* seemed perfectly content to talk and chant about Allah and their servitude to Him . . . endlessly.

As Louis often pointed out, in day after day of religious discourse we never heard any suggestion that theirs was a god of love, or that He had any particular affection for his creations. That they were His servants who were required to submit to His will was oft repeated. That He was a fierce and jealous god was proudly recalled, but never was there any suggestion of His being kindly, compassionate, loving, or generous. "*Jihad* is our path and death in the service of Allah is our noblest desire!" they would intone, over and over again. Islamic context, or at least their version of it, was the template against which all things were judged, even if it might seem to us that they were stretching that fabric well beyond the maker's recommended stress tolerance in order to make their fierce acts fit within an acceptable theological perspective.

To Louis and me they loved to insist, "Everyone is our enemy and everyone is out to destroy us but we will prevail because we alone are true servants of Allah." And they would maintain, "We fight to die, while you fight to go home to your families. How can we lose?"

They will not, in my opinion, soon be defeated. They seemed to have no trouble recruiting. The youngest among them was seven— even if he was more of a mascot and spent only a few days with us—and the voices of three of the others had yet to break. Parents, we were proudly informed, brought them their sons as "gifts to God." I know of no argument that would convince them to abandon their chosen path.

Perhaps the most telling and to me the most unsettling aspect of our captors' beliefs was their attitude to time. It highlighted the gulf between them and us and offered me the strongest proof that Sam Huntington may have got it a lot more right than most analysts seemed to credit in his seminal article "The Clash of Civilizations?" in *Foreign Affairs* in 1993. I'd had dinner with Professor Huntington in 1999 at a Security Council retreat organized by UN Secretary-General Kofi Annan, and recalled that I had found his thesis—in which he posited that future conflict would be based on religious and cultural differences rather than on economic and strategic interests—alarmist, simplistic, and a little xenophobic. As I pursued my discussions with our Al Qaeda kidnappers, however, and learned more about their beliefs and the intensity with which they were held, I began to develop more sympathy for Huntington's vision of inevitably clashing civilizations, or at least the certainty of a growing confrontation between fundamental Islam and Western values and interests. I was living it.

The utter irrelevance of time to our captors was a cultural hurdle I had some trouble getting past. Time is the enemy of Western societies. We want everything right now and are not prepared to wait. We seem aggressively determined to ignore the imperatives of time-imposed realities (aging, health, education, books, food, newspapers, character, friendship, prudence, trust, professional seniority, politics), always preferring entertainment—fulfilment and action now, no matter how superficial and ephemeral—to knowledge, appreciation, and understanding later. When compared to the fickleness of our addiction to an ever-shorter, shallower, and more tyrannical news cycle and our need for instantaneous gratification in all our endeavours, the profound conviction of our abductors that time was on their side was truly unsettling. Because it is so evidently not on ours.

My AQIM captors didn't care if it took another twenty, two hundred, or two thousand years to achieve their vision. In this, they were utterly serene. They accepted that they would win some and lose some, however long it took, but they knew with unshakable certainty and absolute clarity that Allah's victory would be theirs. It was so written. The *when* just didn't matter. That is a powerful weapon by any standard.

Time *dans ce bas monde* counted for nothing. Happily, they have an imperfect understanding of just how much it matters to us, but they are learning fast. They did not expect to achieve victory in their lifetimes, which they fervently hoped would be brief and end gloriously as they fulfilled God's mission. It did not matter how many short generations of *mujahideen* it would take. When the alternative to their path was fifty thousand years of meticulously detailed and quantified torture in hell, what difference would a few centuries make?

I can only imagine how they would have reacted to President Obama's speech on 1 December 2009 to the cadets at West Point, when he announced the Afghanistan surge by declaring, "I have determined that it is in our vital national interest to send an additional 30,000 U.S. troops to Afghanistan. After 18 months, our troops will begin to come home." I have not left out any of the President's words between those two sentences. A little later, a White House spin doctor, apparently with a straight face, insisted that the Taliban and Al Qaeda "would be wrong to presume that time was on their side."

The AQIM *jihadis'* comprehension of the reality of life in the West was spotty—full of deeply cherished myths about our debauchery, godlessness, and decadence. They did appreciate enough of our attention-deficit-addled politics and society, though, to believe that we simply did not have the heart for a long haul, casualty-heavy, expensive, intense, brutal, no-holds-barred struggle. Particularly, of course, a struggle to achieve objectives that manifestly did not engage our vital interests and were, at best, abstract and mostly obscure to the bulk of our citizens. They drew, and I am certain they continue to draw, great strength from that understanding, just as they revel in playing David to our Western Goliath in Iraq and Afghanistan as their standing in much of the world continues to rise while we get it wrong again and again.

They despise virtually all of our most cherished concepts and beliefs.

"Democracy," my kidnappers insisted, in part because of their perception of our fickle attachment to it, is "your religion." "Do you really believe that 51 percent of your adult population is qualified to select your leaders?" They maintained that there was no limit to the hypocrisy of our commitment to what they considered a godforsaken form of government. "You love democracy when it suits you," they would spit. But never—like the victory of the Front Islamique du Salut, or Islamic Salvation Front, in Algeria in 1992 or more recently, the Hamas electoral victory in Gaza—when it does not. They often asked me to square our love of democracy with our anxiousness to see pet dictators prevail in blatantly flawed elections across Africa, with our support of princelings, oligarchs, kleptomaniacs, and oppressive dictators across the Islamic world, and they would point to other places throughout the globe where the venerable U.S. Secretary of State Cordell Hull's "sons of bitches" continue to prevail.

They hated the words *freedom* and *liberty*, believing them to be pernicious ideas, contrary to Allah's purposes, concepts that inexorably led good, Allah-fearing men astray. Strict Islamic discipline had to be the order of their day, imposed by a jealous, ruthless, and vengeful god. How, they would ask, over and over again, could we find the reasonable application of *Shari'a*-sanctioned punishment (stonings and amputations) so barbaric compared to the atrocities and indignities that occurred in bloated Western prisons?

They detested the concept of anything that might be termed a human right, reserving particular scorn for the Universal Declaration of Human Rights, which they saw as nothing other than an ill-disguised Western weapon in the crusade against Islam. They insisted that all rights belonged to God, and it was an affront to Him to presume His purposes.

❖

What, then, did they like? Where did they get their entertainment, find their fun? Well, aside from Islam, they didn't.

They were not allowed to sing but they would sit, sometimes in full sun, and chant Qur'anic verses for hours on end, occasionally joined by a colleague or two who lent their voices to the monotonous rhythms. The soundtracks of the DVDs played on TV Night had also been filled with war chants, punctuated with the sounds of machine guns and massive explosions.

Ayatollah Khomeini said, "Allah did not create man so that he could have fun. The aim of creation was for mankind to be put to the test through hardship and prayer. An Islamic regime must be serious in every field. There are no jokes in Islam. There is no humour in Islam. There is no fun in Islam. There can be no fun and joy in whatever is serious." Our AQIM captors would not have sought an endorsement from this stern Shi'a cleric, but they certainly walked his talk.

Although our abductors constantly expressed a yearning to return to the "purity of the era of the Prophet" and eschewed all forms of "Western capitalistic excess," they did suffer from an ill-disguised technological inferiority complex. They knew from bitter experience of the wizardry of Western weaponry and often said how much they wished to return to the simpler, more straightforward days of the sabre. I was happy to encourage them in this direction.

While they were quick to insist upon the shallowness of our godless values, the hypocrisy of our political thinking, and the wantonness of the death and destruction they saw us sowing so thoughtlessly about the world, they were consistently in awe of the West's technological superiority and inventiveness, which—ominously—they swore they would use against us. They sought (I thought a little desperately) to make a virtue out of the fact that their weapons and equipment were not sophisticated or new, often saying, "We hope the Americans will come to the Sahara, and when they do, their advanced weapons will not save them from the wrath of Allah."

There must have been a dozen shortwave radios in the camp but we were not permitted to listen. Radio France Internationale, BBC (Arabic), and Al Jazeera seemed to be their principal sources of information, and they quickly focused on the fact that Canada was one of the few countries in the world that did not criticize Israeli excess and the appalling butcher's bill in Gaza. They convinced themselves that Canada provided Israel with $10 billion each year in military assistance and were unmoved by my insistence that, at twice our annual development assistance budget for the entire world, this was nonsense. But here as in most other areas they were not to be deterred from their cherished beliefs.

The Israelis began their punitive Operation Cast Lead against Gaza on 27 December 2008, two weeks after we were captured, and for over three weeks they pounded an area half the size of New York City, killing over thirteen hundred, including more than four hundred children. The Israelis lost thirteen. During this time our guards were glued to their shortwave radios, listening to the impassioned news reports that flooded across the Middle East and North Africa, and recounted to us whatever they heard, however exaggerated, as absolute fact. It wasn't as if the bare facts weren't bad enough. The brothers were beside themselves with anger and frustration.

In much the same vein, our kidnappers were aggressive regarding Canada's participation in the coalition in Afghanistan, but it was Gaza that preoccupied them the most. As the predations in Gaza continued, our kidnappers became more volatile and unstable, and I began to despair about our future, which looked to be short and ugly. They had places to go and people to kill, and we were a distraction keeping them from their destiny. They resented us with ever-greater intensity.

PART THREE

THE MIDDLE GAME

CHAPTER 10

SOLO, PERDUTO, ABBANDONATO IN LANDA DESOLATA! ORROR!

=====

Alone, alone, all, all alone,
Alone on a wide, wide sea!
And never a saint took pity on
My soul in agony.

=====

Extreme fear and worry were the pervading themes of our Al Qaeda captivity: fear to the point of physical pain, fear that it would end suddenly with a sword, in a tent, on a video that would be seen by family and friends, and fear that it would go on and on and we would die of the heat, the food, the snakes, scorpions, or merely of broken wills and hearts.

The first five days were the toughest. The next period, while less dramatic, held its own particular horrors, many of them the creatures of our own overwrought imaginations. For the first weeks at Camp Canada, I was plagued by constipation and insomnia. I just could not get my mind to rest, to stop or slow down even if only for a few hours. I could not quit analyzing probabilities and options and endlessly producing largely unhappy end-game scripts. Each night, wide awake, lying as flat as possible to ease the pain of my damaged back, dark thoughts would churn endlessly through my head.

Surely Canada or the United Nations had seen the proof-of-life video we had made on Day 5 and as a result, our families would know we were alive. So why had we heard nothing? It was hard to escape the conclusion that we had simply been written off even if, rationally, I knew that to be unlikely. But where was the evidence? If somebody were, in fact, fighting our corner, would our kidnappers not have asked us for some explanation or clarification of something? Would our "negotiators" not have asked for further health bulletins or additional proof-of-life?

On Christmas Eve, Day 11, Jack swept into Camp Canada and immediately came to see us, accompanied by his staff and the senior officers in camp. First, as previously explained, he had Ahmed distribute "gifts." Then, with some formality, when all had settled cross-legged in a semicircle around our blankets, Jack announced without preamble, "Your case is 95 percent settled. You will be going home very soon. . . . The remaining 5 percent relates to things our side has to work out. They are not your problem." Our abductors seemed inordinately pleased with themselves. They clearly believed they had pulled off a major coup.

While we were surprised and unable to contain our excitement completely, I did reply that although this news was very welcome, I did not think these affairs were usually resolved with such speed and efficiency. It had been only six days since we made the video, and while we had no idea of the nature of their demands or in fact with whom they were negotiating, I expressed skepticism that either Canada or the United Nations could respond with such alacrity. My fishing elicited no information on either issue and our doubts were summarily dismissed.

Ahmed, he of the most malevolent eyes incongruously linked to one of the widest smiles, looked hard at Louis and said only semi-jocularly, "But given your lack of cooperation regarding your BlackBerry, Louis, perhaps we'll keep you with us a little longer."

Louis had, as instructed, turned off his BlackBerry and handed it over to Omar One just before our hands were tied, thirty minutes after our capture. But in subsequent discussions with Hassan and Ahmed at TV Camp and Camp Canada, he had failed to satisfy them that he had revealed all of its secrets.

Jack and Omar One were quick to wave off this not-so-veiled threat from Ahmed because the occasion was about good news and the end to a quick, efficient AQIM operation. Louis and I were almost certain that there was a short-circuit somewhere in this story, however: that some major and dangerous miscommunication or miscalculation had occurred. We also more fully appreciated the extent to which we had a bitter enemy in Smiley Face.

My first thought, which bedevilled me constantly, was that Jack's gang and whoever was negotiating for us had probably not taken the same negotiating course, had not read the same manual, had not seen the same hostage movies. Thus I worried Jack might not know that the first rule of hostage negotiation is never say no. I speculated that if, say, AQIM demanded the release of a few hundred of Al Qaeda's worst miscreants from a score of NATO jails in return for our lives, our negotiator might have replied along the lines, "Well, that certainly won't be easy, but we'll see what we can manage." I worried AQIM might have taken this to mean that our side had agreed, at least in principle, to a major prisoner release, even if the names and numbers were still to be precisely determined, and I thought that such a miscommunication could cause things to head downhill very quickly.

I had no idea what might have prompted such a major disconnect so early in the negotiating process, what intermediaries may have been involved, or what, precisely, had caused the wheels to come off, but come off they certainly had. Thus on Christmas morning Louis and I shared a dread that something seriously bad had occurred—spiked with desperate, irrational, forlorn hope that it hadn't. At best our captors seemed about to lose a lot of face.

Despite our concerns, an upbeat atmosphere persisted in the camp, and the feeling that we might actually be heading home was dramatically reinforced by what Louis and I termed "the Boxing Day *da'wa*." Little by little we allowed ourselves to believe it might actually be about to happen.

The Islamic faithful, we were taught, are required to perform *da'wa,* essentially what Christians would call evangelism. The term denotes a "call" or "invitation" to follow Islam, and it is the duty of every Muslim to explain their faith to the uninitiated, in effect to ensure that as many people as possible are given an opportunity to embrace Islam and thereby remove any possibility of copping an ignorance plea on the Day of Judgment. In addition, the *da'wa* doer earns credits—something like Roman Catholic indulgences— by performing this duty.

By the time the twenty-seventh member of the *katiba* had been brought to us to perform his *da'wa,* relying upon the ever more strained and economical interpretation services of Omar One, there were no words and phrases we had not heard a dozen times as each sought to explain the glories and marvels of Islam and urged us to sign up. This was the only time we got to hear from Moussa, whom we had dubbed The Veteran, and we couldn't help think that there must be something to Jack's announcement if they were bringing the blind bomb maker and the imam into the act.

After the Boxing Day *da'wa* the positive mood persisted in the camp for a few more days. I came to believe that Hassan was allowed to proceed with his "interrogations" over this period because it was understood that we were on our way home and he had better get what he could out of us (within the norms laid down by Belmokhtar) while it was still possible. Inexorably, though, that mood of expectant optimism among our jailers soon drained away into the hot sand in the absence of any follow-through, to be replaced by sullen restlessness. Our initial apprehension had been well founded. Whatever else it was, it was a false start and our captors became resentful, embarrassed, and bitter. They were also eager to let us know it, though nobody ever explained to us what the business had been all about, and why or how it had come off the rails.

Each night after bidding Louis goodnight, as I retreated into my own turgid mind space, the strains of Manon's despairing dirge— "Sola, perduta, abbandonata, in landa desolata! Orror!" (Alone, lost, and abandoned in a desolate land! The horror!)—would fill my head as I lay awake hour after hour. Without sufficient sleep, I was less able to cope with the largely banal challenges of the day. So in the mornings and most evenings I walked hard in the hope that I might become sufficiently tired to allow some sleep, and each afternoon Louis struggled to make our disintegrating loafers walk-worthy.

The constant stress caused in each of us a startling and disturbing loss of short-term memory, to a point at which I seriously wondered if I was losing my mind. It was only when Louis first exhibited and then admitted to precisely the same symptoms that I became less concerned. In the deep recesses of what memory remained, I vaguely recalled reading something about this phenomenon in victims of post-traumatic stress disorder. Having recognized the problem, we made all too half-hearted attempts to rectify it through a variety of mental exercises such as trying to recall the birthdays of each member of our extended families or the words to favourite songs.

While, at least in my case, these exercises tended to confirm the problem rather than mitigate it, they began my compilation of a list of songs—a virtual playlist—that helped release the tension that our predicament generated. Sometimes the selections were blindingly obvious ("Please Release Me, Let Me Go," "Homeless," "Et maintenant," or "Guantanamera"), sometimes wry ("When I'm Sixty-Four," "Dice Are Rolling," and "It Ain't Necessarily So"). There were maudlin entries ("Stand By Me," "Till the Morning

Comes," "Va, pensiero," "Bring Him Safely Home to Me," or "I Just Called to Say I Love You"), bathetic ones ("Are You Lonesome Tonight?" "Heaven Can Wait," "Le dernier repas," and "Find the Cost of Freedom"), stirring entries ("Men of Harlech," "The Holy City"), the chorally inspiring (the *Miserere* and *Spem in Alium*), and the wistful or desperate ("Maybe Tonight," "Someday Never Comes," "Un bel dì vedremo," or "Ready to Run").

And always there was that desolate and haunting aria from Act IV of *Manon Lescaut,* "Sola, perduta, abbandonata, in landa desolata! Orror!" which concludes with the thrice-repeated "Non voglio morir" (I don't want to die). And finally, all too forlornly, Leonard Cohen's "Hallelujah."

I don't know how widely music is recognized to be the favoured window to the soul, but that is certainly the case as far as I am concerned. Nothing is so emotionally evocative, and while I am not a singer, these and many more were comforting, melancholy, and important companions in the Sahara.

On Day 34 I fell into a deep funk and I can recall nothing that might have triggered it beyond the fact that there was so evidently no movement, no developments, no nothing. I came close to convincing myself that our situation would not end happily. Things improved a little the next day, which was wet, windy, and cool, and I contrived to be as active as possible: walking, gathering wood, cleaning up . . . and staring into the middle distance. Louis tried valiantly to buck me up but I could tell he wasn't far behind me as I slipped deeper into the pit. Oddly, this helped. We had rules against that happening, dammit! I was not allowed to infect him with my dark thoughts so I strove harder, in the interests of helping Louis, of course, to avoid going deeper.

But on Day 36, another grey and blustery day with a lot of blowing sand in the air, as we began our walk I saw Hassan digging not very far from where they parked their trucks. Each time we reached a slight rise in our short track, we got a good view through a gap in some scrubby grasses of the masked Ninja Boy methodically, relentlessly, digging. He seemed to be in no particular hurry but as we did circuit after circuit the pile of sand beside him grew, and slowly he dug himself deeper and deeper into the ground.

After a while the taciturn Socks joined him. They took turns digging and every once in a while they walked around what was by now a long, thin, and now fairly deep hole to check out their progress. Hassan was down to his thighs.

I drew Louis' attention to it but he'd already seen what was going on and said nothing—a bad sign. We talked about everything. I hollowly asked why Hassan would be digging. What Hassan would be digging. Could it be another cache? But there was nothing beside him that needed burying, no fuel or water drum, no bag of shoes, or tent.

"It's our grave," I offered, and Louis just balefully stared at me and resumed walking—no challenge, no rebuttal, no happier alternative. So we walked, and for five or six paces every minute each of us in turn got a full view of the emerging grave. Once I had articulated the solution to the riddle there seemed no other answer. Hassan hated us. He had been particularly aggressive and abusive over the past week. He would know we could see and would so enjoy our turmoil as we became aware of what he was up to.

We had been taught about the rules guiding ritual Islamic slaughter, rules I often thought would be applied to any kind of slaughter. Inhumane treatment of the animal went against fundamental principles of Islam, but that would not bother Hassan. A very sharp knife must be used to facilitate rapid and painless cutting. Hassan wore his eighteen-inch fighting knife at his waist at all times. We had been told that the slaughter should not take place in front of the other animals and that the animal being slaughtered should never see the knife, but Hassan would want us to see the knife . . . and the grave.

I was certain, absolutely certain, that some time soon—within the next twenty-four hours or so—we would be brought to a tent, blindfolded, our throats sliced open, and our bodies tossed into that hole. There was no doubt. There could be no other interpretation. It had been decided. Thus the fear was not about an immediate execution. It was not minutes away, but it would happen soon—that evening or the next morning—and these were our last living moments. What a waste! How ignoble an end! No goodbyes, no closure, just a hole nowhere in the Sahara desert.

So we walked and Louis stopped marking our progress. How could that matter? And, straight out of the book of clichés, each of us sought to make peace with ourselves and, a little to my surprise, that was precisely what I managed to do.

I reviewed my life. Took stock of what had gone well and not so well, considered the happy relationships and the less so, reviewed the things I was proud of and not-so-proud, and then I adapted my evening ritual and bade farewell to Mary and the girls and their husbands and children. And at the end I did find a kind of sad peace. There had been a lot more good than bad. I determined that my life had served some purpose, that perhaps the world was a little better for my having passed through it. That I had a marvellous wife and family who were also doing good things. So I was ready—not accepting it, not resigned to it, but ready.

But then strange things started happening around the grave. First, long sticks were bent over the hole in high hoops and then Hassan began weaving grasses among the hoops. Odd for a grave. Then, as it started to drizzle, Hassan stretched a sort of poncho over the hoops and climbed inside. It was a hooch! He'd built himself a shelter from the rain and wind. Talk about taking counsel of one's fears!

We were drained, emotionally wrung out. We couldn't even talk for some time. We had been certain, but we'd been wrong.

Despite this experience, despite having been there before and having so misjudged the circumstances, I decided on other occasions that the game was up and I am confident in the belief that it very nearly was. None, however, was quite as traumatizing as that first time on Day 36. And, of course, we had the making-peace-with-yourself routine all worked out.

I remember nothing about Day 37. We were in shock. It took a while to reconcile ourselves to the fact that the whole near-death experience had been a fabrication of our own less than stable minds. While we believed our captors were entirely capable of killing us, and it was all too clear some of them wanted to get on with doing just that, what had happened the previous day was only indirectly related to them and far more something we had done to ourselves—and that took some getting used to.

Then Day 38 was the pits. I became angry and despondent. How, after more than five weeks, could Ottawa leave us in such misery, in such appalling circumstances, without getting us some sign, some message that a fix was coming? This was the same old self-indulgent stuff: nothing like as deep and wrenching as Day 36 but still down, still wallowing in self-pity, though at least this time with a greater degree of self-awareness. Finally, I snapped myself out of it. Louis and I talked about the need for a very strict application of the rabbit-hole-avoidance rule and the obligation of the one who was further out to extract the guy further down, immediately. From then on we were a lot more successful in applying this practice.

As Days 34, 36, and 38 had been bad, I—the non-superstitious one—could not shake the apprehension that, henceforth, even days would be bad and odd days would be better. It was idiotic but at least had the advantage of implying that 50 percent of the days were destined to be not so bad. At about this time I began to run scripts in my head that always concluded with someone telling us " . . . and, therefore, we have decided to free you." There were countless variations on the scenarios that preceded this phrase, literally hundreds, and I would run them back to back. It was clearly obsessive behaviour and I'd have almost to slap my own face or pinch my arm to extract myself from these delusional loops.

❖

On Day 43, 25 January, Omar Two came by to gloat. With ill-disguised glee he boasted, "We've taken four more!" I sensed that his furtive side glances probably meant that he was not supposed to be telling us this news, so I pressed him for as many details as quickly as possible before he changed his mind. Bit by bit the story emerged, but I decided that he was telling us what he had gleaned from Radio France Internationale or Al Jazeera rather than passing on information that had come through the AQIM communications network.

He told us that three days before, four European tourists had been captured while leaving the Anderamboukane festival of nomad culture on the border between Mali and Niger, about two hundred kilometres north of where we had been taken: a Swiss couple, a German, and an Englishman. They had, he said, been taken by an AQIM sister *katiba* in the Sahara and, ominously, he told us for the first of many subsequent times, "You are really fortunate that you were taken by this group because there are many others that would treat you very, very differently, where it would go very hard for you." And then, with a snarl, "We would really like to be cutting you into little pieces, but Khaled will not let us."

With that, he stalked away and didn't come near us for two weeks. Louis and I were convinced that was because he knew he had overstepped the bounds by giving us tactically useful information and he was worried we would reveal his indiscretion to *les frères,* which, of course, we did not. The information was very precious. It was new, current, and highly relevant to our circumstances. Endlessly we discussed its implications. Was it part of a widespread initiative? Were Westerners being grabbed across North and West Africa?

Clearly our situation had just got a lot more complicated. Now three more Western governments were involved and they had widely differing official stands and track records on the pay or never-pay spectrum. We knew the Brits were, at least officially, among the more inflexible, while it was widely reported that money had been paid to get the German, Austrian, and Swiss tourists out of Groupe Salafiste pour la Prédication et le Combat (the predecessor to AQIM) captivity in 2003. Also, it was alleged that a ransom had been paid to secure the release of the two Austrians, Wolfgang Ebner and Andrea Kloiber, in October 2008. As our situation had become more complex it would probably take longer to resolve, but seven hostages from five different countries (four Western and one African) might bring collective pressure to bear, and collective decision making.

Recalling the horror of our first few days, we had enormous sympathy for the anguish these four people would be suffering, but our minds were immediately, and rather selfishly, flooded with the implications of all this for our predicament. Were the others close by? Would we all be brought together? Was that likely to be good or bad for us? How, precisely, would this complicate or facilitate our eventual release?

We had far too much time to worry about such issues and even in normal circumstances I tend to be compulsive in my analyses. After a couple of days I concluded that it was unlikely we would be brought together with the other hostages as our kidnappers would want to keep their assets in separate baskets. Further, I expected that the three new countries would spend a lot of time talking and fretting as they attempted to find common ground with Canada on negotiating with terrorists, ransom, and exchange of prisoners, but in the end each would make its own decisions.

I considered that the additional hostages would also make the calculations in the relevant capitals relating to rescue options much more complex, and that any attempt to rescue the seven of us would be much more risky. I thought that this new development would very likely prolong our ordeal. However I also believed (or, perhaps, hoped) that it might also militate in favour of a happier outcome, at least for Louis and me.

One additional calculation was but a shadow of a thought—too sensitive, too disturbing to grapple with directly, but too important to completely ignore. Louis and I were always aware that one or both of us might be killed by our Al Qaeda abductors once they decided they didn't like the direction that negotiations were taking. With the capture of the four Europeans, the pool from which the short straw might be drawn had become larger, even if we knew that they were unlikely to execute a woman.

On Day 44, the day after Omar Two revealed that AQIM had taken four European hostages, I spent a lot of time thinking of the 444 days that fifty-two staff members of the American Embassy in Tehran had spent in captivity between November 1979 and January 1981. It was ten times what we had just been through, and I didn't think I could manage that.

On Day 52, 3 February, Louis and I were sitting in the shade around midday when Omar One approached to announce, "Good news, the Canadian Embassy in Bamako wants proof-of-life."

Shortly afterward, Omar One escorted the man we would come to know as Omar Three to our position and, with some deference to O3, introduced him to us as an important fellow, a close collaborator of Emir Khaled. We had seen him around for a few days but always at some distance. Omar Three was clearly a senior officer, more senior, I suspected, than anyone else in camp. He told us that the Canadian Embassy in Mali had asked for another video. As we were talking, a tent was being erected. Omar Three said that we were essentially to perform as we had for Video One on Day 5, but this time there would be three of us, for "The UN has insisted on seeing Soumana—not the government of Niger, which doesn't care about him—but the UN."

I asked what the message was to be and he repeated, "It will be the same as before. Mr. Robert, you will speak first, then Mr. Louis. You will say who you are, when we took you, who we are, that you are not suffering and, if they want to see you alive, there are to be no military actions against us. That is all." I said that we would also want to speak to our wives and families and O3, waving his hand dismissively, said, "Sure, sure."

As we approached the tent, Omar Three drew me aside and said, "You must tell your colleague, Louis, to get hold of himself. We do not want to give people the impression that we are abusing you." Louis was indeed visibly nervous, so we had a quiet chat as I repeated Omar Three's concerns, which we both took as perhaps the most positive sign we had been given since the outset of this horrible adventure. As we entered the tent, I asked O3 when Soumana should speak and he dismissively replied, "You, then Louis. Soumana will not speak!"

The set-up for Video Two seemed to be precisely the same as for the first one. The black Al Qaeda flag with white Arabic script was again pinned to the wall of the tent. Behind us were four *mujahideen* in black turbans, festooned with ammunition belts, three of them with machine guns and the fourth, standing right behind my head, holding a sword, his hand on the hilt. I do not recall these people being there when we walked into the tent, certainly not the menacing one with the sword, who would have received my full attention. So I expect that they did not come in until after the three of us were seated facing the camera.

With little ceremony Julabib, who again sat cross-legged in front of me, signalled: three, two, one, and—pointed. Without preamble I repeated pretty much what I had said forty-seven days before: who I was, what had been my UN mission (getting the title of my employer right this time), when and where we were taken. I said that we were being held by Al Qaeda in the Islamic Maghreb and that we were being treated honourably or correctly, I don't recall which. I stressed that climatic and living conditions were getting tougher and noted we were experiencing health issues. I urged Canadian and UN authorities to put an early end to our captivity without resorting to violence.

I then addressed myself to Mary and the girls (even getting the number of my children right), telling them how much I loved them and how I regretted the pain our situation must be causing them, and turned things over to Louis, who went through a similar routine. That was it. When we got outside the tent, Hassan, wishing to put an end to our upbeat mood, sidled up to us and said with a sneer, "Don't think for a moment that this means anything. This is by no means over." Well, he sure got that right.

The directors, Omars One and Three, however, seemed pleased. Soumana was led away before we could exchange more than a few friendly words, but he seemed pleased that he had been included and, of course, that his family would learn that he was alive and looking well. Once back at our tree we were brought pen and paper and told to write in English and in French what we had just said and to sign and date these statements. Each of us wrote a little more to our families but was careful to stick fairly close to the agreed script.

Once completed, these statements were handed to Omar Three, who was in his truck and on his way within moments. Both Louis and I took great comfort from the seriousness with which our captors seemed to take the production of this second video and the urgency with which they wanted to get it to market. From Hollywood, I had learned that the production of evidence of well-being ("proof-of-life," in the kidnapping lexicon) was usually demanded at the outset and again just before liberation, so we thought we might be on that track; so too, quite clearly, did most of our kidnappers.

That said, we were confused. Aside from the happy addition of Soumana, we had just done on Day 52 what we thought had been accomplished on Day 5, and we couldn't figure out why it had been necessary. What would Ottawa learn from the video message we had just made that we had not told them seven long weeks before, beyond the fact that we were still alive? Was it possible they had not received the first message? It seemed as if the clock had just been reset to zero, that in fact, nothing had been achieved over this period. I think this may have been a fairly accurate assessment.

On Day 62, in a scene out of *The Bridge on the River Kwai* or *The Great Escape,* I demanded to see the camp emir, Abdul Rahman, to request adequate clothing and footwear. At the end of that unproductive meeting, we were informed that we would—after fifty-six days—be leaving the hell-that-we-knew, Camp Canada, the next evening to venture into an even more uncertain future. "We will leave tomorrow, at night," said AR with great seriousness, "so that the flies will not follow us." From his evident frustration, however, it was clear that the move would not be in the direction we hoped so fervently to be going.

We left after dinner and after dark on Day 63 (Valentine's Day) but after travelling only about an hour we suddenly stopped in the middle of nowhere—no rocks, no trees, just undulating sand. Thus, Camp Outside. Our blankets were thrown down at our feet and we were told we would be spending the night. We slept on one side of three tightly grouped trucks and they bedded down on the other. Sentries were posted and everybody was asleep in minutes.

The next day we set out just after dawn. Louis and I were assigned to the truck driven by Abdul Rahman. It was a surprise to be travelling with the camp emir, and I had the impression that this severe and taciturn man wanted to tell us things without having to rely on the doubtful mercies of Hassan as interpreter. However, it was going to be difficult as AR had only a smattering of French. After nearly an hour of travelling in complete silence, he rummaged in his robes and wordlessly handed us each a tiny pair of folding scissors, the kind you get in the higher-end Christmas crackers. Evidently he was trying to be accommodating. I think it was to offset the fiasco of the meeting the previous evening, during which Hassan had refused to interpret AR's long answer to my question about the state of negotiations. It was a confusing but not unwelcome gesture. After that, with hand signals, a few dozen words of French and palpable frustration, he explained that he had no idea where the negotiations stood. This at least told us that there were negotiations.

Elaborating further he noted, "The Canadians tell us that there is always another meeting . . . always somebody else who needs to be consulted," and, yes, that sounded like home. Bitterly, he told us, "A special emissary was to come to a meeting with us, but he never showed up." We had no inkling of what that might be about.

We drove until noon, when we stopped in a very different landscape from Camp Canada. This was harder, harsher desert: almost no greenery, a couple of stubby, thin acacias around which they made their camp, and we were told to use the shady side of one of the trucks. However, as it was near midday, with our backs against the truck we had only a strip of shade about fifty centimetres wide in which to cower from the sun. We rigged our bit of blue tarp to various points on the truck and found what shelter we could. When we asked how long we would be at this site, Hassan, swelling in his role of acting hostage manager in Omar's absence, replied, "a few hours or maybe weeks." But the whole arrangement seemed transitory, temporary—as if they were waiting for something.

Louis had sensed something fishy and in pretending to fiddle with the tarp, he spied an operating tape recorder wedged between the door against which we were leaning and the seat. He told me about it as we were off collecting rocks to hold down the tarp, and we considered spending a couple of hours detailing the thousand ways Hassan was a prick—but prudence prevailed. I don't think this gambit was tried again, but who knows?

Around us were seven rather phallic, hoodoo-like rocky outcroppings rising from the desert floor and, in the middle, one softer, rounder formation (we'd been in the desert a long time), so we named that camp Seven Brothers and One Sister. Once the recorder ploy had failed, we were directed to make camp on the far side of a small dune, separating them from us, with no cover whatsoever. We convinced our guards to let us have four metal tent poles and then attached "our" rug at the four corners to create a canopy that offered a reasonable amount of shade. Hassan, no doubt annoyed at the failure of his attempted bugging, arbitrarily rejected our first

two walking tracks and then screamed at Louis for repeatedly staring at the brothers. "We know," he shouted, "you are collecting
information for Western intelligence agencies and this behaviour
must stop now or there will be severe repercussions."

This was a serious and dangerous accusation and I needed to
put it to rest fast, or a Louis-the-spy infection would spread among
our jailers. I took Hassan aside and walked with him far from
Louis and the others. When I insisted that I didn't know what he
had been talking about, Hassan said that Louis had them under
constant observation and was clearly filing data away in the hope
that one day he might be able to use it against them. I retorted that
Hassan clearly didn't like Louis and was making things up to generate ill will toward my friend and colleague.

Hassan vigorously rejected my claim and demanded that I
watch Louis myself and come to my own conclusion. In the meantime, and until Louis desisted, Hassan blustered rather under-
whelmingly, there would be no more access to the Belgian high
school history books.

So I did. I watched Louis to see if he was staring at them,
and . . . he was. But it was so very clearly, at least to me, not to
"observe and report" but simply because they were our entertainment. What they were up to was the only diversion available—
more interesting than staring into the empty desert. There was no
doubt, though, that Louis would sit and stare, sometimes without
even seeing, just letting his mind wander while looking in their
direction. Obviously, this had to stop. Our kidnappers were quite
paranoid enough.

I explained all this to Louis and he gallantly agreed to try to
observe himself. Soon he allowed that he did spend more time looking in their direction than in any other. So we contrived, whenever
possible, to put his back to wherever they were and I'd quietly snap
my fingers when he resumed his vigil. Eventually he largely weaned
himself from this source of passive entertainment and our captors
became less aggressive.

In the evening of our third day at Seven Brothers (Day 66), we had just made up our bed when out of the blue one of the children brought us a litre Tetra Pak of mango juice. It was the most wonderful drink I have ever had. We savoured every drop, swishing the nectar around in our mouths. We had a long discussion about how much we would consume then and there and how much we would save at least for the morrow. The morrow option didn't do very well.

An hour later, as we were sitting on our blankets watching the stars, Omar Two of all people showed up with a bag of candies, another Tetra Pak of juice, a package of some kind of sticky, sweet pastry, and a large, stuffed-full plastic bag. We looked up at him uncomprehendingly. With a grimace, which we took to be the best smile he could manage, he simply said, "These are for you," and left. We had no idea what was going on. We wolfed down the sticky sweet thing, reserved the juice, and tore open the bag. Inside were two brightly coloured and very cheaply made tracksuits—but no shoes, socks, or underwear.

We were, of course, pleased with these goodies, but what did they mean? At this point—and it was really the only time I fell up a rabbit hole—I put together the facts that we had suddenly left Camp Canada with little warning, that for the past four days we seemed to have been waiting for something external to the camp to happen, and that a truck had clearly just come in bearing these welcome supplies and possibly news, and concluded that we had received our "liberation suits." We had seen the news clips: the hostages emerge from a vehicle wearing spanking new, identical tracksuits and are handed over to the Red Cross or some other group of smiling authorities. I really wanted to see that movie and concluded that we were about to star in it.

Louis didn't completely fall for my logic, but needless to say, he liked the idea. We drank off half of the second litre of juice in celebration of our imminent release. I stayed awake all night in a state of euphoria. Loving the stars, loving life, so very excited about seeing my family.

The next day we broke camp early. There didn't seem to be as much excitement in the air as I had expected, but they did smile at our having changed our rags for the bright, new, itchy, and utterly incongruous-looking tracksuits. We travelled all day and covered a lot of ground: lots of speed across wide flat spaces. But there was no mood of something significant about to happen. My euphoria began to ebb. Soon there was nothing left but a sweaty, chafing, and silly tracksuit whose zipper had already broken. By the time we reached a camp we called Thornhill (for obvious reasons), I was in another deep and disappointed funk and I swore that thenceforth I would never again indulge in such self-delusion.

This camp was not unpleasant, even if there was a surfeit of thorns hiding in the sand. We were situated far from our jailers and had an outstanding walking track—seven circuits to the kilo-metre—but unfortunately a number of other creatures were also in residence. Omar One later reported that six vipers and nine scorpions had been dispatched over the two weeks we spent at Thornhill, in addition to our own kills.

I was again plagued by constipation (perhaps it was the prospect of squatting over desert vipers), and just as I feared we would have to deploy "the instrument," Omar One returned from his traditional cure on Day 80. He asked how we had been bearing up, and I told him of the return of my bowel problems. The next day he showed up with a dog-eared package of appropriate pills but gave no hint from where or how long they had been available. There were twenty pills in bubble packaging and after endless calculation, I broke one in half, chewed it, and—as advertised on the package—within twelve hours everything worked. So, I had thirty-nine further chances to defeat the problem before again resorting to mechanical means, and that was comforting. That package became my most valuable possession. I never went anywhere without those pills secreted somewhere in my clothes.

❖

Around Day 81 (4 March) at Thornhill, in the context of a game of Twenty Questions, Hassan told me, "We are seeking the release of twenty of our brothers in return for your freedom," and by that it was clear—even if I cannot remember what made it so—that he was referring to all seven of their captives.

I then asked, "Is it a reasonable list; that is, one the relevant governments could possibly agree to?" Smiling, he allowed that it was. Without further elaboration I had the impression that we shared more or less the same understanding of what constituted "reasonable." I couldn't figure out whether Hassan's transmittal of this information was sanctioned.

While Louis and I talked about everything, we inevitably ended up discussing some aspect of what it would take to get us out of there. Those were rarely very uplifting conversations. The essential issues—those that determined whether we would live or die and, if we lived, in what kind of shape we would emerge from this ordeal—were, from my perspective, neither numerous nor complicated. I was utterly preoccupied with these pertinent questions. Would the United Nations and Canada be able to work out an arrangement for effectively handling our case and avoid getting in each other's way? Would the Canadian government take a stand on principle (tough, inflexible: "We do not deal with Al Qaeda"), in which case we would die, or would the Prime Minister be pragmatic and instruct the public service to find a way to get us home without offending such principles? Would the right person be put in charge within the bureaucracy, with the right authority to cause our case to be managed in our best interests? Would a clear and informed decision be made over which agency of government was given the lead responsibility for knitting together and reconciling the diverse and sometimes conflicting strands of our situation? Would Canada work well (that is, in a manner likely to bring about our release) with our friends and allies and their various agencies, as well as with our African partners in the region? And, so very important, would our families be properly and sympathetically briefed, involved, and protected, and would our friends at home and abroad support them?

Louis and I debated endlessly—literally ad nauseam—what it would take to gain our release. We calculated all the permutations and combinations of the extent to which the United Nations and its current Secretary-General, Ban Ki-moon, would be influenced by the UN aristocracy (the five permanent, unelected members of the Security Council), and concluded that this sort of conjecture was unlikely to improve our sleeping patterns.

Louis believed that eventually—perhaps only after many, many months—our abductors would tire of the costs and risks of holding us, leading them to release us in some form of "humanitarian gesture." I simply did not believe that Al Qaeda did humanitarian gestures, and insisted that they had a rep to protect as the meanest buggers in the valley. There was no room in their raison d'être for generosity. In short, I believed—no, I knew—that they would have to get enough if we were to be released. I agreed with Louis that they would not bear the costs and suffer the inconvenience of holding us for a great length of time, but disagreed that this would inexorably lead to our release. He, perfectly reasonably, wanted me to explain how much was enough, and I said with increasing exasperation that I had no bloody idea. But that didn't mean my analysis was wrong.

One afternoon at Thornhill we saw half a dozen of our guards drag a huge bag across the wide-open space between where they camped on the other side of a dune and our designated spot. In the middle of this football field–sized space they began to dig and were at it for a few hours. Eventually they dumped the bag into the hole, filled it in, and were at pains to flatten and smooth out all traces of their excavations. It seemed obvious to us that they were caching supplies of some sort—we later learned they were hiking boots—but we had never seen them do it like this before and it unnerved us to know that they did not mind our observing the whole thing.

Similarly, Hassan had taken to showing up at odd times, always wanting to talk or, rather, to spar. Often we saw him wrapping his scarf tightly around his head and face as he approached. Were we just imagining it or was he becoming more careless about the possibility we could subsequently identify him?

And then there was the matter of where Soumana was. In previous camps we had been able to see him. Now we could not. Had he been freed? Killed? Was he sick? We asked, but the answers seemed increasingly evasive.

Little things took on greater significance and small frustrations exacted a heavy toll. I first lost my spoon at Thornhill. I have always been a fastidious eater and I didn't want to eat—like them—with my hands. I spent hours on my hands and knees excavating our entire area in my version of an archeological grid, but to no avail. Everything disappeared into the sand. Leave it on the ground for thirty seconds and it was gone. Our captors were always losing tools and utensils. Twice I saw them perform a two-jack tire change and then drive off over one of the jacks, causing it to disappear into the sand.

I sat down and traced every movement we had made that day in my mind. We had moved our sleeping position, and while I had covered both comprehensively, I recalled that our habit after eating dinner was to stick our spoons, handle first, into the sand by our heads so we could find them the next morning. Returning to our first position, I lay down where I thought I had been the night before and, with eyes closed, stuck my imaginary spoon in the sand beside my head and between the roots of an acacia—and there it was.

I was to repeat this whole routine a week later and then again a few days after that, but then it would not be found. I asked for another and was curtly refused. So I was reduced to shovelling whatever mess of rice or pasta was on offer out of the bowl and into my face, in the dark, with my 77 mm Canon lens cap, which had been in my pocket when we were taken twelve weeks previously. Eventually I petitioned Jaffer, who had been newly appointed camp commandant to replace a weary and burnt-out Abdul Rahman, and without a word he pulled a spoon out of the pocket of his *jelabiyah* and handed it to me.

As we wandered about the Sahara, our movements dictated by no pattern or rationale we could discern, we faced a variety of other trials, but by far the most taxing were the ravages of the psychological roller coaster that racked us back and forth between hope and despair.

From Day 3, at the Board of Directors, I considered suicide a valid option among the few available to me, and I tried to ensure that I had or could get the means to end my life should I deem that it had become intolerable. I'm glad to note that I was never seriously tempted, and despite my extreme depression and confusion in those early horrible days and nights, I knew that such an act would have to be weighed exceedingly carefully against the devastating impact on my family and, most immediately, on Louis. I agree with those—like Mary—who hold that suicide is an essentially selfish act in all but the most extreme circumstances, but from my late teens I've deemed it nonetheless a legitimate choice, the ultimate act of free will.

Our fanatical captors, however, while anxious, even impatient, to get past this veil of tears and into paradise, consider suicide among the most heinous and unforgivable of sins. Therefore, any such option had to be surreptitiously preserved and never telegraphed, even to Louis. I was careful to protect the tiny pair of folding scissors that Abdul Rahman had given to each of us as we left Camp Canada and was loath to lend them to Louis even when he could not locate his own, and despite the fact that he was working on our constantly deteriorating shoes. Those centimetre-long blades offered cold comfort against the possibility of extreme suffering, but comfort nonetheless, even if it would take some doing with such an instrument.

At times I came very close to losing heart, when my reserves were nearing empty and I generally considered our situation all but irredeemable, but hope never deserted me completely. From the outset, I believed that the likelihood of our emerging alive from such a trial would be, as the Duke of Wellington said about Waterloo, "a damned nice thing—the nearest run thing you ever saw."

On occasion I wondered if in such extreme circumstances I ought to reconsider a lifetime of committed atheism and seek—though I knew not how—comfort or inspiration from the god to whom Louis prayed. But God just wasn't there for me. I have never had any religious beliefs of any sort, despite a number of well-intentioned people seeking to instil them within me (and, just to be clear, I am not referring to my Al Qaeda proselytizers). God never joined me in that shallow Saharan foxhole and I knew, and was quite serene about the fact, that He was never going to do so.

God was there for Louis, however, offering him support and consolation, and buttressing his penchant for seeing the bright side of things as I meandered about on the darker side. Without doubt, this helped me enormously. When I was unable to drag Louis out of a hole, his God stepped in and helped. When Louis was tempted to join me in holes of my making, his God helped him to avoid such traps. So, perhaps in a way God was there for me too, but we never established any kind of a direct relationship.

CHAPTER 11

BLAISE COMPAORÉ AND HIS
MARVELLOUS GIFT

═══

With throats unslaked, with black lips baked,
We could nor laugh nor wail;
Through utter drought all dumb we stood!
I bit my arm, I suck'd the blood,
And cried, A sail! a sail!

═══

At Thornhill on Day 81, Omar One, rather formally but with real anger and bitterness, announced to us that they'd had it with Canadian negotiators. They no longer trusted them and would have no more to do with them. Their erstwhile Canadian interlocutors, whom he never named, had, he railed, been duplicitous and dishonest. They kept promising things that never happened, he reported, and agreeing to meetings that never took place. It was all about delay, he insisted, and fiercely proclaimed that such a tactic would not work.

This was devastating news to us, with appalling implications, even if we could not avoid the irony of our murderous Al Qaeda kidnappers complaining about our compatriots' dishonesty and untrustworthiness. Further, he told us, once Canada had been disqualified from further direct engagement in the determination of our future, AQIM had sought a regional leader who might "take an interest in your case." However, he spat, everyone they had approached had refused outright. "They all," he said with force and conviction, "were willing to let you die." Observing the anticipated shock in our faces, he added with a theatrical pause, "Save one."

Blaise Compaoré, President of Burkina Faso, was, Omar allowed, the only one willing to step forward and endeavour to save our lives. "Your future" he concluded, "is now entirely in the hands of President Compaoré," and with that he walked away, leaving us to mull over these unhappy tidings.

And I had thought that things couldn't get much worse.

A decade earlier I had worked hard, and with some success, to make President Compaoré an international pariah and had, I knew well, attracted his enmity as a result.

Between 1988 and 1999, the United Nations deployed four peacekeeping and observer missions to Angola (UNAVEM I, II, III, and MONUA) in an effort to limit, if not stop, the carnage in the Angolan civil war, which had been raging off and mostly on over twenty-five years. It was the bloodiest of Africa's proxy wars between East and West. The cost of these UN operations was a few billion dollars, and they achieved nothing because none of the principal players on the Security Council, who had voted these massive and expensive undertakings into existence—just to be seen to be "doing something"—were committed to seeing them succeed. Instead, they sought to ensure that their ponies would prevail in the surrogate contest between capitalism and communism (ideologies that concerned the Africans very little)—the spoils of which were Angola's riches.

When I took Canada's seat at the Security Council table in January 1999, I knew that we could do little about the grand confrontations in the Middle East—most notably the building disaster in Iraq—but I did think that, just possibly, ten years after the Berlin Wall had come down we could put an end to this vestigial Cold

War struggle, in which most outside participants had forgotten what they were doing there but could not bring themselves to stop doing it. It was clear to me that if the seemingly endless Angolan civil war were to be stopped, it would have to be done outside that country; that the answer lay in preventing oxygen from reaching the fire, rather than sitting around in New York designing by committee ever more ineffectual fire extinguishers.

In 1992, the government of President José Eduardo dos Santos had won UN-supervised elections, which international observers had judged to be free and fair. Jonas Savimbi's UNITA (Union for the Total Independence of Angola) did not like that outcome, particularly as his CIA backers had assured him that it would go the other way. So, dropping the pretence of a democratic option, UNITA rebels decided they could do better by returning to the bush and digging up their guns.

By controlling Angola's rich diamond fields, Savimbi could fund his bloody insurrection forever, as neither diamond markets nor consumers seemed to care where the stones came from (despite UN sanctions, which nobody seemed interested in enforcing). Furthermore, arms and fuel suppliers knew that the sanctions prohibiting what they were up to remained as toothless and token as the day they were born around the Security Council's horseshoe table. That said, while the diamond markets in London, Antwerp, Tel Aviv, Mumbai, and New York had yet to appreciate the fact, consumer attitudes were changing, largely as a result of aggressive reports issued by Global Witness and forthright individuals like Alex Vines of Human Rights Watch and Ian Smillie of Partnership Africa–Canada, as they prosecuted their campaign against "blood diamonds." That venerable commodity was just starting to look less and less like the bedrock of the forever business.

For its part, the government of Angola, the internationally recognized victor in those elections and at the helm of the seventeenth-largest oil producer in the world, could afford to resist UNITA indefinitely; thus, it was a perfect civil war. I judged that only through a no-holds-barred, well-researched and well-documented operation aimed at identifying the perfidy of the sanctions busters, and yes, the hypocrisy of many of the main players at the United Nations, who had become so adept at looking the other way, could the paradigm shift and the supply of war materiel to the UNITA rebels be cut off.

To get a genuinely tough report through the Council, however, we needed a mechanism that would be immune from the political interests and pressure tactics that had always prevented pertinent information from being considered. So we created an arm's-length expert panel beholden to no government (including Canada's), and reporting to me as chairman of the relevant Security Council sanctions committee. I then went to Angola and interviewed half a dozen UNITA defectors and learned in exquisite detail where all the bodies were buried.

An awful lot of feathers were ruffled both inside and outside Africa by our two reports on the how, when, where, and, above all, the who of sanctions busting vis-à-vis Angola. But it worked, and also restored a little credibility to the Council's deliberations and, indeed, to the tattered reputation of sanctions as an effective instrument of multilateral diplomacy. Above all, it ensured that the bulk of UNITA's blood-drenched diamonds was denied access to international markets.

On 10 March 2000, I issued the first of those two reports (known, however immodestly, as "The Fowler Report"). For the first time in UN history, it "named and shamed" a long list of those complicit in supporting UNITA, contrary to the dictates of a whole raft of Security Council resolutions outlawing such behaviour. The provisioning of UNITA had sustained the devastating civil war, which over twenty-five years had killed over half a million people, displaced 4.3 million others, or a third of Angola's population, and caused that country to be judged by UNICEF "the worst place in the world to be a child."

With the publication of that report those, such as Russian "lord of war" Viktor Bout, who had been supplying arms and facilitating their illegal shipment to Savimbi, understood that henceforth they would be exposed to public scrutiny and held accountable. Those who had been buying Savimbi's diamonds through the back doors in London and Antwerp came to realize that they were putting at risk the vast and entirely legitimate bulk of their businesses. Eventually, Savimbi could no longer pay the few arms dealers still willing to furnish him with war materiel. He ran out of fuel and ammunition and was soon defeated and killed. Africa's longest war was finally over.

Most prominent among the sanctions busters named in our report were two sitting African presidents, Gnassingbé Eyadéma of Togo and Blaise Compaoré of Burkina Faso.

On the few occasions I ran into President Compaoré between the publication of that Security Council report and my capture in Niger, it was clear that he had not welcomed the publicity I had provided. At one meeting in early 2003 at the Elysée Palace (the French president's office and residence in Paris), President Compaoré, who is a tall, fit, articulate, and handsome gentleman, draped a long, strong arm around my shoulders, his thumb digging deeply into the muscle beneath my collar bone, and said through clenched teeth—and a big smile—"You really must come and see us in Ouagadougou, Mr. Ambassador."

I replied, "But, Mr. President, will I be allowed to leave?" He threw his head back and laughed loudly and then smiled as he walked away, giving me an enigmatic wink over his shoulder.

So, Omar One had just told us that the matter of whether we would live or die now lay in the hands of West Africa's elder statesman, a man whom I had branded an international criminal in a very public manner. All concerned knew that those findings, which had received wide media coverage, were well founded and documented.

Why, then, had President Compaoré taken on such an assignment, if indeed he had? Had no one else been willing to do so? What about Malian President Amadou Toumani Touré (universally known as ATT) in Bamako? What were AQIM's recruitment criteria? Was AQIM simply messing with our heads? If so, to what end? One thing did seem to compute. Many, particularly in Africa, concur with the dictum that *la vengeance se mange très-bien froide* (revenge is a dish best served cold). All Blaise Compaoré had to do to see my captivity prolonged, and have me suffer an unpleasant death, was nothing at all.

That, though, is precisely what he did not do.

The next evening, Day 82, the entire council, led by Abdul Rahman, trooped to our location at Thornhill on a formal visit. They sat in a half-circle in front of us and AR said, through Omar One, "The President has sent you gifts." With a come-hither movement of his left arm, he directed a line of the children forward, each bearing a medium-sized carton. There were eleven in all and they contained quantities of wondrous stuff: vitamins, sardines, cookies of every description, fruit juices, candies, Kleenex, toothbrushes and paste, great bars of soap and chocolate, which, even at nearly fifty degrees, were enormously welcome.

We were at a loss to understand what this was all about, but I was not about to be fooled again. This was obviously no overture to liberation, but nor did it make any sense to give us such stuff if we were about to be killed.

We were urged to open each carton and examine the contents as, quite aside from their evident curiosity, they needed to see what the boxes contained from a security perspective even though we were certain that the containers had already been subjected to some considerable examination.

It is hard to describe how excited we were by those cartons and how perplexed. No Christmas stocking had ever held such valued treasures. We were starving. We immediately opened a package of biscuits and passed them around. Their first reaction, every one of them, was to refuse. "These things," they said lugubriously, "have been sent by President Compaoré to you. They are not for us."

But I could see Omar One salivating. So we insisted, and with some reverence each of these tough, heavily armed, beturbaned, weather-beaten, raggedly clad warriors of Allah slowly and very tentatively reached into the extended package and extracted a rectangular, sugar-coated cookie with the thumb and forefinger of his right hand and began, rather self-consciously, to nibble at the opposite corner, smiling, just a little.

Then, looking embarrassed, Abdul Rahman signalled that he had something important that needed to be said. Obviously ill at ease, he reported that at some point as the trucks were being unloaded somewhere between wherever we were and Ouagadougou—perhaps two thousand kilometres distant—one of the cartons had been dropped. A corner had been crushed. Inside, two packages of biscuits had been pulverized. On examining the damaged carton and discovering the destroyed packages, a few of the younger ones had believed they had the right to eat the crumbs. They were wrong, he sternly said, and they had been punished. It would not happen again, he assured us, and he wished to apologize for such unacceptable behaviour. Then he stared at the ground in front of him, deeply ashamed.

Most of the others seemed equally embarrassed and they stared straight ahead, avoiding any eye contact with us. I could not comprehend what I was witnessing. Here were these vicious desert warriors, dedicated to the path of bloody, no-holds-barred *jihad,* planning martyr operations against civilians and particularly targeting aid and humanitarian workers—but they did not steal cookies. I felt certain that every one of them was not only capable of but in some cases anxious to slit our throats, but they were devastated that some of their number had nicked "our" cookie crumbs. It was at that point I really appreciated the depth and the single-mindedness of their commitment to *jihad* and the breadth of the cultural gap between us.

In the dying evening light Louis and I were surrounded by piles of goodies, not necessarily what we would have chosen if we had been sent into a supermarket and told to fill four or five shopping carts, but wonderful nonetheless. I do not like sardines, but I sure appreciated those rich, oily, salty, very nutritious ones. Nor am I a big cookie fan, but we savoured each one of those suckers in the weeks to come, carefully planning which treats we would allow ourselves over the coming days.

Deciding what to eat ourselves, what to hoard, and how much to share with which of our guards and in what manner became a welcome respite from thinking about when and how they would kill us. It all required management and subtle adjustments. How long would we seek to extend these supplies? Which items would deteriorate in the heat first and which would suffer most in the seemingly ever more random movements across the desert? Cookies, we found, do not respond well to being hurled into the back of a pickup truck under heavy weapons and ammunition with four or five men bouncing around on top. Similarly, waxed cardboard Tetra Paks of mango juice cannot withstand such stresses, to say nothing of those temperatures. And then there were the dozen large bars of chocolate.

For a while, we were fairly parsimonious with our stash, both vis-à-vis our captors and between ourselves, but hunger, attrition, and environmental losses took their toll. So we set our supply-planning horizon to two or three more months rather than the five or six remaining in our original eight-month survival plan. We thought the twelve or fifteen litres of juice would spoil first and, anyway, that stuff was just so damn delicious. We had fraught discussions over whether to enjoy it straight up or cut it with the iffy water to make it stretch. Louis favoured the former and I the latter, not only because that would prolong my enjoyment of those delicious juices but also because even a little made the water palatable.

As the meals became more spartan—just rice or macaroni, twice a day, cooked in powdered milk, again and again and again—we took to sending two or three tins of sardines to the "kitchen" so that they might flavour the common pot. Now and then we would add or substitute a package of cookies. These gestures were much appreciated by some and abhorred by others.

Both Hassan and Omar Two saw these gambits for what they were, efforts by us to curry favour with our kidnappers, and they deeply resented the extent to which the ploy was working. Both tried to get us to stop. Hassan insisted that we husband our resources, asserting, "This could last much longer than you think and you will need these things to keep you alive." Omar Two took a more aggressive stance by simply sending the gifts back with whichever kid was available whenever he was in the kitchen.

But even Omar Two could be tempted. We had received a number of metal tubes of effervescent vitamin tablets—both vitamin C and multivitamins—which we were told President Compaoré had personally insisted be included in the shipment. The vitamins were probably the most important element of this bounty. Whether or not this makes sense from a medical perspective, from Day 82 onward, I was no longer concerned about scurvy.

Every second evening, Louis and I shared a cup of water into which one of these tablets had been dissolved. It became our pre-dinner cocktail. On rare occasions, if one of us was feeling under the weather, we would have another. Omar Two was vividly interested in the containers and regularly dropped by to see if we had emptied one yet. Assuring him he could have them when empty, we asked what he wanted them for. A little defiantly he replied that he wanted to fill them with honey, so that he would have honey with him at all times. Then we recalled that honey was their all-purpose medical response to battlefield damage. Get shot—pour honey into the hole.

Of course Compaoré's care packages were important from a nutritional point of view but, more important, they were vital from a sociological and a psychological perspective. This was—at Week 12—the very first evidence that somebody out there was doing something to alleviate our plight. We assumed, or perhaps just hoped, that all kinds of things were happening in an effort to win our release, but this was the first hard evidence we had received. It was tangible, unambiguous, and so deeply appreciated.

As a result of President Compaoré's largesse, we became less victims, less helpless—more in charge of our own destiny. We had a measure of free will restored. With these assets, we suddenly had choices. We were able to express favour and disfavour, show generosity, demonstrate sympathy or withhold it. Some of our captors allowed themselves to be a little seduced by it, others remained impervious, but all tacitly acknowledged that it altered the captor–captive paradigm.

Over the next few days Louis' special skills again came to the fore as he constructed sturdy web bags from carefully tied together discarded strands of rope so that our precious cartons—which none of the *mujahideen* was overjoyed to see added to the already overburdened vehicles—would not suffer too much damage as we moved from place to place.

As the *katiba* council trooped away from our position into the darkness on Day 82, leaving Louis and me to catalogue this motherlode of delicious stuff, I asked Abdul Rahman how we might thank President Compaoré for his thoughtfulness and generosity, and he replied, "Soon you will speak to him."

CHAPTER 12

CALLING HOME

====

And now 'twas like all instruments,
Now like a lonely flute;
And now it is an angel's song,
That makes the Heavens be mute.

====

The day after we received Compaoré's largesse we again hit the road, but it seemed as if this time there was a little more purpose to our movement and direction. The first leg of the journey was yet again northward. We travelled for eight or ten hours, as always extremely fast over hard, relatively flat surfaces, skirting ever-larger and more impressive rocky outcroppings that soon became harsh, black, forbidding mountains. Eventually, as we could feel the troops becoming more excited, we turned into a deep canyon slicing into the cliff face on our right. It was never more than thirty or forty metres wide and we followed it through radical twists and turns into what seemed to be the very heart of the mountains. We stopped only when we could go no farther.

I was exhausted, but I had the feeling that we were somewhere quite familiar to our captors. They acted as if they were home, but in our entire ordeal I never felt less at home. It was a brutal, ugly place. The surrounding cliffs were composed of crumbling red sandstone, largely encased in an almost burnished, coal-black, thin veneer with vivid red scars across the face of the canyon where the outer black shell had broken away, revealing the sandstone beneath. This was Le Rouge et Le Noir, and it gets the prize for being the most depressing of our camps. One of *les frères* told us it had been their headquarters for more than two years but that they hadn't used it for three or four years. He showed us where they had built a bread oven into the cliff face by embedding a forty-five-gallon drum above a deep opening in which a fire could be laid.

Most relevant to our Salafist captors, however, was that it included a small stand of the fabled arak trees. As we departed the next day, without any order or direction, all the trucks (I think there were four) skidded to a halt in soft sand and everyone leapt out with cutting tools and began hacking at the roots of these small, bushy, willow-like trees. They returned to the vehicles, beatific smiles on their faces, clutching various lengths of twig-like roots, even giving us a couple.

The next day, after another long drive, we reached Wellhead, a camp located near a productive well dug into the bottom of a wide *wadi*. We took on water at the well and then moved down the *wadi* about a kilometre and around a bend to make camp. While the well itself was not visible from where we were camped, we did see, over the banks of the *wadi,* three or four vehicles heading to the well, and I was surprised that our kidnappers were so relaxed about such an exposed location.

On our third evening at Wellhead, Omars One and Three approached Louis' and my exposed position and squatted beside our blanket as the dusk deepened and their faces gradually disappeared into the gloom. They told us that the next day we would be travelling far to a particular location from which we would call our families. We were dumbstruck. However, as the Omars soon made clear, this was no sympathy gesture. They explained that the message we must transmit to our families was the urgent need to reinvigorate the negotiations, which, they darkly added, were essentially at an impasse.

We were desperate to speak to our wives and children, and as I contemplated what I would say to Mary, I was paying less attention than I ought to what they were telling me about the purpose of the call, or rather, their purpose. I had my own. Omar One must have perceived this inattention for he offered us a few scraps of paper and a well-used ballpoint pen and invited us to "take notes" for the forthcoming calls. This moment would be vital, they said, in determining whether we would or would not emerge from this experience alive.

Omar One told us that President Compaoré was arranging for our wives and perhaps one child from each family to fly to Burkina Faso and that they would be speaking to us from there. "It is all arranged," they assured us. Further, after speaking to our wives, we would talk to President Compaoré.

"You must understand," chipped in Omar Three, "that the Canadian government has been very duplicitous. They do not want you back. They are doing everything possible to ensure that you do not return. What you must do is get your wives to make a big noise, to engage the journalists and the politicians to bring pressure on the Canadian government, which will do nothing for you if this does not happen."

While Louis and I had understood from the beginning that something like this was likely to happen, indeed, that like the proof-of-life messages it seemed to be one of those necessary steps in the kidnapping negotiation process, we were conflicted. I strove to separate their agenda from mine and then to construct one that might reasonably serve both. As it turned out it wasn't difficult, but that is because the two agendas were not that different and I have a bright, strong, and effective wife.

I wanted to speak to Mary at just about any cost. There had been no real goodbyes as I stepped into a December snowstorm in Ottawa three months before. We'd had no kind of closure. I did not really think that I would emerge from this alive and there were things I wanted to say—that I desperately needed to say—to my wife of nearly thirty years and through her to our cherished daughters. I needed to put my emotional affairs in order.

Also, Louis and I believed that our kidnappers regularly fed us disinformation but perhaps less than might have been expected. Talk of being conflicted! They took to heart the Islamic prohibition against lying, and while the Prophet, they told us, had specifically allowed the use of certain *ruses de guerre* (actions taken to fool the enemy), that did not offer open season to liars. Even so, we had no reason to believe any of the precious little they said about the negotiating process was accurate or whether the people holding us in these camps had any real knowledge of its progress. We therefore had no reason to believe that we ought to forcefully encourage our wives to pre-empt whatever the government was doing to get us out. I did, however, want to ensure—be absolutely certain—that Mary knew she had my full support should she ever decide to exercise such an option, whatever the consequences.

We knew that we had to avoid inserting ourselves directly into the negotiating process if only because it was unlikely to produce a useful result. Yet we were well aware that this was precisely what our abductors were urging us to do and we could not reject out of hand the possibility that they were right. Maybe the government was not prepared to do whatever was necessary to get us out of the mess we were in. Certainly we had seen no sign of a concerted strategy, but was it reasonable to expect that we would?

Finally, it was evident that the price I would have to pay to speak to my family, and to have any hope of being able to do so again, was to appear to follow the scenario our captors had outlined. In fact, much of the thrust of their message was quite congenial to me.

The timing of and trigger for such an initiative was the essential difference between the AQIM agenda and my own. They meant *right now,* while I would try to say *if and when Mary judged necessary.* I wanted to impress upon her that any decision to make an end run around government action or inaction would have to be her call, and that she could not necessarily trust the government to take all decisions in her (and my) best interests. I wanted her to know that if she believed public pressure should be mounted in an effort to save my life, that without it the government was not going to do whatever was necessary, then she should take such a risk. One cannot spend forty years in the public service and blindly rely on governments to do the "right thing" when thorny issues of political principle are involved. I wanted her to know that I would fully accept the risk she would be taking, so I dutifully set about writing my notes, without, of course being able to see what I was writing.

Early the next morning on Day 87, as we prepared to set out on the remainder of our telephone odyssey, somebody told us to mount up and assigned Louis and me to our respective vehicles. I was getting into mine when I heard a ruckus: the anomaly of loud voices raised in anger, one of them Louis'. I went to investigate and found Louis with his arms full of his share of our baggage standing by a truck looking dumbfounded, with Hassan screaming threats in his face. Hassan had his young posse about him and it looked ugly. Jack was nearby, however, and he quickly strode in and gave everybody a time out.

Jack asked what had happened and Louis explained that he had been about to board his designated truck when Hassan started screaming that Louis was never to approach the trucks without permission, that Louis already knew those rules, and were he to do it again, Hassan had promised, he would "receive great pain." Omar One was there too and told Jack that Louis had been instructed to board. Jack was clearly annoyed and ordered everybody to mount up, and we were off.

It was one of the hottest days we had known, difficult even to draw breath. After about four hours we stopped in an unprepossessing spot to wait out the midday heat. We were assigned a skimpy, ant-ridden tree about a hundred metres from their trucks, and soon the entertainment was the sighting-in of a new sniper rifle. After some time, we were approached by a delegation headed by Jack and including Omar One and Jaffer, who had been named the camp emir the day before, replacing the visibly exhausted Abdul Rahman. Both Louis and I were certain that, at best, we were about to get a lecture.

Before saying anything, Omar offered us each a filthy, hard, thin, flat slab of goat cheese. It was delicious. After some inconsequential remarks, Jack explained that their cause was just but while it was God's work, unfortunately it was performed by men, and men were flawed. Some, he said, warming to his theme, were simply rotten: they "had no honour." Such a man, he allowed, was Hassan. He apologized for Hassan's behaviour and assured us that such an incident would not recur.

After the long midday rest we set off again and this time I was placed in Jack's truck with Omar One. The group emir may have had only one eye but he was a fluid and intelligent driver, anticipating each challenge—and in that environment there were many. No one else came close to exhibiting his driving skills and there were some very good drivers in that *katiba*. But he did not talk much and the usually voluble Omar seemed a little restrained in the presence of the boss. As darkness fell, breaking a long silence Jack snarled—and Omar interpreted in the same tone—"The British and French are mounting a raid to save you," and then added, darkly, "I assure you, they will not succeed."

I found his announcement passing strange, but not AQIM's claim to have such intelligence. (One of their constant refrains was "We have our people everywhere," and they did seem to have some good operational intelligence. After all, that's how they got us.) It was more because I could not understand why the French would involve themselves in such a mission. The Brits, yes, because of the Briton captured on 22 January, but why the French? And of course I also wondered, why not the Canadians?

Obviously there was a reason I had been assigned to Belmokhtar's truck, the only time that happened. He wanted an uninterrupted opportunity to reinforce the message of the two Omars the previous evening about the importance of using the call we were apparently about to make to get our wives to bring pressure on the Canadian government to get us out.

It must have been close to seven in the evening when we saw a light flashing to the east through the gathering dusk, surprisingly high above what I had got used to as the desert horizon. They had clearly been expecting such a signal. Belmokhtar immediately swung off the rudimentary *piste* we had been following and drove toward it, the three trucks behind following in our wake. After a few hundred metres, we skirted a huge, ill-perceived mass on the left and parked beside the two trucks of the advance guard. There was the usual hustle and bustle as everybody stretched after the gruelling drive and gathered weapons and equipment. A lot of sentries were posted, and Louis and I were told to follow Belmokhtar, Omar One, and Ahmed up the razor-backed crest of an enormous sand dune. It was hard going up that steep, soft sand bank. With each step, we slid back about half the distance gained.

At the top of the huge dune were steep slopes in both directions, and being somewhat subject to vertigo, I was glad it was dark. We stood in a line along the crest, one foot on each slope, and they outlined how it was going to go down. We were up there so we could catch the Algerian cell net, the border being some forty kilometres distant. To make such calls from their satellite-phones would be to invite an Algerian air strike, they said matter-of-factly. They were in the main very careful about where and how they used their satellite-phones. So they oriented me toward some distant, invisible tower to the east, explaining that I could not move or twist or I would lose the signal.

Then they announced that I would go first, to be followed by Louis, and eventually by Soumana, who, they said, was somewhere down at the bottom of the dune. Holding the phone, the nasty Ahmed asked me for my phone number. "Where?" I replied. "Isn't she in Ouagadougou?"

"No, no," they replied, waving that off as if it had never been the plan. "In Canada. They are expecting your call in Canada."

"Wait a minute," I exclaimed, panicking slightly, as I came to terms with the fact that I had never considered these calls might be made in the dark. "I need to be able to see my notes," and a very bright LED flashlight was produced. When I directed its beam toward my scrap of paper, I could see nothing beyond blurry brilliant whiteness.

"Here, try these," said Omar One, and handed me a pair of drugstore magnification glasses. To my amazement, one lens worked well; the other made things worse. The flashlight was so bright, however, that it was difficult to read—but of course, I didn't really need to. I was just terribly nervous and the piece of paper was my security blanket. I knew that an awful lot was riding on this call.

"So, what is the number?" asked Ahmed, again. And I didn't know. I could not remember my home phone number. I froze.

Louis then quietly offered me his always appropriate and timely advice at times like these. "Breathe!" he said, "Breathe!"

And I did, calmed down, and remembered the number. In it went and the phone was handed to me. A last-minute correction was made to my orientation and I heard the familiar ring of an Ottawa phone, again and again, until my own voice told me that neither Mary nor I were there so would I please leave a message. So I did: "Hi, Sweetie, I'm calling from atop a huge sand dune somewhere in the Sahara. I am not, repeat not, free but I need to speak with you. I'll call back."

"Call her cell," one of our captors kibitzed, so I did that too. Again it rang and rang until I got her voice mail and left a similar message. Throughout this I pictured her desperately rummaging through her purse (which our family, taking a cue from our eldest daughter, calls her "pit of despair") as she tried and failed to locate the phone before it switched over to voice mail. My blood pressure and frustration levels were by now pretty high, but I'd had my shot and, reluctantly, I surrendered the phone to Louis.

Louis called Mai (it was just after 1:00 p.m. back home) and got her voice mail. He called her cellphone and left another voice message and, with a devastated look on his face, he passed the phone to Soumana, who had just been escorted to the top of the dune. Soumana got straight through to his wife in Niamey and seemed to have a good chat, but as it was in Zarma I understood not a word (though Omar One did). Soumana was deeply moved by the experience and I was shamelessly jealous. I knew we could not perch atop this dune all night.

"OK, Mr. Robert, you try again," said Ahmed. I opted to try our home in Ottawa again, and again struck out. As I took the phone from my ear and damn nearly hurled it into the void, Julabib, who had joined the lengthening and ever less attentive line along the crest of the dune, said, "Send her an SMS."

"A what?" I exclaimed.

"An SMS," he repeated. I had only recently learned how to do that, so a little uncertainly I said, "OK, but let me include a callback number. What is it?" They did not know, or so they said.

"Anyway," Julabib said, "the number will show up on her cell-phone screen." Now that I could read (with one eye), I pecked out, "Darling call me at this number asap great love bob."

As I handed the phone back, Ahmed noticed that the battery was all but dead. So he stumbled down to the base of the dune, hooked it up to a charger in one of the trucks, and soon we heard the familiar "vrooom, vrooom" as they tried to force a charge into the phone.

At this point Belmokhtar decided it was time to call President Compaoré in Ouagadougou. They must have made some kind of telephone appointment as they assured me that at nine o'clock in the evening, the President would be in his office in the Burkinabé capital, awaiting our call. So watches were checked, and after a slight delay the phone was given to Omar to make the connection. I am not entirely sure but I think that, for reasons I cannot fathom (beyond the proven unreliability of the cellphone), we used their satellite-phone. I began to hear faint strains from the "Ride of the Valkyries" and in my mind's eye saw attack helicopters surging over the far horizon out of the northeast.

Omar One spoke for a few minutes with Compaoré's close adviser, Mustapha Chaffi, and then passed the phone to me. Blaise Compaoré has a rich, deep, and quite distinctive voice and I would have recognized it anywhere. Our conversation was brief but to the point. I thanked him for his marvellous cartons, which he shrugged off insisting it was the least he could do. He urged us to keep up our courage and our hope, and twice growled with force, anger, and what sounded very much like a personal commitment: "On va vous sortir de là" (We'll get you out of there). I can't think of any words I would rather have heard.

To my great surprise, President Compaoré said that along with Chaffi he was accompanied by the Canadian Ambassador to Burkina Faso, Jules Savaria, an old friend of ours, and asked if we would like to speak to him. Jules was deeply moved by the drama of the moment. He is a decent, intelligent, and sensitive diplomat, one of the Canadian government's more experienced West African hands. Jules assured us that President Compaoré was utterly committed to extracting us from Al Qaeda's clutches and that the President had told him he would remain personally involved until we were safe, as, Jules assured us, would he.

Jules told me that he would get messages to our wives back in Canada and that our safety would henceforth be his primary concern. This too was welcome news coming from the first Canadian to whom we had spoken during our captivity.

Having heard that Louis and I were talking to a Canadian ambassador, Omar grabbed the phone from Louis and began screaming insults and threats at Jules, to the effect that ours was an untrustworthy country, a gang of hypocrites, which had behaved "dishonourably" at every turn of this affair. He was really working up a head of steam, at least in part for Belmokhtar's benefit, but it became very ugly, with a variety of unpleasant and specific threats being made against us. I can only imagine what it must have been like for Jules at the other end.

When Omar wound down, switching to Arabic, he spoke to

Mustapha Chaffi and as he did so he worked his way down the dune, out of our earshot, and we could barely see him striding in and out of the cones of a truck's headlights at the base, his other arm pumping up and down as he loudly and passionately remonstrated with Chaffi. (Surely, then, we must have been using the satphone.) We assumed that he was laying down terms for our release.

After the call to President Compaoré in Ouagadougou, it was time to try our wives again. Back up the hill came the cellphone, supposedly replete with juice, and I gave it another go. This time I called Mary's cellphone first and she answered on the second ring. "Mary, it's Bob."

"Who?" she replied. Not a good start. Then, surprising me with a skill-testing question, she asked, "What do your grandchildren call you?"

Just as I was about to scream, "Don't mess around!" I understood what must have been going on in her mind.

"Danda," I meekly replied and she sobbed, "Bob, is it really you?" and I choked out something to the effect that indeed it was.

I cannot recall all the details of that call. At first she thought I was free because of my thoughtless drafting of the text message. After I had disabused her of any such hope and Mary had established that I was not some ghoulish prankster, or worse, it was such a relief, so very cathartic to tell her how much I loved her and the girls, of how deeply I missed them, and to take her through my evening ritual vis-à-vis her and members of our family.

Then I told her how I regretted causing those I loved most the turmoil and pain they must be experiencing. I asked how she and the girls were holding up and she reassured me that everyone was well and keeping it together. She told of how they had all (Mary, four daughters, their men, and the three grandchildren) spent the first two weeks camped out in Linton and Rob's small house in Toronto and how, since then, she had constantly been on the move between Toronto, New York, and London to ensure that everyone was supported and remained positive. She reported that the family was stronger and more cohesive in the face of this trial than ever before.

I asked her how my brother-in-law was doing in Vancouver. He'd had a run-in with cancer just as I was leaving Canada and Mary informed me that all was well. She also told me that our friend Daniela was recovering slowly but steadily from a terrible E. coli infection she had contracted in Sudan, where she was the deputy head of the UN World Food Programme operations in that benighted country. Mary then reassured me yet again that she and our larger family were all well.

She asked me how I was holding up, and I explained that all things considered, I was well enough but had experienced health issues. "Like what?" she interjected. I said that I was having stomach and bowel problems and my most immediate fear was of a ruptured bowel. She didn't get it. "You mean, diarrhea?" she said.

"No, quite the opposite," I insisted. Mary knew well that I had regularly battled various intestinal infestations during my many trips to Africa and found it difficult to absorb the fact that nothing like that was the problem.

"Did you get the medication I sent and the letters?" she asked.

"No, we have received absolutely nothing from anybody, beyond some wonderful cartons of desperately needed food and vitamins from President Blaise Compaoré."

"Compaoré!" she exclaimed—knowing full well of his and my history—"Why would he do that?" So I explained that our captors had informed us that all other negotiators, and particularly Canada, had been disqualified in the eyes of our AQIM abductors or had disqualified themselves. Only Compaoré was still in the game. He was, according to our kidnappers, "our last chance."

Mary found this difficult to take in. "Surely you mean President Touré of Mali?" she replied. "Mai and I sent our letters and medicine through him. He has been wonderful." I told her again that we had received no letters. She then insisted that President ATT was fighting hard to win our freedom. It was all confusing and not a little upsetting.

At this point I could feel Omar One, who was standing right beside me, becoming agitated. His body language screamed, "Get to the main message!" I doubted he could hear much of Mary's end of the conversation. (I was having enough trouble myself with the phone glued to my ear as the wind whistled about me, which no doubt made it difficult for Mary as well. Also, I had no idea whether they were recording the whole thing but, of course, I had to assume so.) Omar was nonetheless following what I had to say as well as circumstances allowed.

So I said to Mary, "Listen, this is not just hard on Louis and me but it is evidently stressing our kidnappers to the breaking point. AQIM clearly didn't expect this to last as long as it has. They are not equipped for it. They are becoming ever more threatening and unstable. They say they have lost all confidence in their Canadian interlocutors. You must convince whoever is acting for us in the Canadian government—if indeed anybody is—to pick up the pace, to get this thing over with. I don't know how much longer we can survive in such circumstances and I don't know how much longer our captors can, or will, put up with it and us."

"What, precisely, are you telling me?" she asked. So I went through essentially the same routine again.

"We have appalling food. Both of us have health issues. It's getting a lot hotter and our kidnappers are showing more and more aggressive signs of extreme instability. Canada has got to find a way to end this thing or these zealots will put an end to it themselves."

Then, getting to the crux of the issue, she asked, "What do you want me to do?" I replied that I could not know what was and was not going on in Ottawa or anywhere else, particularly with regard to the status of any negotiations. She had to satisfy herself, I said, that everything possible was being done, and being done expeditiously; that the government was using every channel, every contact, every friend, every wile to get us out of there. If she considered that more pressure were required, she would have to decide whether it made sense to engage our many friends in the media or to approach the parliamentary Opposition with a view to raising the profile of our desperate and increasingly perilous situation.

Turning slightly away from Omar, I carefully told her that only she could be the judge of when or if such additional pressure were required or would be useful, but I wanted her to know that I was giving her my full proxy to take that decision. I told her that I would fully accept whatever risks such a course entailed. I asked her if she was getting advice from our friend Ted Johnson, as I believed that his counsel would be of great help to her as she contemplated a perilous and last-ditch public pressure route. She assured me that he was playing just such a role.

I knew that Mary understood what I was and was not saying. I suspected that she would know that I was saying it because my captors needed to hear me do so and also, and rather differently, because I thought there could well come a time when the government would go no further unless severely prodded. In such circumstances, it would be a very risky venture with the potential for all sorts of unforeseeable consequences, but even those risks, she would understand, might be preferable to doggedly pursuing an unproductive tack to its unhappy conclusion.

Mary had been a journalist. She knew that there could come a time when such pressure was required, and now she knew she had my moral power-of-attorney. I had placed the decision entirely in her hands.

What she told me on the phone, however, was that the effort being mounted on our behalf was massive. Our many friends in the public service and the foreign service were rooting for us and working tirelessly to get us home, giving up time with families over Christmas and weekends, and they would, she said, get it done. "But," I asked, "would it be in time?"

She told me the Prime Minister and the Foreign Minister were directly engaged and that many of our friends in other countries and the UN system, current and retired, had offered support. Kofi Annan had been among the first to offer to do anything that might prove useful. Needless to say, this was what I wanted to hear, but I also wanted her to know that she was "weapons free" to deploy any tactic she thought was required, whenever it was needed.

I also asked her to ensure that whoever was doing the negotiating was aware that President Compaoré was playing a central role, at least as far as our abductors were concerned. He had managed to get us a deeply appreciated shipment of essentials, which could not have come at a more opportune moment, and she should let others know that I had just spoken to him and that the President had assured me he would get us out of there.

She then surprised me by telling me she was in Florida but would be immediately returning to Toronto to tell Linton and Justine of this remarkable call and would then by phone fill in Ruth in New York and Antonia in London. I urged her to stay in Florida for a few more days, insisting that she not allow her life to be utterly dominated by these difficult circumstances—but she said she needed to be with the girls.

With considerable regret, I told her that I ought to let Louis have another crack at phoning Mai, but in case that did not work asked Mary to phone Mai to let her know of the call and that Louis was as well as could be expected.

As I signed off I said something to the effect that I was sorry I'd miss Henry's third birthday. Our New York grandson's birthday was in two weeks' time, which was symbolic for Louis and me as it would fall on Day 100. And I added, "In case I don't see you again, I'm so glad I have had a chance to tell you what a wonderful wife and mother you have been, how happy you have made me, and how very lucky I have been."

Her reaction to this mawkish moment was swift and uncompromising, "What do you mean, *if you don't get back?* Of course you are going to get back. You would not believe the enormity of effort being deployed to get you and Louis home. We *will* bring you home, probably in time for Henry's birthday. Don't you let your guard down now." Mary asked me to try to call her back once all other essential calls had been made but I said that I doubted it would be possible.

I knew that despite being a formidable woman, Mary did not necessarily have the capacity to ensure I would be home in thirteen days but I was heartened that she was so positive, so assured, so very determined to make it so. Her passion and spirit were salutary and I felt better, more confident, and more determined than I had felt since 14 December.

When I handed back the phone to Ahmed, he checked it and declared that there were insufficient phone credits to permit another call. "No problem," added Julabib. "We'll get some more." And with that he skipped down the dune, hooked up his laptop, and e-mailed somebody in Algeria to instruct them to buy more credits. This took a fair amount of time, which left me to reflect on the conversation I had just had with my wonderful and inspiring wife. It also left Louis to stew over the fact that he had still not enjoyed such an opportunity. I could see the toll it was taking on him and my assurance that Mary would let Mai know he was all right did little to ease his disquiet.

Over an hour later the phone came back up the hill with more credits and again it was Louis' turn to give it a try. He got through to Mai at their home almost immediately and had a good long chat with her and their eldest daughter. I moved along the dune a few paces to give him a little privacy. At the end of his conversation, I could see from his face that he too had found an element of closure.

At this point Belmokhtar asked us, rather breezily, "Would you like to call anybody else: journalists, politicians, anybody?" I looked at Louis but he signed no, so I said that I would like to speak to my wife again. Sure, said Belmokhtar. But again Louis' call had used up the available credits.

Then out of the blue someone, I think it was Ahmed, said, "Why not try this?" and handed me Louis' government-issue BlackBerry, which we had not seen since just after our capture. With my newly acquired one good lens I checked its battery charge level, which was fully topped up. I punched in Mary's cellphone number and within moments was talking to her again.

Since the last call, she had returned to Ted and Sharon Johnson's condo, packed, and waited for a taxi. When the cab arrived she explained that she was in a terrible rush to catch the last flight to Toronto. The cabbie was gazing at her strangely. Looking down she realized she was still wearing her bathing suit, which required a further delay as she grabbed the suitcase and went back in to dress. This time I reached her in the back of the taxi just as she was approaching Orlando airport.

Mary and I really did not have a great deal more to say to each other beyond, that is, everything. I reiterated that she should tell somebody about the Compaoré connection and mentioned that, however strange, AQIM had threatened to send us to Afghanistan, "where," Omar One had insisted, "they really know how to deal with people like you." And yet again I asked her if she thought the government was doing enough to win our release, and again she said yes. Not being able to help myself I reiterated our earlier conversation to the effect that we had had a good life together, we had made and brought up great kids, and that I loved her deeply and would forever.

She put a stop to such maudlin wallowing once more by insisting that there were lots of things we still needed to do together, places to see, more grandchildren to behold, and I must not give up the belief that soon we would be doing those things.

She then said, "They won't let me through security with my cellphone to my ear, and unless I go through now, I'll miss the plane." So what, I thought. This conversation (which I thought could well be our last) is more important than any damn plane, but at the same time I understood that we had really said all we could usefully say, that anything more was likely to reduce us both to further tears, and that she did need to find refuge in the support and comfort of our daughters. So we said goodbye again and cut the connection.

I handed the phone to Louis but he had made all the calls he wanted to make. So I asked if Louis' trusty BlackBerry might be used to call my eldest daughter, Linton, in part because, among our daughters, her memorable number was the only one I could recall. Belmokhtar waved, sure, sure, so I called her in Toronto. She was just walking in with a bag of groceries in each arm, and when she heard my voice she cried, "Who?!" Then she shouted, "Dad, Dad, I've been waiting so long for this call."

With a large gulp, I had to reply, "But darling, this is not that call, so let's just chat." I explained that I had just been speaking to Mary, who was on her way to Toronto, but I had been allowed another call and wanted to let her know I was okay. She was confused and so palpably distressed it nearly broke my heart. But she had her wits about her.

Linton asked "Are you alone?" and I replied, "No, I'm with Louis and our driver, Soumana."

"Nobody else?" she inquired, and finally the penny dropped.

I carefully replied, "No, that's it. There are just the three of us. I've seen nobody else." From that point on I knew that a rescue scenario would become a distant, *in extremis* option, for Ottawa would now know for certain that we were not co-located with the four Europeans taken on 22 January. The managers of our case would understand that the likelihood of simultaneous rescue missions launched against two separate targets being successful was almost nonexistent.

There followed a short, almost chatty conversation during which she brought me up to date regarding what had been going on within her family, focusing on her two little girls. Then the pauses got longer and the choking began at both ends. Neither of us could summon any further enthusiasm for small talk. I said, "You've made me a very proud dad," and asked her to tell her sisters the same thing, and then goodbye.

She said, "I know, . . . I know, . . . I understand, goodbye."

I replied with a stifled, "I know too," and we faded apart and I handed the phone to somebody and stumbled up along the dune's summit and felt utterly, completely devastated. I had no reserves left, just an aching emptiness, and was overcome by a profound sorrow.

For weeks I hated myself for putting Linton through such torment but eventually became reconciled to the positive aspects of our conversation and was glad we had spoken. Aside from upsetting her, at least the call had served to transmit the fact that the seven hostages in AQIM hands were in two wholly separate locations.

When I handed the BlackBerry back to Ahmed, Belmokhtar told Louis to call somebody in the Canadian Foreign Ministry, "somebody in the government." Louis told him that all government offices would be deserted at that hour. (It was probably around 8:00 p.m. in Ottawa.) "That doesn't matter," said Jack, "Leave a voice message." Louis thought about this carefully and dialled his former boss, Scott Proudfoot, the head of the Sudan Task Force at DFAIT. When the phone switched to voice mail, Louis began to leave what must have been the strangest message Scott had ever retrieved from his voice mailbox.

Before he got very far, Omar snatched the phone away and began to shout into the phone a threatening, menacing message, something not dissimilar to what he had said to Jules Savaria a couple of hours previously: Canadians were liars, they had not been negotiating in good faith, there would be dire consequences for Louis and for me, our blood would be on their hands, and finally an all too evidently improvised "We are contemplating sending them to our friends in Afghanistan where they know how to deal with people such as this."

After the calls, we all made our way unsteadily down the dune and milled about as the sentries were brought in and everything was packed up. Nobody seemed in any particular hurry. It must have been nearly three o'clock in the morning when we set out and I was drained. I had been assigned to a truck driven by the camp emir, Jaffer, who spoke not a word of French, and we were joined in the cab by New Guy.

After bouncing against each other for an hour or so, as we shared the passenger bucket seat, New Guy turned to me and said, in passable French, "You don't recognize me, but your friend does."

Confused, I replied, "Without my glasses, I wouldn't recognize my own children," and he let the matter drop. Then, as I knew conversation was possible, we exchanged a few innocuous words about the night and the desert, and I stayed well away from the personal questions such as what his name was or where he was from. He could see that I was still discombobulated from the phone call and I was surprised to see that he clearly wanted to extend some sympathy.

Suddenly he said, "Allah will ensure it will be all right. You are not to worry. It will end well." I sneaked a look at Jaffer at the wheel. Either he had no idea what we were discussing or he did not care. This was one of the most unambiguously positive statements we had heard from one of our captors. Of course I knew that this generously proportioned *mujahid,* who was obviously not part of the command team, had no idea how it would turn out, but I was touched that he would wish to diminish our worries. Without any prodding from me he said he had committed himself to *jihad* following "Bush's crusade" (the 2003 invasion of Iraq) as he had found this further and unprovoked "invasion of Muslim lands" intolerable and the stated purposes unworthy of consideration. And then we talked of—what else?—God, and soon he was seeking to add me to the multitudinous slaves of Allah.

Some hours later, when the drivers simply could go no farther and we had come closer than ever before to pitching into deep ravines, we ground to a halt. Everyone piled out and bedded down around the trucks in the open desert, and we were soon asleep. This was Camp Nowhere. Louis and I were so exhausted that we could hardly summon the energy to talk about the most important thing to have happened in eighty-seven days: our phone calls. Just before dropping off, we assured each other that all was well with our respective families, and I told Louis that Mary was fully engaged, threatening to have us back by Day 100. I then recounted the bizarre comment from New Guy: "You don't recognize me but your friend does." Louis shrugged his shoulders, saying he did not know what the hell he was talking about, and was asleep in an instant.

A couple of weeks later, apropos of nothing, Louis had a slap-yourself-on-the-forehead moment: "I know where I saw that guy! It's all very clear. It was outside the Grand Hotel in Niamey as we left for the visit to the mine." This had been early in the morning on the Sunday we were taken. Suddenly everything clicked into place, confirming what we had already suspected but been unable to confirm. New Guy had been an AQIM spotter that morning, and we had in fact been under observation from the morning of the day we were grabbed.

Waking up at Camp Nowhere was a pretty bleak experience, but there was just enough time for our daily walk before we were given the order to mount up. We drove well into the heat of the day before stopping in a group of scrubby, thin trees. The heat was crushing and we were left alone to wilt under another designated tree. As we expected, after lunch the group prepared to split up. Belmokhtar and his staff, along with New Guy and a crew, would be going one way, while we would be taking some other direction.

The council members were sitting in a circle about fifteen metres west of the trucks while all the others save the sentries were clustered into a sliver of shade in the lee of the trucks. Louis and I were about thirty metres to the south of the truck park. Someone was pulling at the load on one of the trucks when there was a great whoosh, followed, a few seconds later, by a mighty, flat BANG! I was convinced we were under attack.

I looked toward the trucks, which were wreathed in white smoke, as Sideburns staggered out, his hands clapped to his ears. New Guy was sitting on the ground on the other side of the truck slowly shaking his head back and forth, and the officers were all standing staring into the desert to the west, where a plume of smoke was rising in the still air, and then back to the trucks. Nobody was racking rounds or aiming weapons or preparing to repel an attack. Jack strode over to Sideburns, pulled his hands from his ears and examined each one, then walked back to the trucks and checked out the shocked group under the nearby tree. New Guy was still sitting shaking his head on the other side.

Half an hour later Omar Two approached us and said in his best deadpan, "Here's your blanket," thrusting it into our hands and walking away. It was still smoking, having been holed and burned in a number of places. Apparently, a rocket-propelled grenade had just been fired through it. The warhead had passed about twenty centimetres over the head of New Guy, who had been bending over to fill his canteen on the far side of the truck, at the business end of the RPG launcher. The round had flown straight over the group of officers and exploded at its self-destruct range, about a kilometre out in the flat desert. The back blast had washed over the group sitting beneath the trees.

Nobody had been hurt, although a few were shaken up and suffered some hearing loss for a few days. Apparently one of them, Sideburns I believe, had wanted something from the tied-down load in the back of one of the trucks. He had been pulling at our blanket, which was wrapped around the RPG launcher, and somehow the motion had dislodged the safety and fired the weapon (or the safety had not been set properly). There seemed to be no recriminations. Allah had decided that nobody was to die that day.

Soon after that, the seven trucks split into two groups and were on their separate ways. In four trucks we drove late into the evening, and when our captors were unable to raise anybody on their short-range walkie-talkies at the camp to which we were headed, we stopped just outside, again in the open desert (Camp Anywhere), rather than surging forward in the gathering darkness and risking being shot up by sentries.

The next morning they were able to make contact with the

camp a few kilometres away and we entered a deep, wide *wadi,* which we called Camp Cut Finger, so named because the surly young AR2 sliced the length of an index finger as he was helping in the kitchen. There was a lot of blood but no great concern. We sent him a packet of cookies, a gesture again welcomed by some and resented by others. AR2 didn't know what to think—but he ate the cookies. Louis and I worked much of the next day to improve our position at Cut Finger, removing the thorns and stones from the place where we had slept badly the night before, and just as we were about to settle in for our second night, we were told we would be leaving in five minutes.

I had been suffering through another long bout of constipation and, despite the order to prepare to leave, I suddenly felt what Louis termed "signals." I had not used the pills, as we had been constantly on the move, spending ten or twelve hours at a stretch in those trucks on the trek to and from the telephone dune. The trouble with the pills was that when you had to go, you had to go. Trying to manage that as we sprinted across the open desert would have been at best problematic.

I was determined to seize the moment. When I received the nod from the sentry permitting me to go *loin* (by now we were no longer accompanied), I was off. I found the right kind of suitably discreet spot and to my considerable relief everything happened as it ought. When I got back to our position, Louis' arms were again full of our baggage and he was heading toward the trucks. As I approached, he asked the distressingly routine, "How did it go?"

Rather than responding with the habitual "nothing!" I replied, with a smile, "Actually, rather well," and he burst into tears of fragile relief. I had not appreciated the extent to which my health issues were also his, that he was suffering the same deep concern about my serious gut problems. It was a touching moment occasioned by the most pedestrian of circumstances.

As we boarded our assigned trucks, I saw Jack talking earnestly to Hassan, his arm around his shoulders, walking him back and forth nearby, and instinctively I knew that the emir was about to send Hassan away. Less than a week later he was gone, at least for a while, and our relief was immense.

We drove deep into the night, across some of the roughest terrain we had yet encountered. We barged our way through huge dunes, twenty times the height of the vehicles, over mountain trails and stretches of flat desert strewn with huge boulders. Some of the assaults on the dunes were terrifying, made worse by the darkness. I was driving with Omar One and it seemed as if his nerves were taking a beating. Each of the trucks became *ensablé* a number of times, but finally we emerged at the top of a long, steep slope—a ramp, really—winding down sharply from the high ridge on which we were perched toward the seemingly limitless desert floor stretching beneath us, bathed in cold, bright moonlight.

We camped on that steeply sloping ramp—Camp Moonbeam. It was a breathtaking sight yet daunting, for arrayed before us was an endless procession of formidable dunes in great lateral wrinkles across the desert below. Soon I knew we would try to bash our way through them all. I hated those dunes, fearing constantly that there would come a time when the trucks could not be extracted and we would die stranded in place. It was cold, and to cheer ourselves up Louis and I drank a litre of President Compaoré's mango juice before crawling, exhausted, beneath our newly ventilated blanket.

CHAPTER 13

SOUMANA DISAPPEARS—
CONVERSION—AND LETTERS
FROM HOME

====

O happy living things! no tongue
Their beauty might declare:
A spring of love gush'd from my heart,
And I blessed them, unaware . . .

====

As we left Moonbeam at dawn, the view was even more dramatic. I was assigned to a truck driven by Omar Three, and Soumana sat by the window. This was the first occasion since our capture that I had been able to spend with him. He was dejected, tentative, and seemingly afraid. Before we left, the brash, swaggering AR2 stuck his head in the passenger-side window and sternly warned Soumana and me yet again against talking to each other. Ahmed reinforced that message a few minutes later but I had the impression that the warnings were directed more at Soumana than at me.

Omar Three, unique among our kidnappers, was usually solicitous of our well-being and morale. He would regularly wave a cautious good morning and seek tiny, subtle ways to offer hope. We were particularly sensitive to any possible signals coming from him as we had the strong impression that he was the closest to Bel-mokhtar, or at least to his way of thinking. Others, like Ahmed and Ibrahim, Abdul Rahman and Jaffer, shared Jack's warrior camara-derie—a type of relationship the portly Omar Three did not enjoy— but from an intellectual or strategic planning perspective, Omar Three seemed to have a privileged relationship with the commander.

A few days earlier, pointing to my much-repaired shoes dur-ing a midday stop, he had said with a smile, "They will make an interesting souvenir of all this when you get back to Canada." This vigilant observer had seemed genuinely anxious to indicate that everything would work out all right.

During the day-long drive from Camp Moonbeam on Day 91, Omar Three, ignoring the various orders we had received prior to departure, chatted as best he could with Soumana and me in his rudimentary French. I forget precisely how it began but soon all three of us were talking about our children, how many, and the extent to which we had or hadn't seen them recently. Omar and Soumana were appropriately dismayed yet delicate about my shameful failure to produce a male heir, and with tolerant, know-ing smiles they listened to my insistence that I was more than satis-fied with daughters. Soumana and I were asked about the ages of our children and they were a little shocked to learn that my eldest daughter would be forty in early July.

Then, after a longish silence in the middle of this gentle, social chatter, Soumana, who was not supposed to be talking at all, defi-antly and with vehemence interjected, "You will be celebrating that birthday with her, I am sure." Omar Three, to my even greater surprise, rather than summarily shutting up Soumana, murmured something to suggest he thought Soumana was absolutely right. The whole exchange was so bizarre that the three of us were stunned into silence, nobody daring to explore the subject any further but all of us glad that we'd had the moment.

Late in the afternoon, as we approached what seemed to be the next camp, Omar Three declared, "You will recognize it." And it seemed to me that we were passing through an area that closely resembled the environs of Thornhill, which we had left only a week before. Just as I was thinking that perhaps we would be able to get some new footwear from the buried cache, Soumana suddenly pointed to the lead truck and said, "The left rear tire is about to go." Insofar as I could see, there was nothing wrong with it, but twenty seconds later the truck lurched to the left and shuddered to a stop. It was a soft, quiet afternoon with a slight breeze chasing away the heat of the day. Changing the blown tire would be difficult as Omar One had not been able to get to hard ground before he had to stop.

The heavily laden truck frame was resting on the sand by the blown tire. Immediately, Omar One's crew freed a spare from the maze of ropes, baggage, fuel, water, and weaponry in his truck bed. Omar rummaged endlessly in the passenger floor-wells, which served as tool boxes in all the trucks, and eventually came up with three hydraulic jacks but only one jack handle. Someone else began to dig around the tire, quickly to be shouldered aside by Omar One, who grumpily insisted on looking after his own truck. Louis and I met up and moved off a way and shared a cookie and some water, each of us still beset with the emotional turmoil of the telephone calls and the epic trek back.

Soumana sat alone fifty metres away on the other side of the tightly grouped vehicles looking miserable. He seemed again to be cradling his right forearm, which had been hurt in the initial grab ninety-one days previously. I knew that we still had some of the arthritis pills sent in the shipment from President Compaoré, which we had twice before tried to get to Soumana through intermediaries. We knew we hadn't asked for them and we wondered if they might have been sent in response to some complaint of his, in much the same way we had put in our own, largely unfilled, orders. So I sorted through one of the tattered plastic bags that served as our luggage and, finding the pills, began to approach Soumana. At that point the young AR2 (whom we now called "Cut Finger") intercepted us at a run, screaming, "No speaking, no speaking," and aggressively gestured that I was to return to where we had been. I sought to give him the pills, indicating with hand signals that he pass them to Soumana. But he would have none of it.

I set off to find someone who might straighten all this out. The first candidate, Omar Two, was not the one I would have preferred but I didn't have much choice. I asked him to give the pills to Soumana but instead he said, with his usual sardonic smile, that he would take me to Soumana so I could give them to him myself. Seeing the two of us approaching, Soumana looked truly distressed. I handed him the pills, saying that I believed they must have been intended for him and in any case they would, I thought, probably ease what I assumed was his joint and muscle pain. In some confusion but with force Soumana refused to take the pills, saying over and over, "You keep them." Omar Two displayed his sinister smile, but this time for Soumana's benefit, and led me away.

Perhaps half an hour later, the difficult tire change had been accomplished with lots of digging and multiple jacking. Al Zarqawi, whose aggressive attitude toward us had begun to thaw just perceptibly, had cadged the last strawberry and coconut cookie. He remained irreverent and cocky but less calculatingly nasty. He no longer strode over our blankets, whether or not we were beneath them.

We were loaded back into the vehicles for what was billed as a short drive to the next camp. Louis was instructed to join me in the cab of Omar Three's vehicle and Soumana was directed elsewhere. That was the last time either of us set eyes on Soumana.

At dusk, about an hour later, the trucks pulled in among some trees and bushes. While it looked somewhat like Thornhill, it wasn't, though that place may well have been only a few hundred metres— or a few hundred kilometres—distant. Thus it seemed we would get no shoes. Night was falling and we were directed to a spot without any kind of cover, close to the trucks. We were exhausted after a long, rough, and hot drive, so we made up our bed and prepared to crash, not knowing and not caring if there would be anything to eat.

Soon, out of the dark emerged a very jacked-up AR2, who started yelling well before he reached us. In this fourteen-year-old's rudimentary French, delivered with too much hate and not enough grammar, we were once again being given hell because we had spoken to Soumana. I was tired and had had enough of screaming teenagers, so I went off toward the trucks in search of an adult. First up again was Omar Two. In fact, he was so readily available I wondered if he had put the lad up to the whole thing. Undaunted, I explained that I'd had it with AR2; if someone wished to upbraid us, could it be someone in some authority and someone we could understand? Further, Cut Finger seemed to be exercised about my talking to Soumana, when the last time I had done so had been in Omar Two's presence an hour before, so what the hell was the fuss about?

Omar Two could not have been less sympathetic. AR2, he barked, had all the authority he needed to say anything to us he wished. He was right to have reminded us to stay away from Soumana. We needed to remember that we were prisoners of war and we had no rights whatsoever. In effect, get out of my face. Not a fruitful encounter.

Twenty minutes later, the entire council emerged out of the dark—all the senior members of the group. They were led by Jack, who must have just arrived for he had not been travelling with us over the last couple of days. At first I assumed it to be an escalation of the AR2 incident. Then I noticed that someone had plunked down two well-stuffed, medium-sized, black nylon backpacks in the middle of our blankets. They all sat cross-legged around the edge of those blankets, though not actually touching them.

Belmokhtar opened the discussion, Omar One interpreting. He said that the backpacks and accompanying letters were from our families, delivered through an intermediary working on behalf of the President of Mali. We were dumbstruck. First the cartons from Blaise Compaoré only nine days before, then the emotional turmoil of the telephone calls four days previously, and now tangible things from those we loved: the very stuff Mary had mentioned during our phone call, and via President Touré as she had said.

Jack encouraged us to open our "presents." I would very much have preferred to do this in private but they obviously wanted to see what was within. I suspect that they also wanted to gauge our reactions to each item as they sought to determine whether a locator device had been secreted into anything. I had the impression, as per the cartons from President Compaoré, that all these things had been well vetted prior to delivery to us but not necessarily by Jack's *katiba*. Thus the shipment might have been in AQIM hands for some time. The backpacks bore bits of tape on which were scribbled "Louis" and "Robert," so, like kids opening Christmas stockings in front of their parents, we unzipped them and began to haul out marvellous things.

There was clothing, medicine, books, and sundry other bits and pieces. Some of it seemed out of place, like the new black nylon knee-length dress socks and rather elegant summer-weight formal slacks with knife-edge creases and prominent, sand-collecting cuffs in the precise sizes we had been when we were thirty pounds heavier, but no belt. There was an extremely welcome safari-type long-sleeved shirt, and each of us received a fetching short-sleeved Lacoste golf shirt (but, dammit, Louis got the nicer colour!). Then there was the underwear. Someone had known, no doubt from the lists we presented so persistently to our jailers, that we really needed underwear. But that person was obviously not a family member; the embassy in Bamako, or perhaps psychiatric profilers in Ottawa, clearly had been forced to grapple with the existential dilemma of whether we were boxer or jockey guys. In best bureaucratic fashion, we had each been sent both.

We received an interesting selection of four paperback books, two in English (*Ursula, Under,* by Ingrid Hill, and *The Shelters of Stone,* by Jean Auel) and two in French (Nicole Fyfe-Martel's *Hélène de Champlain* and *L'homme-ouragan,* by Lucie Dufresne). Not necessarily how we would have made our own desert-island selection, but we were grateful nonetheless. *Les frères* scrutinized each of the books with great care, riffling through the pages and closely examining the front and back covers and spines. After he had studied them, Omar One disdainfully threw them back on our blankets and asked, "Are there no male authors in Canada?" If there were, he wanted to know, why had all four books been written by women?

At the conclusion of the show-and-tell they took away the books. They were returned some days later with the promotional photos of the authors methodically defaced (no depictions of women were permitted). The entire cover of Nicole Fyfe-Martel's book, bearing the familiar "courtesy of the Canadian Embassy in Mali" sticker inside, had been ripped off as it had displayed an artist's depiction of Samuel de Champlain's twelve-year-old wife, Hélène, in a not-particularly-immodest *décolleté* dress. Even reading with one eye through Omar's unreturned glasses, I was happy to discover that our censors had not delved sufficiently far into the book to discover the shenanigans of the randy Mme de Champlain.

There was a store of pills from Mary. On my previous trip to Niger in September, I had contracted the most lethal form of malaria, *Plasmodium falciparum,* the same cerebral malaria strain that had come very close to killing me forty-four years previously in the Congo. Unlike *Plasmodium vivax,* which I'd had a number of times, if *P. falciparum* is not properly and promptly treated, the prognosis is terrible. The Canadian peacekeeping contingent in the Congo in 1960, utterly ignorant of tropical medicine, had put four sick soldiers on a ship bound for the UK and all died long before they arrived. Mary seemed to be worried that this would be my fate during captivity for she had sent me a huge supply of Malarone, used for both preventing and treating malaria. While floodwaters occasionally course through the *wadis* for a few days after a heavy rain, there is no standing water, so there are no mosquitoes and, thus, no malaria in the Sahara.

There was a satisfying variety of antibiotic pills for everything from the intestinal bug giardia (a real threat) to bronchial infections. They were great to have, offering considerable comfort even though some carried stern warnings that sunlight had to be completely avoided. Indeed, the items that caused the greatest worry and attracted particular scrutiny on the part of our kidnappers were the sheaves of photocopied literature that accompanied each prescription drug. They seemed to think that all this English-language technical data must contain some sort of secret message, so they took it all and returned it about a week later with evident frustration. I doubt very much if they were ever able to follow all that pharmacological jargon and legalese. It's challenging enough for native English speakers.

Mary had sent me many of the elements of a fairly complete medical kit (without the sharp edges). There were nail clippers, lip balm, vitamins, and a very welcome industrial-sized container of heavy-duty sun block. We received toothbrushes and toothpaste, soap, antibiotic cream, eye drops, huge wraparound sunglasses that made little sense after weeks in the harsh Sahara light, but, alas, no prescription glasses for me.

Also, we each received a pack of playing cards, which looked to our captors suspiciously like fun, but they grudgingly let us keep them. So began the Great Sahara Cribbage Tournament. We played most days, usually in the late afternoon as the temperature became more bearable and the wind often died down. We were not entirely sure of some of the more arcane rules and, of course, I regularly accused Louis of creative accounting, but those games gave our minds a rest from the endless worry that had been our lot up to the delivery of the backpacks.

Finally, still surrounded by the council, Louis and I set aside our stashes and, with great care, our letters, for subsequent private scrutiny and further caressing. Belmokhtar—no doubt picking up on the disruption caused by the endless would they or wouldn't they convert speculation on the part of his troops—chose this moment to lance that boil in an attempt, I suppose, to restore a little order and tranquility to his *katiba*.

After the final TV Night at Camp Canada—one in which Adam Gadahn, "our American brother, who we love more than our own sons," had been particularly prominent—Omar Two had suggested that with my much-admired grey beard and venerable bearing I could become "the Bin Laden of America." I gently suggested that I thought it wouldn't work out that way.

The pressure on us to become slaves of Allah had been intense from the outset, particularly from the two Omars, but soon almost everybody was into the recruiting business. Each of the children, if passing us on the way to and from sentry duty, would ask, "Have you decided yet to become our brothers?" and our kidnappers were assiduously ambiguous about the acceptability of such an act taking place *sous le sabre* (under the sword).

We suspected that each time Jack visited, he was given reports on our health and state of mind as well as on our religious education. Probably with breathless tediousness he would be advised of our impending conversion. While I have no way of verifying this, I imagine that his own very strict interpretation of what was permissible in such circumstances combined with a wholly understandable desire to put an end to this annoying and distracting undercurrent of our imprisonment. In any case, Jack chose the moment of the delivery of our backpacks on Day 91 to inform us—in the hearing of all the senior members of the group—of the circumstances of a legitimate conversion.

He began by reiterating that he and all the brothers would be happy to welcome us into the Muslim fold, the *ummah*, but, he very carefully added, "We cannot and will not attempt to force such a decision upon you." He then explained to us (and everybody around him) the import of the Qur'an's "no compulsion" verse, something that had been lacking in our religious instruction to date.

Jack underlined that such a grave decision could only be the result of a pact between an individual and Allah. Nobody and nothing of this world could force such an undertaking. He hoped that our hearts would open to Allah but, looking attentively at each of his officers assembled around our blankets on that starlit night, he stressed that conversion could occur only if God willed it. It could not be imposed by men, no matter how well intentioned. Further, he reiterated the fundamental principle of the *da'wa,* whereby it was every believer's duty to expose the unbeliever to the word of God, but like horses led to water the infidels could not be made to see the light.

I offered a judicious reply, noting that the brothers had been generous in taking the time and making the effort to inform us of the teachings of Islam. I said we would consider the matter thoroughly and, when we reached home, would closely study the relevant texts and consult Muslim friends and imams—and then it would indeed depend on whether Allah entered our hearts. He stared at me a while and eventually gave a quick nod for all to see and got up and left, followed immediately by his entire crew.

From that point on the zeal of our instructors, older and younger, diminished significantly. Whether or not they had studied the "no compulsion" verse before, it had now been decreed that we could not be bullied, tricked, threatened, or bribed into making this pact with Allah. As a result, even the most zealous among them reluctantly abandoned the view that even if our hearts seemed not about to be immediately engaged, as clearly they were destined to become, such a happy and certain eventuality surely had to allow for a somewhat more flexible interpretation of that verse.

It was a moment that changed our relationship with our captors. It became more arm's length, less threateningly intimate, more menacingly clinical—less religious, more political. It was increasingly "just business."

❖

As the council departed, it was, at last, time for the letters. Louis opened his family's unsealed envelope and began to read by the light of a dying LED flashlight left by one of our guards for use during our dinner in the dark, tears pouring down his face. I reached over and squeezed his shoulder, but we both knew that there was nothing to be said—it had all been said over, and over, and over again. When he had finished reading I asked him if everybody was well and, staring into the night, he nodded. He asked if I wanted him to read his letter to me but I replied, "No, not now."

I had Mary's letter clutched in my hand and it stayed there all night. Unlike Louis, I didn't have the courage to open it, let alone read it. In fact, I didn't read it for nearly twenty-four hours. I carried it around with me waiting for the right moment, by which time Louis had re-read his letter (like mine, a compilation from his wife and children) many more times and was coming to terms with the emotions it generated. I had yet to begin that same journey.

Finally, the next afternoon, using the right lens of Omar One's glasses, which seemed to be on extended loan, I read the words Mary and each of our girls had crafted. It was hard going—and lovely. Eventually I found a kind of imperfect calm. In my darker moments, I had worried that the shock of all this would make Mary ill or kill her and that, if I got out, she might not be there. But her letter demonstrated that she was so evidently alive, active, and vigorously managing the family, keeping it whole, connected, and focused on the positive.

I could tell also that her words had been carefully drafted and tried to read between the lines, with little success, to learn more about what was going on. The letters inevitably brought into stark relief the enormous distance between Louis and me, on the one hand, and everything we cherished, on the other, and rekindled my incessant, obsessive calculations of what it would take to bridge what seemed like a widening gap. It was all too evident that neither a hundred days of ascetic desert existence nor conversations with and inspirational messages from my family had done much to improve whatever bridge-building skills I possessed, because I still could find no way home.

PART FOUR

END GAME

This shot of the Namib Desert, which I took ten years before our capture, evokes the flat stretches of the Malian desert that we crossed at great speed as we headed north following our kidnapping.

The above photograph of the Namib is strikingly similar to what I took to be a sea of impassable dunes on our way to make the third video message, during which—on Day 108—an ultimatum death sentence was issued by our captors.

Our mental and physical health depended on maintaining our regime of walking four to six kilometres each day, but our shoes began to come apart after about three weeks.

Someone tugging at the baggage in the back of one of the trucks inadvertently fired a rocket-propelled grenade through one of our blankets. I thought the cavalry was coming.

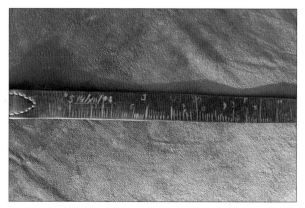

On arrival at Camp Canada, I knew I had to find some way to keep track of the passage of time. Otherwise, I feared I would lose my tenuous hold on reality. Each line on my belt represents a day of captivity.

On arrival at TV Camp, Omar One reverently explained the merits of the arak root, called *miswak*, extolled in the Qur'an and from which we made toothbrushes.

We were each given a pair of tiny scissors, which we used for everything. I always considered that they could, *in extremis*, serve a darker purpose.

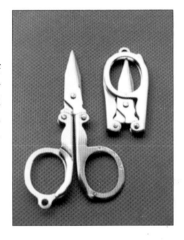

I have every reason to believe that this prosaic invention saved my life by putting an end to my acute constipation.

I have no way of knowing, but I think the *mujahid* making the cell phone call in this screenshot from an AQIM video, above, is doing so from the Ait el Khaoua dunes in Mali, facing Bordj el Mokhtar in Algeria, the same area from which Louis and I spoke to our families on Day 87.

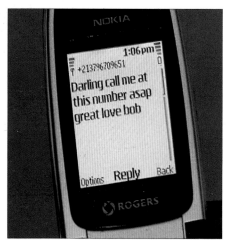

When I couldn't reach Mary on either our home phone or her cell, my captors urged me to send her an SMS. So I did, ineptly phrasing it in a way that caused her to believe I had been freed.

Edwin Dyer was beheaded by Abou Zeid, the thug in the upper-right corner of this AQIM screenshot, a month after our release. I was devastated. So very often had I envisaged that Louis or I would suffer just such an end.

Michel Germaneau, a seventy-eight-year-old French aid worker, was beheaded by AQIM just over a year after Dyer's murder.

Mustapha Chaffi was with President Blaise Compaoré of Burkina Faso when we called from the dune on Day 87. He made four arduous and risky trips into the Sahara to win our release.

Baba Ould Cheik, right, was President Amadou Toumani Touré's chief negotiator with Al Qaeda. Baba made eleven perilous, two-thousand-kilometre round trips into some of the most dangerous territory in the world on our behalf.

In this screenshot, taken from a remarkable video of our liberation deep in the Sahara, I am to the right of the two machine gun–toting figures, beside Louis. Sources in a friendly country forwarded to us the AQIM video recording of our release.

In Bamako, we expressed our deep gratitude to President Amadou Toumani Touré of Mali and his foreign minister, my old friend Moctar Ouane, for bringing us safely home.

The next morning we flew to Ouagadougou to pay our respects to President Compaoré and to thank him, too, for the essential part he had played in bringing our ordeal to a happy conclusion.

In Ottawa, Mary receives my call from Gao, on Wednesday, 22 April 2009, at dusk, to say I was free.

The RCMP insisted on taking a "before" picture, which I dressed for after showering at the hotel in Bamako.

When the aircraft door opened at the U.S. Air Force base at Ramstein, I saw Mary and Mai, Louis's wife, clutching each other at the foot of the stairs. A moment later, I fell into Mary's arms.

From left to right, Linton, Ruth, Justine, Antonia, Mary, and I take a walk in Trier, not far from the Landstuhl Regional Medical Center.

Louis and I say farewell following our arrival in Ottawa on Tuesday, 28 April 2009.

Three weeks later, Mary and I paid our respects to UN Secretary-General Ban Ki-moon.

CHAPTER 14

ULTIMATUM

===

The naked hulk alongside came,
And the twain were casting dice;
"The game is done! I've won! I've won!"
Quoth she, and whistles thrice.

===

A nt Hill Camp was an unsettling place, really three quite different camps. The first was where we spent the night in the open, near the trucks, as we received our backpacks and letters from home. For the second night, which christened the location, we were relocated about a hundred metres to a large, seriously ant-infested tree. Their bites were less annoying than their invasion of every part of our bodies. Then, two days later, we were told to gather our stuff and walk about four hundred metres over a couple of smallish dunes to a group of quite healthy trees surrounded by a wide-open space, which was to be our next prison. There were ants there too, so we stayed under the trees during the day but slept in the open behind a windbreak made of the tarp and tent poles. There were snakes but we saw no live ones.

In the afternoon of Day 95, though we couldn't see our captors, there seemed to be a great deal of commotion on their side of the dune. Then, through a dip in the sand, we saw a heavily loaded truck moving slowly out of the camp. All the children seemed to be aboard. I quickly convinced myself that Jack had decided they were becoming unstable and thus a liability to his kidnapping operation. We were relieved to see them go but, as with just about every event large or small, my paranoia blossomed and I began to develop dark, negative rationales for this expulsion of the young-sters. Were things about to happen that Belmokhtar did not want them to witness? On the other hand, wasn't that part of their *jihadi* apprenticeship?

Suddenly Hassan, whom we had last seen at Cut Finger and who we had not realized had rejoined the group, ran toward us demanding "my books" (finally proving that, as we had suspected, the Belgian high school history texts were indeed his). Louis, handing them to him, had the temerity to ask, "What about my BlackBerry?" but Has-san was already running back toward the fully loaded truck.

He stopped, just before jumping aboard, turned and shouted, "Well, that depends, Louis, which you would prefer, your tele-phone or your head."

After their departure, an eerie quiet descended on the camp. Other than the ubiquitous sentry overlooking our small valley there seemed to be nobody around. Then Ali came over the hill. Aside from the few words we had exchanged from time to time when he was delivering food, mostly as a result of his extremely rudimentary French we had very little to do with him. With a few words and sign language he asked if he might sit. I invited him to do so and without preamble he proceeded to perform an all-but-incomprehensible *da'wa*. By now we understood that he was tick-ing off that box, but why had he chosen that moment?

Early the next day we were directed to gather up our belongings and cross the dune toward their camp. Surprisingly, there seemed to be only one vehicle, and we were told that for the first time we were to ride on the back as Moussa had to travel in the cab. We concurred that a couple of two-handed ancients were probably safer up there than a lone one-handed blind bomb maker.

We clambered on top of the mass of baggage, to be joined by AR and Ali. Jaffer was driving with Omar Three and Moussa inside. AR carefully pointed out where the best handholds were and seemed rather nervous as we set out in a single truck for the first time since our descent into hell immediately following the grab. I was worried about what this would do to my back, but as the stretch of desert we travelled across was relatively featureless, it turned out to be no worse than travelling inside.

We travelled like that for four or five hours and I had to take care not to doze off, for fear I would lose my grip. It was a change and almost any change was welcome. Eventually we slowed as we entered another *wadi,* encountering a few, sparse trees. There were a number of tire tracks converging in the direction we were going. As we worked our way deeper into the trees and brush, our abductors in the back were staring at us expectantly, but it was not until we came to a stop that I realized we were back in Camp Canada.

Little had changed in the thirty-three days since we had last been there. Over that period we had made camp in ten different locations. We were directed back to the tree that had sheltered us for fifty-seven days and our small complement of four jailers plus the blind Moussa occupied the place that had been theirs. It was very much a corporal's guard and I thought that it would be a fine night for the cavalry to come over the hill.

We asked about Soumana, who was so obviously not around, and were told, somehow unconvincingly, that given his undefined illness, he had been sent to another camp where there was a doctor. This did not seem to ring true and we speculated—and hoped—that he might have been or was going to be freed.

Both Louis and I felt an odd sense of nostalgia being back there but it was hard to pin down why. Perhaps it was simply that it was a familiar place. We stayed there for four uneventful days, during which we reestablished our walking track and dared to make it significantly larger. After a couple of days, two more vehicles arrived bearing reinforcements to ease the strain on the exhausted crew who had brought us.

We left on Day 100 (my grandson Henry's birthday) and then, after a dramatic passage through some difficult dunes, spent two days at a desolate camp we called Somewhere, at the edge of a vast plain strewn with large, clinker-type black rocks and sharp, black lava ledges.

On the second day at Somewhere we were presented with a plastic garbage bag containing a couple of pairs of very basic shoes. We were surprised, as we had not noticed the arrival of the truck that must have delivered them. Previously, on any number of occasions, we had provided them with our shoe sizes, so we knew who was to get what. Mine were of the shapeless and supportless desert boot variety, essentially fake-leather bags with a thin, rather rigid sole; a short lace threaded through only two holes a side kept them on. Louis' were large, black and white versions of a flashy, thick-soled running shoe, made exclusively of synthetic materials. Within ten days his new shoes began to come apart. Mine, to our surprise, held up better, but they were never comfortable or good walking shoes. I had failed to understand why they were called desert boots when I was a teenager and now, in the depths of the Sahara, it made even less sense.

On Day 102 we travelled to Grande Allée—so called because we all camped in fairly close proximity along the bed of a shallow, narrow *wadi* with a few trees to one side. To get anywhere, our kidnappers had to just about step over us. We bedded down on a calm, quiet evening but within a short while the wind began to rise. Soon a stiff gale was blowing at, I guessed, well over eighty kilometres per hour. And of course the wind was thick with sand.

It was impossible to open my eyes, because even the thinnest of slits admitted quantities of sand. In any case, there was nothing to see. The night was pitch-black and opaque, and the rushing, howling wind seemed apocalyptic. I felt Louis stirring nearby and he signalled that he was managing. I wrapped my light scarf tightly around my nose and mouth, tied my longer grey, cotton turban cloth Tuareg-like around my head and face, and pulled my blanket over my head, tucking it under me on all sides as the wind threatened to tear it loose. Within a short time I could feel the sand drifting around our bodies and regularly shook and squirmed to stay above the dune building on top of us.

At dawn on Day 103, I shook myself out of a semi-stupor, barely able to move. Some time during the night I had scrunched into a fetal position while I made a tent of the blanket over my head and shoulders, using my forearm as a tent pole as the wind screamed at us from every direction. Literally, I had to dig my lower body out of the dune. As I looked about in the yellowish light of a day still dark and heavy with suspended sand particles all but obscuring the sun, everything looked changed as it does after a major snowstorm. The contours of the surrounding features had shifted, softened, and become rounder and smoother. And it was very quiet as people about us struggled to their feet. They seemed as surprised as we were that it was over and we were all alive.

Three nights later there was another sandstorm, dramatic but not as intense as the first one. This time, though, our captors posted a sentry to sit within a metre of us, mostly, I suspect, to ensure we survived and didn't wander off, never to be seen again. On various occasions throughout that last night at Grande Allée I remember looking out through one of the holes blasted through the blanket held firmly over my head to see that sentry, within arm's reach yet only barely perceptible as he sat immobile, lashed by the sand swirling around him, his turban wound tightly around his face and head, and his arms around his Kalash, which was jammed between his raised knees. I never learned who it was.

We were not sad to leave Grande Allée, but just before we did we met two new *mujahideen* whom, it appeared, Jack had brought in to replace the children. These were obviously experienced, steady, thirty-something, sergeant types, Abou Mujahid and Abou Isaac. We had little to do with them; they were all business and seemed to have no interest in us.

The next camp was no treat either. After a long day on the move, our captors had looked for a suitable spot for over an hour and this was the least bad place they managed to find. There was little cover and soon it began to rain. We were able to unroll our tarp relatively quickly and were therefore only a little clammy. Our kidnappers, though, were drenched. A number of them, glowering and muttering at us, clearly resented the fact that we had the tarp. We called the camp Air Compressor because the tires had taken a terrible beating over the previous few days and the air compressor ran—loudly—all night as they levered tires off rims, patched, sealed, and sought to restore them and the many spares to a semblance of operational readiness.

That night a huge argument burst forth among three of them within a dozen metres of where we lay. This had never happened before and it was all too clear that they were really furious as well as being armed to the teeth. I have no idea what it was about, but it was the beginning of a series of similar confrontations that seemed only to get worse. The cause seemed to be a combination of accumulated stress, little sleep, terrible weather, and some kind of disagreement about us, which we could only begin to decipher.

The next one-night stop was Vesuvio. It was named after the tall, volcano-shaped mountain that reared above the camp. Here there was little shade but more rain and this time, when shouting again broke out after dark, Omar One subsequently explained that there had been "a slight disagreement" about our being allowed the tarp while Moussa got soaked. I told him to take the damned tarp. Happily, he refused, allowing that we were more decrepit even than Moussa and as we were the weakest people present, they had an Islamic duty to offer it to us. I did not press the point but we knew there was more to these angry outbursts.

The next morning was hot and bright. As we loaded up, Jula-bib, who had joined the group the previous evening along with Jack and his staff, said to me just a little ironically as he pointed across the flat plain below to an impressive ridge of mountains on the far southern horizon, "That is our Tora Bora."

We left Vesuvio shortly afterward and within half an hour we reached a high pass that funnelled sharply down toward a long, open-ended U-shaped valley criss-crossed from edge to edge with enormous dunes disappearing into the distance. All three trucks stopped at the lip and the drivers met to consider their best route through this endless array of serious obstacles in precisely the same manner as my canoeing pals back in Canada would climb the banks of a raging northern river to scout and ponder how to negotiate a particularly challenging stretch of white water. To my untrained eye the problem was insurmountable. The dunes were simply too steep, with insufficient space between them to allow enough of a run from one to breach the crest of the next.

To my dismay, Omar One, to whom I had been assigned, launched forward with great bravado and almost immediately became *ensablé* before fully entering the maze. With some digging and pushing he was able to reverse, turn, and scoot back up the pass. The three trucks then scouted along the overlooking ridge at the back of the "U" and eventually found a practicable ramp down that skirted the left-hand wall of the valley, but the going was very hard. Soon we turned left into a canyon in the valley wall and, after more challenging driving, came to a stop at the point we could go no farther. Yet again we were led to a poor, thin tree, and left alone.

Before long, however, we heard the dreaded sound of steel poles being hammered into hard sand and knew there was to be another tent event. Sure enough, about an hour later, Omar One, looking very sombre, arrived to tell us that there would be a third video. Canada and the United Nations, he said ominously, needed to be encouraged to work harder for our release, needed to know the extent to which AQIM was deadly serious. It sounded horribly like a death sentence had been pronounced on one or both of us, and I was sorely afraid.

This time, he explained, we would have no speaking role. We would sit blindfolded, with our hands behind our backs. They would then read a statement in Arabic that explained the gravity of our situation and demanded an immediate response.

At best I thought they were about to issue an ultimatum, but I saw no point in discussing that with Louis. We were taken to the tent and told where to sit. Their black flag was pinned to the wall behind us and the side we were facing was open. Then we were blindfolded. I cannot recall whether the classic backdrop of turbaned, armed *mujahideen* was in place when we arrived, but at one point there was a lot of shuffling behind us, then a terrifying silence. Eventually, a rather soft, singsong voice (I think it was Jaffer's) started expostulating on and on, with plenty of forceful references to *jihad, mujahideen,* Allah of course, and the Qur'an. I don't really remember if I heard *Shari'a* but it ended with a lot of *Allahu Akbars.* Clearly it was either well rehearsed or he was reading from a script.

When he stopped there were noises behind us and I wondered if this was it, but they soon began to fade as everybody left the tent. Finally Omar undid our blindfolds and, almost without speaking, led us back to our tree. We saw nobody throughout the afternoon and heard almost no noise. It was unpleasantly still and surreal.

As evening fell, we prepared a sleeping position and were about to turn in when Omar One appeared to say that we would be given something to eat shortly and then would be moving out. Within thirty minutes we were on our way through those dunes in the dark, which did not make our passage easier.

We travelled far into the night. At one point the satellite-phone on the dashboard rang and Omar, incongruously, appeared to give an interview. In a pleasant and modulated voice he seemed to be answering a series of questions in Arabic, smiling and nodding into the phone held in his left hand, steering with his right as he drove into the night at speed, without lights, his AK held in the crook of his left elbow and pointing out the window. From time to time he would glance a little furtively in my direction. The interview lasted at least twenty minutes, but when it was over he said nothing. Much later, we stopped because the drivers were exhausted, but there was no kind of cover and a little rain.

As the sun came up we were given a cup of powdered milk and everyone congregated around the three tightly grouped trucks when I heard, very distinctly, a snippet of what was clearly the BBC International Service (thus, BBC Camp). It took me a moment to appreciate that it was in English. I assumed, therefore, that it must have been from a radio belonging to the Nigerian from Kano, Obeida. Before it was turned off, I realized it was about us and heard something about a threat to our lives having been issued.

Again I was riding with Omar One and once underway I asked him about what I had just heard. He did not lie well and insisted gruffly and without looking at me that I must have misheard. But he was shifty, uncomfortable, and uncharacteristically taciturn. We drove almost completely in silence through the morning and, around noon, arrived at a spot where, as at Thornhill, we were widely separated from them by a flat, open space. We were directed to a treeline perhaps 150 metres away, and Omar warned us that the thorn trees under which we would be sitting were poisonous; if pricked, the small wound would inevitably fester. Thus on Day 109 we stayed at Camp Poison.

Once we were settled, Omar set off back to his truck, which we could just glimpse through a break in the trees, with a sense of grim purpose and self-importance, and we realized that his crew had not unpacked and were still aboard. He immediately swung behind the wheel and was off, we knew not where, but he seemed to be in a hurry.

While it offered almost perfect shade on an excruciatingly hot day, we didn't like the thought of those poisonous thorns dangling above our heads so we boldly set out in search of a better campsite. We found one a fair distance away on the other side of the same treeline, where the long, sharp thorns looked more familiar.

In fact the whole thing looked familiar and at first we wondered if we might have been here before. Soon, though, we determined that while we had not, somebody else had. Someone had made camp much as we would, clearing a patch of ground of thorns and stones, and setting up a small windbreak with rocks, twigs, and grasses. Staring at these archeological remains we wondered which other hostages could have languished here and what had been their fate.

CHAPTER 15

SOMEONE WOULD DIE

===

There passed a weary time. Each throat
Was parch'd, and glazed each eye.
A weary time! a weary time!

===

Louis and I speculated throughout the remainder of that day, 1 April, what Omar might have gone off to do with such determination, and convinced ourselves that it had to be concerned with the negotiations. His language skills and knowledge of the wider world, however flawed, might be required to put the finishing touches on whatever deal was, we hoped, brewing. We really had no idea what, if anything, was going on or whether we were about to enter some kind of end game. Nevertheless, when early the next day we moved to another camp, we called it Great Expectations.

Getting there was challenging in itself. Allowing that Khaled had been annoyed to learn that Jaffer, AR, and Omar Three had casually risked us a couple of weeks earlier by trundling such valuable commodities perched precariously on the back of the truck, they were apprehensive about having us do it again. They were nevertheless again down to a single, overloaded vehicle, so Louis and I sat high on top of the load in the back, only this time they had rigged a sturdy rope down the middle for us to clap on to. It was a beautiful day and despite a couple of long tire changes in full sun, I could not control the optimism that our speculation about Omar's possible mission caused to continually bubble to the surface. After only an hour we approached another fringe of vegetation at the edge of the open desert and at the foot of some high rocky outcroppings.

We were shown to another tree and they established themselves behind a screen of bushes. It was a good tree but at the very edge of the desert, where we were exposed to sun and wind. The noon period of virtually no shade seemed particularly long at this location.

Omar One had said he would be back on Monday, 6 April, Day 114, but we didn't put much store in that. By Wednesday, however, we began to worry. So, evidently, did our remaining guards. Omar Two, of whom we had seen little over the preceding couple of weeks, had been deputized as the person in charge of hostage liaison, something that never inspired trust or confidence, but he was preferable to Hassan. Omar Two had largely given up his conversion brief, but he was still curious about what made us tick. He was also preoccupied by the all too evident presence around the camp of a very large hyena, whose fresh paw prints along our walking track each morning were only slightly smaller than my hand with fingers splayed.

By Thursday (Day 117), the tension in the camp had become so acute as to cause Omar Three and Abdul Rahman to disappear for the day, presumably to make a satellite-phone call or travel directly to wherever the action was taking place—most likely wherever Jack was—to seek information. They returned after dark and joined the others, who were already at dinner behind those bushes, perhaps thirty metres away from us.

Suddenly, voices were raised in extreme anger in the pitch darkness, first one (which we identified as Omar Two), then in response, another (probably the usually reserved AR). Soon others were joining in and it was pandemonium, much louder and more aggressive than anything we had heard to date. Soon everybody was shouting and there seemed to be some scuffling. Then the space between the shouters seemed to widen as if others were physically drawing the opposing parties apart. Late into the night we continued to hear loud outbursts as the argument flared, died down, and then rekindled.

It was terrifying for us, less the anger and emotion itself than what we imagined it portended. We felt like little kids listening to raging, battling, parents and we knew we might suffer ugly consequences from this confrontation. I do think, though, that we were able to put together a plausible explanation. We speculated that AR and Omar Three—who along with Jaffer were the most senior people in the group and Jack's closest collaborators—had brought back news of what was probably the final or nearly final result of the negotiations. It was no great stretch to assume that Omar Two's initial outburst was a rejection of the terms for our release as reported by Omar Three and AR.

Omar Two had perhaps insisted that such a deal was inadequate compensation for the costs and risks—not to say unpleasantness—of the seventeen weeks they had spent minding us, and might have gone on to suggest that accepting such terms would demean their cause and cheapen their commitment to *jihad*. Of course, we did not really know, but this all made sense on the basis of his posturing over the previous four months. I think it perfectly plausible that he might have argued it would be better to kill us and get nothing than have a miserable settlement forced upon them by the apostate oppressors with whom they were at war, indeed, that their honour and the sanctity of their *jihad* demanded such forthright action. Certainly I can easily imagine Omar Two taking such a line, strongly seconded by Hassan, were he there, but Jack had ensured that would not be the case.

Believing that we understood what had happened did not make it any easier to absorb. The next morning, Good Friday, Day 118, AR and O3 again left the camp, presumably to tell Jack he had a problem in the ranks. They did not return until mid-morning on

Saturday, 11 April, followed about an hour later by Omar One and his crew. Shortly after that, Jack and his full headquarters complement rolled into camp. None of them made any contact with us.

After everyone had eaten lunch, Jack summoned his full council—nine of them, including Omar Two—to sit beneath a distant tree across the flat open space behind our designated prison, perhaps three hundred metres distant. There they sat talking for five interminable hours. Without a doubt, this time it was indeed the jury that was deciding our fate. Jack obviously felt he needed to get formal buy-in from his senior lieutenants and that was not coming easily.

While the jury was deliberating, Louis and I discussed the extent to which any of them were really in our corner. There were clearly two schools within the group: one believed that whatever deal was on offer should be rejected, with cataclysmic consequences for us; the other held that it was better than nothing and we should be released. I believe that Omar Two led the first faction, probably supported by Imam Abdallah and Ahmed, while Omar One and Omar Three and possibly Al Jabbar championed the second. The remainder of the in-camp staff, Abdul Rahman, Jaffer, Ali, Obeida, Abou Isaac, and Abou Mujahid, were probably fairly neutral, content to do what they were told and leave the policy decisions to their emir.

I never could read where the relatively happy-go-lucky Ibrahim and the ever-curious Julabib (who may have wanted to film a beheading) stood: probably wherever Jack was. But that was not the case for other members of Jack's staff, most notably Ahmed, who had wished us ill from the outset.

Eventually, in the gathering dusk, the members of the council trooped back, right past us, without saying a word or acknowledging our presence in any way. They had their habitually quick dinner and all was quiet. We were on tenterhooks. What had been decided?

A couple of long hours later, Omar One emerged from the dark and hunkered down before us. He did not appear happy, but we couldn't tell if he was angry at us or with some of his colleagues. He was sure as hell angry at Canada. He began by reiterating how perfidious Canada had been throughout the negotiations, stressing the lies he said they had been told and the unfulfilled promises made. He repeatedly insisted, stabbing his finger at me, "They do not want you back. They do not care the least about you. They hope you will stay with us, or, more likely, that we will kill you." But—and then I suddenly paid close attention—"We will not do that. We have decided to free you, and by God, Canada will feel our wrath." And I have no idea what else he said but it went on for some long time.

This annunciation, on 11 April, probably about 10:00 p.m. on Day 119, was the perfect enactment of one of my myriad obsessive mantras: " . . . and, therefore, we have decided to free you." It had just been said.

We were to be freed; nothing else mattered a damn.

When Omar departed, Louis and I shared a cautious, long, firm two-handed handshake. We had been waiting four months for that moment. Usually we were pretty leery about believing anything they said or promised, but somehow I was confident that these were straight goods.

I had no idea what Omar's preambular screed was about or whether any of it made any sense. I didn't care. It was irrelevant. We were going home. Paraphrasing Keats just a little, that was all we knew and all we needed to know.

The next day, Easter Sunday, Omar struggled toward us dragging the big, black, plastic thirty-litre water container and told us to clean ourselves up. That was of course welcome because we had not been able to wash for more than three weeks but, more relevant still, it seemed to prove that Louis and I had not simply entertained the same fantasy the night before. We had assumed this would happen prior to the liberation moment.

I said to Omar, "This washing invitation is great but we don't want to squander this valuable water, so should we save it for a few days or use it right now?" He knew precisely what I was about, of course, and with one of his relatively rare smiles replied, "Use it now."

❖

On Monday, 13 April, Day 121, nothing was happening and the negative body language of our abductors was eloquent. Louis was despondent. Within a short space of time Louis and I convinced ourselves that, yet again, everything was going to rat shit. Notwithstanding our rules, I attacked Louis for creating the biggest damn rabbit hole ever, and then dived spiralling down after him. He was usually better at avoiding these free falls but not in this case. In an effort to escape the mood of growing despair, I began doing hard laps on our track in the full heat of the day, thereby undoing the salutary effects of the washing the day before. Eventually, I returned to where Louis sat under our tree and we talked ourselves back to the rational surface.

It seemed to each of us, simply through reading the mood of our abductors, that the promise of freedom was about to elude us again. We began to assess what could have gone wrong, for clearly, although they had not said a word to us, a wheel had come off somewhere. We reviewed everything we had seen and heard over the past few days to determine whether we could have missed or misunderstood some vital element. Eventually we concluded that, yes, something had gone wrong, but no, the decision to liberate us had not been faked. So there had been progress, and even if the moment of our liberation were to be significantly delayed, we strove to convince ourselves that we remained on a positive track.

On Tuesday and Wednesday, Days 122 and 123, time stood still. We hardly saw our captors. Great Expectations was eerily quiet. Before dawn on Wednesday, 15 April, I awoke to a loud crunching sound and a huge wet muzzle drooling onto my face, as a large camel chewed away on the thorns a few centimetres above my head.

Then on Thursday, mid-morning, a phone rang shrilly somewhere behind those bushes. It was something we had not heard for more than four months and it sounded just like home. I wanted to shout, "I'll get it," but someone got there first. About twenty minutes later our abductors began to gather behind the screen of bushes and trees separating us, and then a couple of them emerged into the empty space in front of us and emptied their AK magazines into the mountain beyond. Without a look at us they returned behind the bushes. Five minutes later we saw them mounting the heavy machine guns on two of the three trucks then in camp, but they were in no hurry and seemingly without purpose or provocation.

While this was happening, the taciturn Ali emerged from the bushes to our right with his ever-present PK machine gun on a sling over one shoulder and a belt of ammunition flapping from the breech. He worked the charging lever and began to spray the open desert behind us with fire until, after ten or twelve rounds, his gun jammed, whereupon he retreated back behind the bushes. A few minutes later, Abou Isaac could just be seen above the bushes, standing, feet wide apart, in the bed of one of the trucks loading the heavy gun. Then he pointed it toward the top of the nearby mountain and started to blast away: pom-pom-pom, small clouds of dust erupting from the cliff face just below the summit, perhaps 350 metres distant. Eventually, the same thing occurred from the other truck but that gun seemed to jam after three or four rounds.

All this was pretty bizarre but utterly unthreatening. Eventually Omar One strode to where we were sitting under our tree to remark, without any conviction or sincerity, that he wished to apologize for the disturbance. He explained that he was sure we would understand that every now and then they had to cook off old, deteriorating ammunition. "Come on, Omar," I replied, "do you really expect us not to recognize a *feu de joie*?"

With a faux-sheepish grin, he allowed as how it was indeed a *feu de joie*—albeit the most dispirited and desultory one I could conceive of—and, of course, we pressed him to explain what it was about. Without much further prodding, he told us, "The delegation is on its way from Bamako with your negotiators."

"What delegation and what negotiators?" we asked. "Do you mean the Red Crescent?"

Now smiling mockingly, he replied, "Why would we have anything to do with those Western stooges? No, they are the negotiators sent by the presidents of Burkina Faso and Mali, and they are coming to get you. We will be leaving in ten minutes." With that he walked away, leaving us to contemplate this surprising and happy news. Soon, but in more than ten minutes, we left Great Expectations with little haste for what we assumed would be some kind of desert version of Checkpoint Charlie.

We drove far and for most of that trip I remained in a euphoric haze. We stopped as evening approached in a pretty exposed place, which we confidently named Last Stop. But by then we really should have known better. The next morning Louis and I did our full four-kilometre walk over an innovative track and at its conclusion, with a little formality, we shook hands, believing that it was our last walk.

Shortly after we set off that morning—Louis and I both assigned to Omar One's truck—we were handed blindfolds and told that soon we would be required to wear them for our own protection as there were things we really did not want to see, for seeing them would place our lives in jeopardy. We said we understood and soon, for the first time while in transit, we put on blindfolds. Omar verified that they effectively prevented us from seeing anything. I don't think we wore them for much more than an hour but I can't be sure.

When we stopped around noon Omar said we were in Algeria, but I have no reason to believe that was the case. He then explained with more menace than we had heard from him in months that this location was extremely dangerous and we had to be very careful indeed about not exposing ourselves to scrutiny. We had seen no other place like this one, much closer to a bona fide oasis with lush, healthy acacias and high, sharp grasses and bushes. The three-truck convoy had trouble working its way into deep cover. We couldn't see "their" camp from our designated prison but it was no farther away than usual. We christened this camp Not Yet.

That afternoon I went *loin* and at a critical juncture I perceived movement in what in a car would have been my blind spot. Turning my head slightly, I saw a large camel's knee at my lowered eye level, less than a metre away. Following the knee upward, not surprisingly, I found the camel and perched way up there was a Tuareg in full regalia staring down at me through a very narrow opening in his turban, an ancient rifle strapped across his back. He watched what must have been a remarkable sight for a while, then slowly, soundlessly, and in stately fashion moved through the oasis and out onto the heat-blasted plain.

After I had finished, I reported to the sentry what I had seen and Omar was sent out to investigate. Perhaps twenty minutes later he came to ask me for some antibiotic pills as the camel-man had a child who had a severe bronchial infection. I knew that if what appeared to be our looming liberation did not pan out we might well need those pills, but I really didn't have a choice in the face of a sick child, so I handed over a handful of the pills Mary had sent me.

In the early evening, Omar passed by on some errand or other and I stopped him and asked, "Any news?"

He exploded. Without preamble or explanation, he began screaming at me for the first and only time: "You have no right to ask such questions. I told you that I would let you know if there were news. You are prisoners in our great struggle to do God's work, and rid our lands of your vile presence, yet you keep trying to extract valuable tactical information from me. This will not be tolerated. There will be consequences!" And with that he stalked off toward *les frères*.

With a worried look on his face, Louis approached and asked, "What the hell was that all about?"

"I've no bloody idea," I replied.

A couple of hours later we saw a row of figures working their way slowly toward us through the tall grass. It was the council—the seven senior members of the group present in the camp. When Jaffer, the camp emir, reached us, he said—through a very sombre Omar One—we needed to have a serious discussion. So once again we all sat and they formed another semi-circle around us. Jaffer began, "Omar has told us of your unacceptable question—it cannot be tolerated." As I opened my mouth to respond he raised his palm toward me, shutting me down. "We have treated you well, but that will change all too quickly if you continue to show disrespect for our rules and seek to violate our trust," he continued. "You know that our religion prohibits us from lying and yet you continue to probe for information, information which would be damaging to us and indeed to you. Should such behaviour be repeated, there will be instantaneous consequences. You must stop trying to wrest operational details from us at this extremely tense moment."

Nobody else said a word, and seeking to defuse the tension, I assured them that had not been my intention and promised we would ask no further questions of this sort. They seemed satisfied that they had made their point and trooped off, but as they left I thought I saw Omar Three give me a conspiratorial wink, as if to suggest things were not really that bad.

On Saturday, Day 126, after our walk Louis disappeared *loin*. Waiting, I believe, for such a moment, Omar One quickly approached me and, not looking at me directly, announced, "In view of Louis' *mauvais caractère* the brothers have decided that should things not work out as planned, and as I indicated they would last week, it will go very badly for Louis. He will pay a very heavy price, very heavy—it has been decided!"

I was aghast and reminded Omar that it was I, not Louis, who had been the cause of the incident the previous evening. With a dismissive wave he said, "That's been settled! It is of no importance. We thought, however, you should know what we have decided."

I have no idea why they felt I should be apprised of such a decision. It could be simply that they wanted to unsettle me, but somehow I think it was more than that. In all his stories of battles and honour in the field, Omar had made much of the fact that war could be undertaken only once a clear declaration had been issued. In the same vein, I knew that it was standard practice for Al Qaeda to issue warnings, however vague and general, to their intended targets. I think that the transmittal of this appalling decision was therefore a declaration of this nature. In effect, I had been given due warning so that I could not subsequently claim surprise or even that I had been duped or deceived. I also have no idea whether they expected me to transmit this news to Louis but again, I do not think that was the point or that they cared much one way or the other.

Throughout our captivity I had thought it was likely our Al Qaeda kidnappers would consider killing somebody in order to truly get the attention of those with whom they were negotiating. I had heard the stories, read the books, and knew more than I really wanted about the history of "extreme kidnapping."

The branding of Louis for expendability—in a manner that would justify his subsequent execution—did not have anything to do with whether they liked him or respected him less or me more. Rather, it was a cold calculation based on their own cost–benefit accounting. If, in order to attract the requisite world attention, effectively *pour encourager les autres,* they needed a bloody gesture, they would start with their least valuable asset. And I was certain that if Louis' murder didn't achieve the desired effect, it in no way would protect me from a similar fate further down the line. This had been done before and would be done again.

Also, these thugs needed to demonstrate that they were prepared to go the distance to protect their newly acquired Al Qaeda trademark. They had to demonstrate to their "great emir" in the Tora Bora and *jihadi* brethren throughout the world that the Al Qaeda franchise in North Africa was strong and in good hands.

They also, however, felt the need to offer some ersatz Islamic justification for their decision and selection. Their rationale was idiotic, unfounded, and brutal, but the underlying logic was unassailable, however disturbing. First had been Louis' alleged Jewishness, which had begun in the context of the ongoing Israeli Operation Cast Lead in Gaza. Then they had attempted to build a catalogue of trumped-up offences to demonstrate that he had a *mauvais caractère*—coughing all too obviously when I was going somewhere he thought I shouldn't go in a discussion with one of them (which, incidentally, made me feel like whacking him), hurling a dish in (justified) anger at Ant Hill when they had issued conflicting instructions. And there had been very recent, equally ill-founded accusations that he had been peeking beneath his blindfold in the truck. But these were only justifications for what they had decided to do anyway.

On that Saturday morning, 18 April, at Not Yet, I sought rather desperately to convince Omar that Louis' character was very respectful and gentle, more so than mine. I allowed that while Louis would on rare occasions get frustrated and then freeze up, becoming increasingly inarticulate and seemingly aggressive, he remained a decent, sensitive, God-fearing individual. I insisted that Louis was genuinely interested in Islam and had time and again demonstrated sympathy and understanding toward our captors.

Omar was uninterested in what I had to say. He had come to deliver a message, not to debate it. Their minds were made up.

As soon as Louis returned, Omar beat an unusually hasty departure, barely acknowledging Louis, who clearly sensed something was amiss. For the first time in eighteen weeks, during which there had been total, sometimes brutal, honesty and absolute frankness between us, I prevaricated. I brushed off his inquiries by explaining that Omar had wished to follow up on the council's visit the previous evening to further insist we avoid asking "tactical questions."

I was terrified, literally short of breath, powerless to stop what appeared to be an avalanche thundering down upon us. Louis had five kids, two of them still in high school. Mai didn't work outside the home. I was eight years older than he was. My kids had left the nest. Mary had an outstanding employment record. Half of my pension, in addition to hers, and my life insurance would not be too shabby. It was not fair. It made no sense but I understood all too clearly that there was nothing I could do to change their logic.

Further, a week previously we had been told that we would be given our freedom. We were so very evidently involved in some pre-release dance, but the music seemed to have stopped. If they were telling me this, then surely something had happened that our kidnappers did not think would be soon recoverable. But I couldn't discuss any of this with Louis.

I knew that, given the enormous and building strain to which this interminable end game was subjecting us, such dark knowledge could not possibly be of any benefit to him. Further, I was not at all sure he could handle such information. Who could? And with any luck—a commodity that had been in short supply—the wheel would be repaired, whatever problem had developed in the release scenerio would be solved and the whole episode could be written off to my own overly fertile imagination. I am not sure if I should have withheld such information from my friend but I justified it to myself on the basis that, had the circumstances been reversed, I hoped he would have made the same decision.

The lesson I took from this episode was that as soon as I determined that our passage to freedom had been well and truly blocked, it would be time to update our rather inchoate escape plans. I also realized that at some likely not distant point I would have to share this information with Louis in order to convince him that escape was worth the all too evident risks.

❖

Late that evening the whole camp was moved from deep within the oasis at Not Yet to its edge. A huge, absolutely flat and empty expanse of desert stretched before us. Our sleeping position was right beside theirs on the edge of this sea of sand. They were extremely vigilant, and the heavy machine guns were mounted and manned throughout the night. For the first time, we saw distant lights moving about across the desert.

On Sunday, 19 April, Day 127, we travelled three or four hours to Still Not Yet as the tension vis-à-vis our captors became all but intolerable. On arrival, as we began to pace out our walking track, Omar intervened to say there would be no "sport" until further notice. He instructed us to move around discreetly and talk quietly. It was unbearably hot and his admonition was easy to follow. At night, though, it was cold. Beyond Omar's instructions we had no contact with our kidnappers. Adding to our worry, a phone rang in camp half a dozen times on Monday, 20 April, as everybody held their breath in the blistering heat and waited, and waited.

We knew next to nothing about the identity of our negotiators. We had been told at Great Expectations on 16 April that they were on their way into the desert, and I feared they would be unable to sustain themselves for very long in the hostile Saharan environment. It was hard to escape the conclusion that were they, for whatever reason, to leave without us in tow, it would be a long time before we could catch such a train again. As of 18 April, it was also clear that at least one ticket to that train would not be reissued.

CHAPTER 16

LIBERATION AND THE FLIGHT
TO FREEDOM

===

With sloping masts and dipping prow,
As who pursued with yell and blow
Still treads the shadow of his foe,
And forward bends his head,
The ship drove fast, loud roar'd the blast,
And southward aye we fled.

===

I awoke serene on Tuesday, 21 April, Day 129. When our breakfast milk was delivered we were told we could resume walking. Even before this news I was sure that everything would be all right. I don't know what made me so confident other than that the change in the mood within the camp was palpable. I felt as light as air and completely tranquil. As we walked, there was a growing bustle around us and just as we completed our last kilometre, Omar approached, smiling, to say, "Now, you will be liberated. So many of the *mujahideen* have gathered. You will not believe it."

Omar was calm and assured. It was as if the tension and turmoil of the last dreadful days and the pronouncement of a death sentence against Louis had not occurred. There seemed to be no nervousness, no guile in his attitude, no conditionality, no uncertainty.

We loaded up, Louis and me in the same truck with Omar, and there were no blindfolds. At one point, as we nestled into a tight ravine awaiting instructions to make our final approach to where all those *mujahideen* were supposedly gathered, Omar left the cab to make a sat-phone call. I squeezed Louis' hand and whispered, "I think this really is it."

Then there were lots of short stops as we zigzagged toward what was obviously not a distant destination. There was a final flurry of very brief sat-phone exchanges. Then, only about an hour after our departure from Still Not Yet, as we headed toward a far distant line of greenery across a flat expanse, the walkie-talkie on the cluttered dashboard crackled into life and there were joyously excited answers to Omar's "Arak, Arak" call sign, as, I assume, he told them that we were incoming.

Soon we saw a number of trucks parked at random among the approaching vast clump of acacias and bushes and, amazingly, lots of people were milling about as we drove toward the thickest concentration. There were a few cries of "Allahu Akbar!" as we approached, but they were not triumphalist—not like those that greeted us as we drove into Board of Directors 126 days previously.

Omar jumped from behind the wheel, the boys in the back having leapt into the crowd long before our vehicle came to a halt. Omar threw his arms around a series of identically armed and dressed, black-bearded clones of our AQIM abductors, people we had never seen before. There was lots of smiling and laughing and what seemed to be the pretty classic back-thumping, how-the-hell-have-you-been greetings common to long-lost comrades in arms, happy to find each other still alive.

Louis and I remained in the cab of Omar's truck for perhaps ten minutes. We knew in our gut that all this probably spelled excellent news but were nevertheless a little surprised that we had been forgotten. I suppose we had become used to being the centre of attention, no matter how malevolent that attention had been.

Eventually, Omar returned to the truck and, gesturing around, remarked, "Didn't I tell you that there would be lots of *mujahideen*?" He backed his truck out of the mass of assembled AQIM warriors and drove around to the back of the oasis, where he found a stand of a few closely grouped acacias and pushed his truck among them. Our blankets were thrown to the ground and we were told to sit. Shortly thereafter Omar pointed to another group of trees, about fifty metres distant, and instructed us to take our backpacks and change into our Western clothes.

This too we had anticipated, but not quite what was to follow. I decided in favour of the full monty and donned the torn and weathered ball cap that I had not worn for months. Louis opted for the more practical turban, to which we had both become accustomed. We were swimming in the clothes from the backpack delivery almost six weeks earlier, destined as they were for people forty pounds heavier. I returned to the vehicle a little self-consciously clad in my iron-creased and cuffed dress pants, snappy safari shirt, and preposterous desert boots.

Omar summoned us to the sunny side of his truck, where our blankets had been relocated. The black AQIM flag had been attached haphazardly across the side of the truck. We were told to sit with our backs to the truck. Four metres away, squatting in the sand facing us, was Julabib, his camcorder strapped to his right hand and at the ready. Omar explained we would be making a final video message but was quick to allay our pretty obvious fears. There was no armed backdrop, no fearsome tent, just the two of us sitting in the sun in front of that damned black flag.

"What's it about this time?" I asked Omar.

Very relaxed, he said, "Just say how pleased you are to be going home; how glad you are to be freed despite your government's desire that you remain with us; how you were not mistreated and how happy you are that some people rose to your defence." This was not a script that would be difficult to follow.

I don't recall precisely what I said in this fourth and final video recording, in such a relatively unthreatening environment, but since no coercion would be evident to any viewer, I decided to deploy my emergency code word, which Mary and I had long agreed I should use if ever I wished to surreptitiously indicate that I was not speaking freely. Given the heavily armed tableaux arrayed behind us in each of the three video messages we had recorded previously (Days 5, 52, and 108) there had been no need to spell out that I had been speaking under duress, but this time it was less clear, and also evidently less threatening.

The word Mary and I had settled upon was "golf." As I'm not a golfer, we thought it unlikely that the word would slip inadvertently into a statement. So I managed to say something along the lines of, "Our lives over the past nineteen weeks have not been easy. We have not been visiting some golf club." I said that it appeared we were finally headed home and allowed how marvellous that was, adding that I was pleased to learn from our captors that some non-Canadian friends had made our liberation possible. In conclusion, I noted that I would be eternally grateful to those people, whoever they were. Louis was quite happy not to speak.

Afterward, we moved back to the shady side of the truck and soon a crowd of teenagers gathered to gawk and giggle until there were over a dozen of them. Their jostling and snickering soon became too much for Omar and he shooed them away. As Omar moved between us and the main throng a couple of hundred metres distant, our guard was the quiet and gentle Ali, who, with sign language, asked if he might clean his machine gun on our blanket. Happy for yet another sign that things were really changing, we indicated he could proceed and he methodically and wordlessly field-stripped his weapon a hand's breadth away from me, cleaning each bit with a carefully protected oily rag.

Omar had returned and was snoozing behind the wheel when Hassan, whom we had not seen since Ant Hill, thirty-four days previously, swaggered toward us, barking at us to empty our backpacks and pockets so that he might inspect the contents to ensure we would not be taking out with us anything that might have intelligence value. Before he got very far, Omar emerged from his truck and, with a growl, sent him packing too. That was the last we saw of Hassan.

As our meagre possessions now lay in a heap, I asked Omar if we might keep our RPG-holed blanket and stainless steel cup, and he said, "Yes, you will need them on the long way back." It did not look like a helicopter option was in play.

After a couple of hours, a runner approached Omar with a message, and one last time he gave us the order to mount up. We drove to the edge of the gathering clans and were stationed beneath yet another acacia. Here too we attracted the curious, but this time they were the senior cadres of other groups. Each was introduced to us proprietarily by Omar using some *nom de guerre* or other for the newcomers, none of which I remember. All of them performed some kind of *da'wa* to get that ticket punched and then strove to engage us in conversation, sometimes in fractured French or English, and once in what Louis averred was reasonably fluent Spanish.

Time drifted on into the afternoon. There was a call to prayer and according to what I am convinced was all part of the plan—for they tended not to improvise much—they lined up in one long north–south line, facing east, some twenty metres in front of us. This allowed me to methodically count them from one end to the other, no doubt so I could report that there were an awful lot of them. In fact, there were ninety-six in that line. In addition, there were two sentry trucks with heavy machine guns mounted on small flanking hills on either side. Assuming a minimum of three in each to man the guns and vehicles while the others prayed, that meant at least 102 present in nineteen armed trucks. All I could think was that the gathering represented an extremely high-value target and we were at its epicentre. I knew that if Algerian helicopter gunships popped out of the sun behind us, their 30 mm cannons would not worry about Louis' and my whereabouts.

Finally, the *mujahideen* were chivvied forward and lined up perpendicular to their prayer line in front of the line of armed trucks.

A very self-important, forty-something, short and stocky *mujahid* pulled up in a shiny white four-door Toyota pick-up, a few metres away from where we were sitting. He ignored us, but we were told he was Abdelhamid Abou Zeid—who, along with Belmokhtar, ran AQIM operations in the vast southern Sahara region. Eventually he drove off to the far end of the line of vehicles to our right. Suddenly, there was a loud and sustained *feu de joie* as everybody fired weapons of all kinds into the air, and a couple of new pick-up trucks appeared and then immediately disappeared behind some trees to the left.

Then Omar ushered us forward where, after just a few paces, we were joined by a brace of PK machine gunners on each side and rather ceremoniously escorted, as if in review, down the line of AQIM *mujahideen* arrayed in front of their trucks. At the far end Abou Zeid's four-door was waiting. I had my backpack over one shoulder and was carrying our most valuable possession, our plastic water container. Louis was carrying a large plastic bag containing the blanket and other bits and pieces.

As we proceeded down that line, we kept hoping that this was really it and not some cruel joke. If it was, it was an elaborate and expensive—not to say risky—prank, and I didn't think that AQIM was into that sort of thing. Then, out of the corner of my eye, rather far away, I saw Julabib with his small video camera filming the whole thing. I never imagined there might come a day when I would see that recording of our liberation ceremony, but it is now readily available on the Internet.

Once we were loaded into the back seat of Abou Zeid's spanking new Toyota, we were driven a full two hundred metres to a clump of trees to the left, toward which the two pick-up trucks had been heading. A few rugs were spread on the sand, and standing on them in front of their vehicles were three men we had not seen before.

As we exited Abou Zeid's truck and were directed toward the rugs, the eldest and smallest of the three stepped forward and said, turning to each of us, "Mr. Fowler, Mr. Guay, welcome. Has anybody told you that you are free?"

"No, not lately," I replied warily, to which he responded quite formally, seeking and getting eye contact, "Well, then, let me do so. You are free." It sounded pretty good.

I asked him for his name and he quickly and softly said we would discuss all that a little later. Recognizing his voice from the phone call, I replied, "As you wish, Mr. Chaffi."

He laughed, extending a hand and saying—very quietly— "Mustapha Chaffi. I represent President Compaoré." Chaffi was a slight, fairly light-skinned gentleman with closely cropped hair who seemed to be in his forties. He was extremely well spoken, with naturally gracious, almost courtly, manners. Despite his efforts to disguise the fact, he was nervous and seemed to be out of place in the tableau in which he found himself.

Baba Ould Cheik, whom Chaffi introduced as the representative of Mali's President Touré, was entirely different, clearly an operator. He was a big-boned, fit-looking, no-nonsense Arab who was perhaps in his early thirties. He spoke little French and was clearly focused on getting it done and getting out of there as expeditiously as possible. That was encouraging.

I felt a little dizzy and was still not entirely sure all this was as it appeared. All kinds of people armed to the teeth were moving about and talking among themselves and, from time to time, with those claiming to be our liberators. I couldn't tell the good guys from the bad. Among them were most of the council of Jack's *katiba* but also two or three times that number of equivalent-looking and -ranking fighters from, we assumed, other groups or *katibas*. Baba disappeared as soon as we had been introduced. The third of our liberators was a tall, thin, weathered African who was not young; he was presented to me by Chaffi as a lieutenant in the Malian Special Forces and was the driver of Chaffi and Baba's second truck.

After what seemed an hour but was probably twenty minutes, I saw Jack approaching with a thunderous look on his face. Without any interpretation, he asked, "Can I have dysentery pills? Women need." I had no idea what women he was referring to.

We had not seen a woman in 129 days, but I said "Sure," rummaged in my backpack and handed him a container of the pills Mary had got through to me forty days earlier. He set off, almost at a run, toward a distant truck I had not noticed before.

I turned to Chaffi and with what I suspect was a pretty evident what-the-hell-is-going-on-here look on my face, asked him, "Did you not say we were free?"

He replied, "Yes, yes, but there's a problem."

Of course there was a goddamned problem—here we go again!

Chaffi pointed to the truck, perhaps two hundred metres away, and reported that it contained two "European women" who, in his words, were "in abominable shape." They had been held, he explained, along with two men, by the Abou Zeid group. And he pointed to Abou Zeid, who was sitting about twenty metres from us engaged in intense, agitated conversation with Baba Ould Cheik. So there it was. Chaffi looked frustrated and very nervous.

Turning to Omar One who, as ever, was hovering close by, I asked, "What's going on?"

"The negotiations for the release of the European women, which were to have been completed many days ago, seem not in fact to have been concluded." Abou Zeid, Omar explained ruefully, was refusing to allow them to leave with us. The last ten days were slowly coming into focus.

He also told us, though with a little less excitement than I might have expected, that at some point during her captivity the German woman, Marianne Petzold, had converted to Islam. But while we had yet to set eyes on Marianne and Gabriella Burco Greiner, those who had were not crowing over this fine Islamic victory. When I did see them a few hours later, I understood why. A few of the young and foolish among the assembled *mujahideen* boasted of the conversion victory but those with any sense knew it to be utterly hollow or much worse. Belmokhtar's troops were aghast. They had spent all that time explaining that Islam did not wage war on women, children, or old people, but here were these two women, both sick. One of them—old, frail, and confused—had clearly been horribly treated even though she had chosen to become their Muslim sister. It was evident in Jack's face that he found Abou Zeid's handling of these women unconscionable.

After some long time—perhaps an hour—Jack quietly gathered a dozen of his senior people around the Baba/Chaffi truck, which Louis and I had been told to board: me in the cab and Louis volunteering, in deference to my damaged back, to ride in the truck bed. The Malian Special Forces lieutenant, at the wheel of Baba's second vehicle, was told to place his truck immediately behind the one we were in. Then Jack ordered the distant truck containing the two women to be brought up, bumper to bumper, behind our second vehicle. All this took place quickly and with a minimum of fuss.

Louis got settled as best he could in the bed of the first vehicle, seated again on barrels and blankets but with a lot more room than on the AQIM vehicles. The European women were carried from the third truck to the cab of the second. I again sat in the middle position in the cab, but this time I had Chaffi to my right and Baba, who had left Abou Zeid sitting with a couple of his fighters about twenty metres away only moments before, was now at the wheel. Belmokhtar's troops, fully armed, pressed around all three vehicles facing outward. As soon as the women were loaded, Belmokhtar, standing beside the driver's window, ordered Baba with a sweep of his hand, "Leave—immediately!"

Suddenly Omar One knocked on the passenger window. When Chaffi opened it, Omar, wagging his finger at me, reminded me that on the Day of Judgment I needed to be very clear in my meeting with my maker that he, Omar, had tried valiantly—if unsuccessfully—to guide me to the straight and true path.

Then to my utter surprise, Omar Two, who had refused even to acknowledge our departure moments before, thrust his hand through the window and grabbed mine, saying "I will give you the benefit of the doubt and assume that you will find the true path, so I offer you my hand believing that you will become a brother."

Then, as the truck started to roll, Chaffi leaned across me toward the driver's window, looking worried, to ask whether Abou Zeid had agreed to release the two women. Belmokhtar angrily growled something and gestured "Just go, now!" Baba needed no further encouragement. He slammed the truck into gear and off we rumbled in a lonely two-vehicle convoy, leaving a hundred Al Qaeda warriors in our wake, uncertain whether we were leaving or escaping.

A few minutes later, Chaffi and Baba confirmed that in those last moments Belmokhtar, by word and deed, had indicated he was taking the decision to free all four of us out of Abou Zeid's hands; the deal for his hostages (Louis and me) had been done for almost two weeks and he would not abide seeing the two women left behind to die while Abou Zeid haggled over details.

I suppose, too, that it was a matter of face. First was the fact that he had made his deal and would see it honoured, and second was the issue of whose vision, value system, and authority would prevail among AQIM forces in the southern Sahara. Moreover, this struggle for status and leadership was being played out before the eyes of the assembled clans, and Belmokhtar could not blink. In Chaffi's view, as confirmed by Baba, Belmokhtar had made clear to them that his will would be done, by force if necessary.

After about an hour of hard driving, with me sandwiched between Baba and Chaffi, and Louis perched on two spares, grasping a couple of tie-down ropes as if he were clinging to the rigging of one of Nelson's frigates in a gale, we suddenly crunched to a stop in the deep dusk. Baba tersely explained we would be making some phone calls. He said he had made a deal with our abductors that he would not fire up his satellite-phone until we had travelled thirty kilometres from the place at which we had been liberated. Now that we had come that distance, it was time.

We would not, however, be calling Mai and Mary, as Louis and I had fervently hoped. That would have to wait—for reasons I still do not fully comprehend—until we entered the cellphone net on the outskirts of Gao, in southern Mali, some thousand kilometres to the south.

While Baba got on his sat-phone, I left the cab and walked back to the second vehicle, where for the first time I saw the two European women. The shock was physical. I recoiled with horror at the sight of those small, troubled white faces, twisted with pain and concern, wispy hair askew. They were in evident distress. The older woman, Marianne Petzold, was by the window. Despite what she had just been through, she whispered a courteous introduction as she sought to allow her companion, Gabriella Burco Greiner, to exit the truck from the middle position.

Gabriella was in urgent need of going *loin*. They explained that they, along with Gabriella's husband, Werner, and their fellow hostage, Edwin Dyer, had contracted a virulent form of dysentery some weeks previously and had all been suffering terribly. Abou Zeid had refused to give them the medicines that their governments had provided. It did not look to my untrained eye as if Ms. Petzold would last another hour, let alone sixteen to eighteen hours of hard driving across the trackless desert.

In a brief conversation with Gabriella, I learned that Marianne was a seventy-seven-year-old retired French teacher from a small town near Hamburg. Gabriella, a city official from Zurich in her early fifties, and her husband, Werner Greiner, a fifty-seven-year-old lawyer who practised in Zurich, were Swiss citizens. Their fellow captive, the Briton Edwin Dyer, originally from Buckinghamshire, was the sixty-one-year-old manager of a plumbing supply business in Vienna, where he had lived for forty years.

Baba signalled that the calls were about to go through. As he passed me the phone, he told me that he had been unable to reach President Touré so instead I would be speaking to the head of Mali's Security Service, to whom Baba was reporting on this assignment and who had been designated by President Touré as the senior officer managing our file. When he came on the line, I thanked him for having liberated us and asked that our deep appreciation be passed to President Touré. For his part, he congratulated us on our freedom, telling us that the President would be informed we were free and assuring us we were in good hands with Baba and Chaffi. This helped, but not completely. Louis and I were both still not absolutely convinced that we were indeed free and clear.

The satellite-phone was then passed to Chaffi, who called President Compaoré and got straight through. That same deep, distinctive voice I had last heard precisely six weeks before from the top of a dune by Algeria's border offered similar congratulations, and I finally believed that it was true. We were free, while remaining in perilous circumstances. I told President Compaoré that his cartons had nourished our bodies and his "On va vous sortir de là" had sustained our wills. I said we would be eternally grateful, for he had done exactly what he had said he would do. I hope he understands the extent to which that remains true.

As I was talking to the President, Ms. Burco—not a tall person—was jumping up in front of me shouting, "Help my husband—you must save my husband!" as she tried to wrest the phone from my ear. While I had deep sympathy for her appalling dilemma, I also needed to complete my call with President Compaoré. Eventually Baba placed himself between her and me and when I had finished, Louis had a chance to thank President Compaoré. Louis then handed the phone back to Baba who, a little reluctantly, passed it to Gabriella. She then pleaded the case for her husband, urging President Compaoré to do everything in his power to get him and Mr. Dyer out as well.

Once the calls were completed, and we were on our way again, I took the only turn Louis would permit me in the back of the truck on our run to freedom, giving him the chance that I had just enjoyed to talk things over in the cab with Baba and Chaffi.

The night was cool but not cold. The spares and lots of bedding made a comfortable seat. There were ropes against which I could brace and I was free. I felt like that woman in the bow of the Titanic but didn't much like the image. It was a delicious time and I savoured every moment, including a spectacular sunset, glimmering almost purple through a building sandstorm on the western horizon. Finally, I could appreciate its startling beauty. Soon the stars shone brightly, the wind was sweet against my face, and I could release all those carefully corralled thoughts about my family now that, once again, it seemed we had a future together. Furthermore, no one could see my tears.

But dammit, the stars revealed that we were heading due east and not south as I knew we must. Inexorably, nagging doubts seeped back into my troubled mind. Might we have simply been passed on to some other group of miscreants who would seek to extract their pound of flesh? Sure, Compaoré and Baba and Chaffi talked a good game and seemed to be still doing so inside the cab with Louis, but was all as it seemed? After about ten minutes of this I simply decided that I would not allow my mind to go in those directions yet again. So I closed down the second-guessing instinct honed so carefully over the preceding four and a half months. Half an hour later, we turned sharply south, never again straying from that bearing.

After another few hours Baba drove a few hundred metres off the rough track we had been following and we pulled in behind a small rise. I asked why we were stopping and he said he thought that the women travelling in the second vehicle simply could not take much more; an argument I could hardly disagree with, even if Louis and I were anxious to put as much distance as possible between us and the AQIM horde.

Chaffi handed Louis and me a Tetra Pak of juice to share, noting that it was the last one. They had brought lots but a week wandering about in the Sahara had all but eliminated their supplies. "Those women drank almost everything we had," he said ruefully. Not surprising, I suppose, given their dysentery, but a little worrying. The lieutenant prepared a very simple meal, distressingly similar, in fact, to the standard fare of AQIM, but I didn't care and I wasn't hungry.

Marianne was in terrible shape. In addition to dysentery, she was impossibly thin, had cracked a couple of ribs, and only a few days before had been stung by a scorpion. When I saw the damage it had inflicted, I appreciated more fully how lucky Louis and I had been to avoid such a fate. Her arm was hugely inflamed between hand and elbow with a large, shiny, black, very painful-looking swelling that looked as if it were about to burst. I was later told she spent six weeks in hospital in Germany receiving skin grafts to replace the necrotized flesh.

As we prepared to get some rest, Marianne asked if Louis and I would sleep close to her and Gabriella and, of course, we agreed. Each of us took turns helping her to stand up, sit down, and eventually lie down. Gabriella looked after her when she had to go *loin* and explained to us that throughout their captivity Edwin Dyer had performed all these tasks; Gabriella and Werner had looked after each other but Dyer had done everything for Marianne.

The wind had been building for some time and as we started to prepare our sleeping positions a sand-laden gale was blowing, visibility was down to a metre or so, and anything not tied down or tucked beneath us was soon cartwheeling across the desert into the night.

I don't think anybody slept much. At about four o'clock in the morning Louis and I got up and started walking about, the wind having significantly abated. When we saw that Chaffi was also awake, and that nobody else was sleeping, I suggested we get underway. He agreed. By the time we'd had a little to eat and drink and had loaded up, the first signs of a brilliant red sunrise were showing in the east.

We had no choice about where we were as AQIM captives, but Chaffi and Baba did. They had put their heads into the lion's mouth time after time, taking significant personal risks. On our long drive to freedom on 22 April, I sat between them as Louis hung on, hour after hour—refusing all relief—in the back. They told me that Baba had made eleven trips deep into the desert to talk to our captors and, not incidentally, to bring us the backpacks. Chaffi had made four, including one to bring us President Compaoré's eleven cartons. They were each asked to take on these perilous missions by their respective presidents, but they did not have to do it, did not have to put their lives at risk for us. Of course they had been compensated in some manner or other for their remarkable services, but that does not mean they were any less courageous or that we owe them any less gratitude.

Baba spoke limited French, so much of our conversation was interpreted by Chaffi. They were neither friends nor rivals, merely professionals who had been through an awful lot together on our behalf.

Baba Ould Cheik was a rough frontiersman type. A Malian Arab from the northern wastes, he was neither subtle nor sophisticated. He was the mayor of the tiny desert village of Tarkint, on the edge of the Sahara, and had been involved in the negotiations leading to the release of German tourists in 2003 and of Austrians in 2008. To get us out of there, he and Chaffi had to deal with some hard and unforgiving men. He knew them because he had dealt with them before and they trusted him. President Touré gave that mission to just the right guy—however rough around the edges—and thank heavens for that. We are very fortunate that the President of Mali took such a vivid interest in our welfare, because Baba was also a politician of sorts, and not among his supporters.

Baba travelled the desert with a battered, well-oiled, and well-used AK-47 always close to hand. A little disconcertingly, he had our captors adjust the firing pin while we awaited permission to depart following our liberation. He needed to be certain that it was in good working order as he considered it entirely possible that we might meet some different nasty folks on our run to freedom, people who would recognize marketable commodities when they saw them. Chaffi, on the other hand, brought along a beautifully chased, single-barrelled, twelve-gauge shotgun, not the weapon I would choose when venturing into Al Qaeda–land.

Mustapha Liman Chaffi was a very different kind of negotiator and perhaps both types were required to get the job done. Chaffi told me he was Mauritanian and had been doing "special tasks" for President Compaoré for many years. He was a deeply intelligent, subtle, tenacious, and courageous person.

On our long drive out of the Sahara we talked of many things, and I quickly realized that I was dealing not only with a West African political practitioner of enormous experience but also an extremely sophisticated observer of the broader African scene. So I asked him, "What's been happening in Africa over the past four and a half months?"

"Where in Africa?" he replied, presuming, perfectly reasonably, upon my ignorance.

"Well, start in Tangiers and when you get to Cape Town, stop." He laughed good-naturedly, took a deep breath, and proceeded to do just that. He knew who had done and was contemplating doing what to whom in every nook and cranny of that great continent.

Africa is huge (20 percent of the earth's surface—bigger than the continental USA, Western Europe, China, India, and Japan combined). Chaffi knew many of the secrets, successes, and failures of its fifty-three extremely different governments. He knew a lot of the key personalities and a great deal about the continent's rich linguistic and religious make-up, which make Africa more diverse than any other major region on the face of the earth. His exposé was masterful and I wish I could have recorded it.

We talked of my UN mission in Niger and he offered informed

insights into the challenges I had faced there. Both he and Baba strongly shared my suspicions that we had effectively been handed to AQIM by the government of then President Mamadou Tandja of Niger.

I asked him to tell of his first meeting with AQIM and he recounted this harrowing tale:

After our phone call with President Compaoré and his discussion with Omar One on 10 March, there had been further calls and eventually Chaffi was invited to go north to meet with Belmokhtar. He was given a set of precise coordinates and told to be at that location, deep in the Sahara, at a certain hour on a certain night. He and a colleague, I think from the Burkinabé armed forces, surged north over a few days until his GPS told him that he had arrived at the right spot about an hour before the agreed time.

He left the lights on, as instructed, and waited . . . and waited. Four interminable hours after the designated rendezvous time vehicle lights flashed in the distance some hundreds of metres away. He waited as he had been directed for somebody to approach him. Two hours later lights flashed again but from a different direction. Then another wait, following which lights flashed from the four points of the compass and then all four vehicles drove in close. Somebody approached his window and, without a word, handed him a slip of paper with another set of coordinates and a new time for the following evening. Then abruptly, all four vehicles departed.

He got out his GPS and determined that the new rendezvous was far distant, so far that he was not sure they could make it. They drove for most of the next twenty-four hours. Then at the next rendezvous they went through essentially the same routine. At the point when four vehicles revealed themselves, he was relieved of phones, GPS, and all other electronic devices and was told to follow them. For some hours he tore after them until they reached a camp, where he met Belmokhtar the next morning. Not everybody would find that fun.

On the trip that had secured our liberation, his fourth into the Sahara, he and Baba had been wandering about the Sahara for ten days—far more than we had thought—as Abou Zeid stewed about whether or not he would release the Europeans and on what terms. Chaffi confirmed that our deal had been done—fully settled—when our abductors told us on Saturday, 11 April, Day 119, that we were to be freed. Over the intervening ten days Baba and Chaffi had moved from bleak spot to bleak spot, using up their fuel, water, and food and trying their health and patience as Belmokhtar and Abou Zeid wrestled over the details and our big liberation show was being brought together. He was not surprised when I described our perilous end game and did not consider my worries unfounded when I told him I believed that had he and Baba left the desert because either their supplies or their patience had been exhausted, it would probably have spelled the end for us.

The most distressing moment in that long drive south out of the Sahara came when Chaffi spoke of the trip Compaoré had asked him to make to "negotiate away the death-threat ultimatum" immediately following their receipt of the third video, made on 31 March, Day 108. Once deep in the Sahara, he had again been put through the stressful vetting procedure to ensure he had not been followed and that Belmokhtar was not being set up. When he finally arrived at Khaled's camp late in the evening, he had been told that the emir would not see him until the next morning. Negotiations opened early and had been confrontational and difficult from the outset. Chaffi said it had been like talking to a stone wall. He could not get them to budge on any issue. Finally, late in the afternoon, Jack abruptly stood up, declared the discussions were at an end, and instructed Chaffi to leave the camp immediately. Chaffi asked for a few more minutes but Belmokhtar just walked away.

Chaffi returned to his vehicle and began very slowly to pack up and then stopped. He spread out his blanket, sat down, and began to read. Various of Belmokhtar's lieutenants passed by and asked him why he had not gone, why he was disobeying their chief's orders, but Chaffi engaged them in innocuous conversation, regaling them with all sorts of stories that had nothing whatsoever to do with the reason he was there. Bit by bit he won back their interest and then their confidence.

Soon Jack walked by and observed, "You're still here!" However, rather than again sending Chaffi away, he sat down with the others, saying little, and Chaffi continued his inconsequential stories, seeking to nurture some kind of rapport.

Eventually, Belmokhtar sent all save Ahmed away and said something along the lines of "Where were we?" And seamlessly the negotiations resumed, to conclude four or five hours later, as they all sat in the absolute darkness of the desert well past midnight. Chaffi returned to Ouagadougou over the next two days, the ultimatum having been lifted and an agreement in place that the third video was deemed no longer to exist and would never be aired. I believe, however, that portions of the audiotrack may have received some subsequent distribution. It is reasonable to assume that had Chaffi left Belmokhtar's camp as originally ordered, we would have been nourishing hyenas in the Sahara shortly thereafter.

After an extended silence in the course of our long sprint to freedom, Chaffi turned to me and, giving me an uncertain look, asked, "Would you like to know how they would have done it?"

"Done what?" I replied.

"How they would have killed your friend," gesturing with his thumb back toward where Louis sat on his tires in the back of the truck, "and then, perhaps, you?" I was not at all sure that I wanted to hear this, but he was clearly anxious to tell me, so I nodded.

To sharpen his focus during those long hours of negotiation, they told him that they had decided they would kill Louis first, in order to get the attention of Canada and the United Nations, before they decided whether I should get the same treatment. They explained that they would have stuffed our mouths with cotton wool and then put tape over our lips to prevent unpleasant sounds being heard on the video and to ensure that there would be no unseemly eruptions of blood from the mouth when the sword was drawn—some practitioners insist that it be done slowly—across our throats. It's a story that tends to stick in the mind.

Throughout that epic nine-hundred-kilometre run south to Gao on Wednesday, 22 April, Louis refused to cede his position in the back. Shortly after our pre-dawn departure, we left whatever track we had been on the night before and set off cross-country. Baba was a genius at the wheel. He eschewed use of a GPS, navigating in this featureless moonscape by memory and feel and with confidence and aplomb. But neither he nor Chaffi was relaxed and, as we smashed southward into the morning, the truck with the two women kept falling behind, to the evident annoyance of Baba. On the third occasion we had to stop and wait for them to catch up, I went back with Baba to see how they were doing. The answer was: not well.

Marianne was again by the window and in addition to her other injuries and problems, the bouncing about had opened up a gash in her scalp, which was bleeding down her small, skeletal face. Gabriella explained that Marianne could not hold herself down with only one hand (well did I remember that problem), particularly as she strove to protect the damage caused by the scorpion sting on her other arm. Gabriella could not simultaneously protect herself and Marianne from the extreme buffeting. Baba immediately grabbed some rope and despite feeble protests from Marianne proceeded to lash her into her seat. It was unpleasant but it worked, and at the next stop she allowed it was a distinct improvement.

Clearly Baba and Chaffi believed we still faced considerable risks. They noted that were we to take longer rest stops in an effort to ease the strain on the women—particularly Marianne—the risks to all of us would rise exponentially. In addition, sitting in a truck at fifty degrees would only further sap her strength and there were no oases around. They explained that they believed there was a real possibility that Abou Zeid might change his mind and come after us, particularly as he had never really decided to let the women go the previous afternoon when Belmokhtar had ordered us to leave. All the other denizens of the Sahara shadow world made our negotiators nervous too: the gun and drug runners, people movers, and classic smugglers, to say nothing of Ibrahim Ag Bahanga's Tuareg renegades, all of whom would be vividly interested in us.

So we bulled our way through similar obstacles to those we had endured on the way north 130 days earlier: through vast fields of high, treacherous dunes (getting stuck only once) and across baking stretches of hardpan desert and everything in between. But this time, at least, we were not tied and despite renewed damage to my back, we were free and going home. Nothing could make that anything but wonderful. We drove for twelve hours due south, again furiously, infused with the palpable fear and concern of our negotiators.

It was not until we had passed some unremarked point perhaps a dozen hours into our journey out of the desert and much closer to Gao, that Baba turned to me and, with some formality, said, "Now, you are probably safe." Drunk with the glory of our freedom, I had not fully comprehended the extent to which our rescuers believed until that moment how significantly unsafe we had been.

About a hundred kilometres north of Gao, we surged out of the desert onto a rough dirt track that allowed us to pick up our speed a little, which only increased the strain on my damaged lower vertebrae and coccyx. Marianne Petzold was probably suffering worse punishment in the second truck. As we approached Gao—perhaps twenty kilometres out—in the gathering dusk, we saw a truck parked by the side of the road with a few men milling about alongside. Without hesitation, Baba veered off the road, accelerating into the desert and giving the scene a wide berth. I've no idea whether it was a genuinely threatening situation but clearly he was taking no chances.

When we rejoined the road five or six kilometres later, the second truck was no longer behind us, but Baba blasted forward as he tried to raise its driver on his cellphone. He kept losing the connection, however, and on the outskirts of the town he moved very reluctantly to the side of the road and waited for them to catch up. After twenty minutes, he could stand it no longer. Nor could the long-suffering and sandblasted Louis, who was still refusing to cede his place in the back. Both of us were tortured by the thought that all this screwing around would again cause freedom to elude us.

Recalling we had passed a fork in the road a few hundred metres back, we retraced our route, took the other fork and still could not find them. Finally we got a clean cell connection and the Malian lieutenant directed us to a tiny two-man police post some distance along the road we were now on. It was a relief to see their truck beside a waiting police officer who seemed to be about sixteen. Baba roughly demanded that the other truck follow him and, this time, keep up. Just before he hit the gas, however, policeboy demanded to see his papers.

This elicited something that was probably not polite in the local dialect and as the kid's AK came up, Baba thrust a letter at him signed by the President of Mali demanding that the bearer receive any and all assistance. But the kid couldn't read. So, grabbing the letter back, Baba shouted that he was off to a rendezvous with half the nation's security police, who were waiting a short distance away. Then, covering the policeboy in a hail of gravel, our small two-truck convoy was on its way again. The centre of my back felt exceedingly hollow and I considered that being shot by the Malian police would be an odd way to end all this.

Roaring ahead on an increasingly populated road in the gathering darkness, Baba established a good cell connection with a Malian Security Services colonel who talked us into a small clearing a little way off the road. There were half a dozen large black SUVs in a rough open circle and yet again a lot of guys with guns. We were introduced to the colonel, further official proof that we were safe.

Chaffi approached me with a cellphone, as he had promised he would do what seemed to be a lifetime ago, and invited me to call my family. I punched in the number of Mary's cellphone, and a gruff male voice answered immediately. Confused, I asked for Mary, but first I had to convince the RCMP officer looking after her that I was who I said by answering another skill-testing question, to whit, "What do you eat when you take your granddaughter Alice to get your hair cut in Toronto?" When I answered "sushi," she was passed the phone and I told my extraordinary wife that I was free, in safe hands in Gao and that, indeed, as she had promised, she had guided me home and we would be able to enjoy all those dreams together.

Our daughter Ruth had come up to Ottawa from New York to be with Mary a couple of days earlier, when she had been told we might actually be freed, so I was also able to have a happy and all too brief chat with her to celebrate my freedom, before passing the phone to Louis.

Once Louis had spoken to Mai, the now quite large convoy made its way to the Governor's residence in the centre of town. After contacting the Canadian team in Bamako—and downing three tepid Cokes—we were ushered with some formality into a vast guest suite with an equally large bathroom and told, triumphantly, "You may wash." I am quite convinced that anyone who came near us would have thought that was almost as fine an idea as did we. However, when we turned our first taps in four and a half months, there was no water.

At dinner, in a scene straight out of *Charlie Wilson's War,* when the Governor asked what I would most wish to drink, I wondered only a little shamefacedly if a beer might be possible in this Islamic and therefore officially dry country. There was an exchange of furtive looks. At a curt nod from the Governor, an extremely gracious and engaging former army colonel, one of his aides scurried into the night and quickly returned bearing a brown paper bag, which he handed me whispering quietly and not a little surprisingly into my ear, "It's not a [Labatt's] 50, but I hope you will enjoy it."

Aside from the beer and many wonderful fruit juices and soft drinks, I did not have the stomach for the very freest range chicken that was on offer. This worried our host. So the Governor leapt to his feet declaring, "I know just what will do the trick," and disappeared into the kitchen to return a few minutes later with a bowl of . . . rice and milk. I sat transfixed with horror as Louis explained that this was the staple we had eaten twice a day for 130 days that had been a major contributor to my near-terminal constipation. The Governor immediately understood, sending the bowl back to the kitchen, and allowed that he had assumed (like everybody else) that my stomach problems were quite the opposite and that I was in need of a culinary cork.

While we enjoyed the Governor's hospitality there were more calls back to the Canadian team at the embassy twelve hundred kilometres away in the capital, Bamako. We also got to speak to our families again—this time enjoying more relaxed and normal conversation without the need to first establish our identities— and we learned that they were already assembling for the flight to Europe, where we would shortly see them.

Startlingly, the team in Bamako proposed that one of us travel with Chaffi the roughly twelve hundred kilometres over a very poor road to Ouagadougou, while the other proceeded over an equally poor road a similar distance to Bamako accompanied by Malian security officers. Apparently, the reasoning was to allow one of us to thank one of our benefactors while the other thanked the remaining one, and in the process take a road trip the equivalent of Toronto–Winnipeg, Detroit–Los Angeles, or Warsaw–Madrid. Eventually, saner heads prevailed and we were informed that a plane would pick us up in Gao around midnight to fly us to the capital. A few hours later we were flown out, but the two Canadians who came on that plane to fetch us, a thousand kilometres from Al Qaeda–land, never set foot outside the aircraft in Gao, a city of sixty thousand and the administrative capital of eastern Mali.

As we left the Governor's residence for the airport, I went to talk to Marianne, who by this time was covered in blankets and securely strapped to a stretcher atop a wheeled gurney. On seeing me she sobbed, "Bob, you abandoned me," and it was true—as I made those calls while swilling half a dozen different juices, soft drinks, and that glorious beer, I had in fact lost sight of what might be happening to Marianne. I regretted my thoughtlessness. Gabriella had dined with us, but as she'd had to leave her husband, Werner, behind in the vicious clutches of Abou Zeid and his gang of thugs, her celebration of freedom was a severely muted affair and her being lost in her own thoughts was all too understandable.

I stayed by Marianne's side, but once we were aboard the aircraft I was caught up in the red tape of my freedom and an onslaught of police debriefings. She and Gabriella were met in Bamako, as were we, by their respective national representatives, and I never saw them again.

AFTERMATH

CHAPTER 17

BAMAKO AND OUAGADOUGOU, GERMANY, AND HOME

===

He went like one that hath been stunn'd,
And is of sense forlorn:
A sadder and a wiser man
He rose the morrow morn.

===

Around midnight we boarded the special flight and a little more than two hours later landed in Bamako. Most members of the Canadian interdepartmental team that had been managing our situation at the African end, along with their Malian counterparts, were at the airport in those wee hours to greet us. What a joy it was to see those people on the tarmac! At this point I had been awake for three days, so I was barely coherent. We were taken to the Radisson Hotel, which had become Task Force Headquarters, arriving around 3:00 a.m. I still could not sleep, however, so I pottered about my vast hotel room touching normal things, finding all the stuff I had left in my Niamey hotel room 131 days previously, and trying—and failing—to make some sense of it all.

Of all the joys of that hotel, the greatest was the shower, to which I kept returning. It took five magnificent long, steaming sessions before sand ceased to cover the floor of the shower stall. The

RCMP insisted on taking a "before" picture in which I am finally clean but wearing what I put on when Omar One directed me to don my Western clothes for the liberation ceremony, deep in the Sahara.

The next day there were gracious, thoughtful, calls from Prime Minister Harper, UN Secretary-General Ban Ki-moon, Jean Chrétien, and many others. And then a very pretty young hairdresser was ushered into my room to see if she could make me look presentable for our call on President Amadou Toumani Touré that afternoon.

I decided to keep the beard, at least until the family convened the next day in Germany. So she hacked off most of it, along with much of my wild hair, leaving a reasonably trim white fringe around my tanned, weather-beaten, and stress-lined face. The first look in the hotel mirror had been pretty shocking. For his part, Louis chose to keep his sumptuous patriarchal beard, which his clan promptly voted off ten minutes after our arrival in Ramstein. The Fowler girls, however, had grown up with a bearded dad, as I'd worn a beard from age twenty to forty, so they voted to keep it.

In the afternoon we called on Malian President Touré and his Foreign Minister, my old friend Moctar Ouane. It was such a pleasure to express our deep gratitude to them for bringing us safely home. Indeed, had it not been for the generosity and steadfast affection for Canada on the part of Presidents Touré and Compaoré, their deep personal engagement, their political courage, and the willingness and determination of their brave negotiators, Baba and Chaffi, to assume considerable risks on our behalf, we would not be revelling today in our freedom and in the joy of our reunited families. The Fowlers, and here I can confidently also speak for the Guays, will be ever grateful to such fast friends of Canada and indeed, of ours.

I had met ATT a few times prior to these events and knew Moctar well. He and I had served together at the United Nations. When Mali was elected to the Security Council in 2000, I had already been representing Canada on the Council for a year and had another year to serve. We became friends. He experienced first-hand my passion for Africa, and I hope I was able to ease his entry into that bewildering club, which, unlike Al Qaeda, takes no prisoners. He returned any such courtesy ten-thousandfold.

These two neighbouring presidents, Touré and Compaoré, have had their differences, but in order to extract us from the clutches of Al Qaeda, they set these aside and worked together to make our release possible. I know that Canada could not have done it without them.

Omar One had told us one morning, with a derisive snort, that Radio France Internationale had reported that President Touré had informed the media in Belgium, where he was on an official visit, that Louis and I were in good health. ("How would he know?" Omar spat.) However ATT had come to this conclusion, we thought it might bring some comfort to our families. He was telling our loved ones what, we later understood, Canada would not, and then he effectively told them that we had received their shipment.

In a 3 April 2009 press report that also had ATT commenting on our well-being, Agence France-Presse noted, "Touré said his country was working discreetly to win the release of the hostages, adding: 'They came to Africa to bring peace. It is unacceptable that their freedom is taken away. . . . Mali and Canada have become closer because of this hostage taking. We are working together diplomatically to find the best solution.'"

In a long piece in the *Globe and Mail* on 24 April, infelicitously headlined "Operation Diplomat," Colin Freeze quoted President Touré as saying, immediately following our release, "Canada never asked us for anything. For once this friend asked us for help. Of course it was Mali's duty to help." I think that just about sums it up. Mali and ATT simply were not going to leave Canada in the lurch.

The next morning we flew to Ouagadougou to pay our respects to President Compaoré and to thank him, too, for the essential part he had played in allowing us to keep body and soul, indeed body and head, together and in bringing our ordeal to a happy conclusion. President Compaoré was accompanied by Mustapha Chaffi, who must have driven all night and most of the previous day to be there in time. We had last seen him in Gao, about forty hours and twelve hundred kilometres earlier.

President Compaoré could not have been more gracious and welcoming. There was no press, no fuss, and an hour later we were back at the airport. Then from Burkina Faso it was on to the vast U.S. Air Force base at Ramstein in Germany.

Linton and Justine had come up from Toronto to join Mary and Ruth in Ottawa, and along with members of Louis' family they all flew to Germany, where they were joined by Antonia from London. All of them were in place at the air base when we arrived from Ouagadougou in the evening of Friday, 24 April.

Prior to our arrival, military psychiatrists had briefed our families on what might emerge from the aircraft and how they should behave. It was explained that after four and a half months of being told what to do by our jailers, of having been deprived of any free will, we would react badly to being given instructions by anyone, even those we held most dear, so they had to be careful about demanding anything. Unfortunately, this wise advice seems not to have stood the test of time.

When the aircraft door opened, I saw Mary and Mai clutching each other at the foot of the stairs and a moment later I fell into Mary's arms and managed to say very little, savouring the moment I had dreamt of all those long months. She was so evidently well, whole, and happy, and I was safe and with her. I looked around for our daughters but they were being held back against the possibility that we would not be presentable. Mary explained that they were all awaiting my arrival at the Landstuhl Medical Centre a few kilometres away, where we were headed.

The girls had been to the base department store and decorated my hospital room with all the things they imagined I had missed: my beloved jujubes, chocolate bars, photos and letters from the grandchildren, a denim shirt, and the current edition of *Foreign Affairs*. It was a wonderful reunion. Finally I knew for certain that we were all to be allowed to have our lives back.

Everyone was talking at once, and my story and theirs emerged in bursts and bits, all of it punctuated by tears and laughter. Eventually, some stern doctors shooed them away to their accommodation across the street at Fisher House, a largely privately financed facility for the families of U.S. service men and women damaged in Iraq and Afghanistan. As she left though, Mary served notice that she would be back at dawn and that she expected to be able to "sleep over" the next night, something she managed to do against all odds.

The medical staff was beyond outstanding, giving Louis and me exquisitely sensitive and gloriously efficient care. Our stomachs were examined and treated, our blood tested and rehabilitated. Everything was x-rayed and the compression fracture damage to my lower back and coccyx was confirmed. The ravages of too much sun were zapped with liquid nitrogen, and industrial-strength drops caused sand to bubble from my ears for days. We were given exercise advice—although we were judged to be in "remarkably good condition," if a little anemic and emaciated—and offered lots of wise counselling by young military psychologists who had seen far worse.

All the while, hospital rules and regulations were relaxed and suspended to allow us to catch up with our families between tests, treatments, and debriefings. In the halls, waiting rooms, and cafeterias, all of us were moved by the sight of so many young soldiers who had paid much heavier prices than had we through their service in Afghanistan and Iraq.

By the end of the third day we were allowed to go out to a local restaurant for dinner, and the Guays and our various minders were understanding about our desire to have this moment *en famille*. At the end of a marvellous few hours, selflessly allowing me the full limelight, Antonia informed us that she was pregnant with her first child, which was the perfect happy ending to this Fowler misadventure.

After a couple more days and further batteries of tests we flew back to Canada on Tuesday, 28 April 2009, where there was a quiet welcome reception in the Billy Bishop Lounge at the Canadian Forces Base portion of the Ottawa airport. Finally—after a warm farewell to Louis—Mary and I found ourselves at the home I had left in a snowstorm nearly five months before, the girls having gone back to their own homes to rebuild their lives with their own families. Suddenly everything seemed so normal, so solid, and so familiar that I couldn't help wondering if it had really happened.

EPILOGUE

FILLING IN THE BLANKS

===

The many men, so beautiful!
And they all dead did lie:
And a thousand thousand slimy things
Lived on; and so did I.

===

I n early November, about five weeks prior to Louis' and my capture, our next-door neighbour, CBC correspondent Paul Hunter,
joined Mary and me for coffee in our kitchen, where we were
discussing journalist Mellissa Fung's recent kidnapping in Afghanistan. Paul knew that I had held a variety of security and international affairs–related jobs in the Canadian public service and was
anxious to get my take on the most appropriate media posture with
regard to this calamity.

He said that the government had urged the CBC to be extremely
circumspect in its reporting of Fung's kidnapping and to rigorously
stick to factual accounts if anything needed to be covered at all.
Paul allowed there had been a lot of internal soul-searching, but
led by John Cruickshank (then head of CBC News), management
had agreed to follow such a strategy. Paul clearly believed that "the
Corp" had taken the right decision, as did I, and was pleased that

the imperative of protecting the safety of his colleague had trumped the need to get the story out.

"Great," I aggressively and not a little uncharitably replied. "It's wonderful you've come to such a wise decision when the life of one of your fellow journalists is at risk, but what will you do when I get kidnapped?"

On my return to Canada at the end of April 2009, Paul, who had offered Mary extraordinary support and friendship throughout my ordeal, told me that he had recalled this conversation almost every day I was away. His steadfast insistence that the CBC refrain from airing any material that could have a negative impact on Louis' and my situation or cause our families extreme worry and pain was influenced by this recollection and his belief that the CBC did have a commitment to be consistent—to treat others the way it had treated its own.

There is no doubt that the CBC decision to stick to factual, non-speculative reporting, and as little of that as possible, was the right one. Further, its intelligent and sensitive approach did influence other journalists and outlets—but by no means all—and that posture helped the resolution of our kidnapping and saved our families a lot of grief.

❖

During a September visit to Niger, two and a half months before our kidnapping, Louis and I had been accompanied to the troubled north by Minister of Defence Djida Hamadou. We got along well. I liked him and I believe the feeling was reciprocated. In the course of that visit he had invited me to be his guest at the celebrations marking the fiftieth anniversary of Nigerien independence, which would take place from 17 to 19 December 2008, centred this particular year in his own political constituency of Tillabéri, 120 kilometres up the N1 highway, northwest of Niamey.

On Friday afternoon, 12 December, as we left a long, confrontational, and unpleasant meeting with Minister of the Interior

Albadé Abouba (known widely as President Tandja's "adoptive son"), I received an urgent request through our accompanying protocol officer from Minister Hamadou to meet him in his office as soon as possible. We went there straight away. When we arrived the usual coterie of hangers-on and supplicants was absent from his outer office. We were ushered into the inner sanctum to find only the Minister, no slouching, bored, and cynical generals, no fawning political assistants.

Mr. Hamadou was evidently ill at ease. He was pacing and did not ask us to sit. He apologized for being brusque but said he would get straight to the point. He had been looking forward to receiving us in Tillabéri the following Wednesday and Thursday, he allowed, but he had just been told by President Tandja that he would instead be representing the government at the local and very subsidiary independence celebrations in Agadez, in the north. Therefore he was sorry but he would not be there to honour his invitation and receive us in Tillabéri along with the President and the remainder of the government. With the attitude of someone repeating unequivocal and unwelcome instructions, he noted that we were welcome to proceed to Tillabéri but that the President's decision was final.

I guess my surprise showed, but he offered nothing more, shrugging heavily with palms raised, as if to add, "What can I say?" I suppose I ought to have read more into it. The meeting was over in less than three minutes and as we retreated from Minister Hamadou's office, confused and not a little annoyed, Louis and I wondered what Tillabéri would be like, surrounded by a palpably hostile government, now that we had been unhosted.

In the aftermath of the 11 December 2007 AQIM attack on UN premises in Algiers, Secretary-General Ban Ki-moon of the United Nations asked its most accomplished diplomat, former Algerian Minister of Foreign Affairs Lakhdar Brahimi, to chair a panel of experts to look into the "strategic issues vital to delivery and enhancement of the security of United Nations personnel and premises and the changing threats and risks faced by it." To that end, the panel (universally known as the Brahimi Panel) produced a report entitled *Towards a Culture of Security and Accountability*, and presented it to the Secretary-General on 9 June 2008, six months before our abduction and a few weeks before my appointment as Special Envoy.

Paragraph 250 of the Brahimi Panel report noted, in part, "The primary responsibility of Member States for the security and safety of UN officials and premises is a guiding principle of the United Nations security management system. This responsibility derives from the inherent function of government to maintain law and order on their national territory."

Perfectly reasonably, the executive summary also noted in paragraph 18, "Member States are not equally well-equipped to provide that security. Indeed, it is quite often in those countries where capacity is modest or lacking altogether that the most serious risks exist. All the UN can and should expect from the host government is that it provides security to the best of its ability. The central element of the cooperation and trust between the two sides is information sharing about security conditions."

The issue with regard to Louis' and my kidnapping, of course, was that the government of the member state in question, that of President Tandja in Niger, detested the United Nations in general and my mission in particular. Not only were the President and his Minister of the Interior not providing me with security to the best of their ability over the weekend of 13 and 14 December 2008 but they were, I believe, allowing or perhaps encouraging information relating to our security to be shared with Al Qaeda.

Utterly germane to our kidnapping—indeed, to everything we learned while being held captive by AQIM—the Brahimi Panel observed in paragraph 60 that "the explicit targeting of the UN by terrorist groups represents a sea-change among the threats the

Organization faces at present and will continue to face in the fore-
seeable future. The UN is being targeted by terrorists for what it is
and what it represents, not because its people happen to be in the
wrong place at the wrong time or for what any part of the Organization happens to have done at a particular place, at a particular
time. As such, this threat is not confined to any one country or
region; indeed, for this specific type of threat—that of al-Qaeda
and similar organizations—the UN is a potential target everywhere
it has a presence."

Of course the government of Niger was fully informed of our
plans for the entire trip, including that fateful weekend. Before leaving Canada we checked on several occasions—as we did each time
we visited—to ensure that the UN resident coordinator's office in
Niamey had provided the host government with copies of our latest
itinerary, and we received assurances that this had been done. We
proceeded in this way to facilitate the organization of our official
meetings and specifically to allow the host government to assess the
security requirements and put in place adequate protection so there
would be no embarrassing incidents.

This responsibility, as noted by Brahimi, is the exclusive prov-
ince of the host government, be it Canada's responsibility for the
preservation of the health and safety of foreign leaders attending
meetings in our country, or Niger's responsibility to protect the UN
Secretary-General's representatives.

Finally, I was at pains to ensure that the Niger government
had our itinerary well in advance of our arrival precisely because I
wanted to provide as little leeway as possible for President Tandja's
government to misconstrue the purpose of my visit or to avoid its
security responsibilities or, indeed, to invoke a lack of transparency
on our part as an excuse to reject my mission and send me packing,
as I knew the President and some of his officials would have dearly
liked to do.

On Monday, 15 December, the day following our kidnapping,
Nigerien Minister of Communications Mohamed Ben Omar told

an Agence France-Presse reporter, "The diplomat had not informed authorities or the UN office in Niger of his trip," a government of Niger line that was deployed for many days following our disappearance and was much reported in Canada. When we arrived in Niamey from Paris, on the evening of Thursday, 11 December, Louis and I were met at the steps of the aircraft by a vehicle from State Protocol and whisked away to the VIP lounge, where we were greeted by the chief of protocol, a representative of the presidency, the acting UN resident coordinator, the World Food Programme country director, and a number of senior officials, without having to worry about any customs and immigration formalities. Then we were taken off to our hotel in the same big, battered, clapped-out Mercedes driven by the same venerable old government retainer who had acted as my driver for the Niamey portions of my two earlier visits. And again a motorcycle outrider, with siren blaring, led the way. Not, I think, the attributes of a private, unofficial, or unsanctioned visit, or one about which the host government and the local UN Office were unaware.

Following the last meeting on Friday afternoon, 12 December, we discussed our weekend plans with our accompanying protocol officer at the Grand Hotel. We explained that the trip to the mine was fixed for Sunday and that on Saturday we intended to drive outside of town to get a feel for the country beyond formal and official encounters. He offered the view that the old Mercedes would not be up to the roads outside the city. Anticipating this, we told him the United Nations had offered us a four-by-four SUV suitable for such conditions and a driver who was a native of the local area and knew the way to the mine at Samira Hill. Further, we stressed that there would be lots of room for the protocol officer in the UN vehicle, where he could occupy the front passenger seat as he had for meetings within the capital.

He said that he would check with his office and let us know that evening. A few hours later, as promised, he called to say that "it had been decided" he would not accompany us. He wished us a good weekend and said he would see us at the hotel at 8:00 a.m. on Monday.

So who handed us to AQIM? Because surely somebody did. It had to be someone who had access to our itinerary, so it could have been anyone in or close to the UN Office in Niamey, or the UN Office responsible for the West African region in Dakar, or even someone at UN headquarters in New York. A number of individuals at each of these locations knew of our plans.

I believe it is much more likely, however, that the government of President Mamadou Tandja arranged—however indirectly—for information relating to our movements to reach AQIM. Aside from stopping the interference of a pesky foreigner from the United Nations, an organization that had so embarrassed Tandja in 2005 by suggesting that his people were starving—when, of course, they were—both he and his enforcer, Albadé Abouba, had every reason to want my mission to fail or just stop. The last thing they wanted was to see an end to the Tuareg rebellion.

The continuing rebellion allowed Tandja and his supporters to claim that the enemy was at the gate, even if the gate was many hundreds of kilometres north of the capital. Further, in December 2008, the President had one year left in his second five-year mandate and the constitution forbade a third term. He wanted to stay in power, and his backers needed him to do so. They had already begun to moot the requirement for constitutional changes that would allow Tandja to stay on. His plans for a referendum on that issue were twice ruled illegal by the Constitutional Court, so Tandja disbanded the court and dissolved the National Assembly. In June 2009, he announced that he was suspending the government and would rule by decree.

While a continuing Tuareg rebellion reinforced his case for such powers, how about Al Qaeda grabbing the UN Secretary-General's Special Envoy at the very gates of the capital? Now that was an enemy at the gate that even Washington, New York, and Paris could not ignore.

Ironically, I think that the combination of deteriorating domestic circumstances, flagrant disregard of parliament and the constitution, the ravages of continuing rebellion, curtailment of the freedom of the media and the NGO community, a worsening food crisis, and perhaps also suspicions regarding our kidnapping—suspicions widely entertained throughout the country and the region—caused growing resentment among a desperately ill-served population. Finally, a coup was launched in February 2010 that deposed Tandja and his government.

The interim Prime Minister was Mahamadou Danda, the former very helpful economics and public affairs officer at the Canadian Office in Niamey. And, most relevant to my mission, the rebellion in northern Niger is over. Various rebel factions talked peace with the interim government and have handed in their weapons. Following my release, I was able to resign my UN appointment knowing that in a rather unorthodox way my mission had been successfully completed. In March 2011, as promised by the coup perpetrators, Niger returned to civilian rule.

As for Tandja, after a year of house arrest following the February 2010 coup, press reports noted he had been sent to prison in the wake of an extensive audit that alleged he may have looted the treasury of one of the poorest countries in the world of some $125 million during his time in office. However, in May 2011, the appeals court ruled that it was impossible to try a head of state after that individual had left office. The court ordered Tandja's release.

On 9 January 2009 (our twenty-seventh day of captivity), Mary and Mai were invited to a meeting at DFAIT, the Department of Foreign Affairs and International Trade, their first since our capture on 14 December. They were met by a small group from DFAIT and the RCMP, and no other departments or agencies were present or allowed to be there. They were told almost nothing beyond the fact that there was no proof we had been killed.

Frustrated at every turn, Mary approached the most senior-level DFAIT official charged with responsibility for our situation to seek more regular and fuller briefings, but she was told that this would not be possible—other Canadians in similar situations could then make similar demands, which could not be accommodated. She pointed out that Louis and I had accumulated seventy-five years of public service between us—most of it with DFAIT—that they had seconded Louis to the UN, and that they had an obligation to treat families of staff members a lot better than had been the case thus far. Further, as DFAIT had demanded, understandably, that the United Nations butt out of the management of our case so as to ensure no confusion would result from the two players working at cross-purposes, DFAIT had effectively assumed full responsibility for me and my family as well. But they would not alter their policy. There would, Mary was informed, be no change in the nature, frequency, or content of the briefings. Happily, Janet Graham was eventually able to get this edict relaxed somewhat.

Some days later, Mary asked DFAIT for a meeting to clarify information about us that was circulating in the media, but she was told no such discussion could take place in the absence of the RCMP, and "the Force" (as the RCMP likes to call itself) was not available to meet with her.

On top of everything else, Mary and Mai were caught in a bureaucratic and financial Catch-22 at the United Nations that had resulted in our pay being frozen the day we were kidnapped. After all, since 14 December we had failed to submit signed attendance sheets.

Finally, to the discomfort and embarrassment of DFAIT, and to the deep annoyance of the RCMP, on 27 January Mary stormed down to UN headquarters in New York, where she had arranged to meet UN Secretary-General Ban Ki-moon and a variety of senior officials to try to sort things out herself and convince the organization that sent us to Niger to assume more responsibility, at least for our families' circumstances. The Secretary-General was shocked when he heard of the confusion and of how little Mary had been told. He promised her that the bureaucratic silliness would be straightened out "before you leave the building"—and it was, completely.

Secretary-General Ban Ki-moon then sat down with her, ignoring other scheduled meetings, and offered her a great deal of compassionate, personal support, sympathy, and practical encouragement. Then he told her, "We have good and explicit reason to believe that they are alive and in relatively good health." Hope soared.

Lying in the hot Sahara sand, having made a proof-of-life video recording on Day 5, I never imagined that it would take forty-five days before anyone told Mary that we were alive, or that the person who eventually passed her such happy news would not be a Canadian.

The fundamental fact of our alive status was well known among those managing our case within a couple of days of our capture. Since my return I have learned that several people with knowledge of our situation discussed it with others in Ottawa who had nothing whatsoever to do with government or the public service, others who had no "need to know" beyond their interest in and, perhaps, concern for us. Groups of people in friendly capitals shared our status with their spouses and friends in a variety of languages, but our families could not be told.

This lack of indication from any quarter that we were alive, coupled with rare and inadequate briefings and breathlessly speculative media reporting about the horrible things that might well have befallen us, led members of both families to begin mourning the loss of their fathers. Our kids confidently believed that were such information available—if my colleagues in Ottawa, among whom our children had grown up, knew we were alive—then surely they would have been told. Unfortunately, such confidence was misplaced.

Mary, however, demanded that our children believe we were alive, insisting there would be time enough for grieving should they learn that we were not. But she acknowledges that there were many occasions (such as when the *Globe and Mail* ran a front-page story on the dragging of the Niger River for our bodies) when she found this brave façade hard to maintain.

How easy it would have been to ease that pain. The RCMP seemed to have decided that our families could not be trusted with the knowledge we were alive. I can only assume they believed our families would handle such information irresponsibly and thereby wantonly put Louis' and my lives at risk. Nobody within the Ottawa bureaucracy seems to have challenged that preposterous assumption.

And how this retentive behaviour contrasts with the conduct of the Mellissa Fung case. John Cruickshank, the head of CBC news, has told me he was called daily, sometimes twice a day, by a very senior and sympathetic government official with a briefing on her situation. So the bureaucracy is capable of getting it right. When I came home, Mary asked me whether—if our situations had been reversed and she had been lying in the desert—I would have been treated as dismissively as she was. Very reluctantly, I had to conclude that that was simply inconceivable.

In fact, no Canadian told Mary that I had survived the grab on 14 December until RCMP officials called her in Ottawa on Day 48 (30 January) with news—"A videotaped message has been delivered in Mali"—and they wanted her to see it. On our Day 51 (2 February), just one day before we made the second proof-of-life video on Day 52, Mary viewed the first proof-of-life video message, the one I had recorded on Day 5.

The RCMP brought a laptop to our house. Mary and Linton were joined by Mai and one of her daughters, and Mary had asked our great friend Ted Johnson to be there as well. The screening was wrenching. Mary could tell that my back was bothering me, that I didn't have my glasses, that Louis and I were both drawn and worried, and generally pretty fragile. Needless to say, the ferocious tableau behind us didn't help, nor did my bizarre lapses about working for "the Secretary-General of the United States" and my reference to having five children. Despite all that, they were so very relieved to see that we had survived the grab. It seemed to them, therefore, not to be about assassination—even if it was all too clearly about Al Qaeda. So perhaps it was a typical kidnapping.

The issue became what had happened to us over the intervening forty-six days. RCMP officials offered no explanation for the delay and nothing about our current status, though I now know they had up-to-date confirmation that we were still alive, information they again refused to share.

Where was DFAIT in all this? Where was the Foreign Affairs department in fighting for the rights and welfare of the broader foreign service family? What about the Foreign Service Community Association, or that most improbable of unions, PAFSO (the Professional Association of Foreign Service Officers), of which Louis was a member? Is this how the families of Canadian officials and aid workers (or indeed any Canadian citizen), sent into harm's way by international organizations or their government to all those challenging, difficult, and dangerous places, expect their families to be treated? Indeed, is it how any self-respecting enterprise ought to handle its staff and families when tragedy strikes?

Everything suggests that Canada had been offered the first video almost immediately after it was made on 18 December 2008, possibly for a price. The RCMP did not trust (good heavens!) the intermediaries and may have refused to pay or even meet with such people until more than six weeks later—as we lay alternately freezing and broiling in desperate circumstances in the desert. Finally, and only when the RCMP saw press reports from Agence France-Presse detailing what others had seen, the video was acquired either directly or from some other service.

I cannot prove this thesis, however, and "the Force" will not talk to me about it. Maybe those inexplicably wasted six weeks offer some clue why, even now, the RCMP steadfastly refuses to give me copies of these recorded video messages; or, perhaps, some thorny issue of Al Qaeda copyright is to blame.

Following my return, I wrote repeatedly to the Commissioner of the RCMP, Bill Elliott, asking for copies of the videos made on Days 5 and 52 and noting that Louis supported my request. The Commissioner wrote back on 16 April 2010—five months later—to say, "The RCMP is not in a position to release the videos to you," and while offering no explanation, he added (however wisely) that were I to apply under the Access to Information Act, the response would be the same.

Mary constantly travelled between Ottawa, New York, Toronto, and London to keep in touch with our children. From 6 to 16 February she was visiting Antonia and her family in London. They had not benefited from most of the support and bonding that the three North American–based daughters had enjoyed and had extended to Mary since our kidnapping. The day before she left for London, on 4 February, Mary met with the DFAIT/RCMP team and had them promise her that they would contact her, directly or through the Canadian High Commission, should anything significant occur.

On 10 February, Mary and Antonia had lunch with our friend Jim Wright, Canada's High Commissioner to the United Kingdom. Over lunch Jim remarked, "You must have been pleased to hear of the new video message, and to know Bob is still alive." Seeing the shock on both their faces, he clenched his jaw and excused himself, returning some time later without a word. Some minutes after that, a member of his staff interrupted to say there was an urgent call for Mary from the RCMP in Canada. She took the call in an adjoining room and learned—surprise—that there was a second video message.

She asked to see it immediately. The RCMP spuriously claimed that "for security reasons" the video could not be sent electronically to London and further, that to do so "would contaminate the evidence." Thus, if she wanted to see it, she would have to return to Canada. Mary declared that to be nonsense, but only after she appealed to a much higher authority did the RCMP concede that the video could be shown to her in London. The next day, 11 February (our Day 60), Mary and Antonia watched the recording at the High Commission—this time only eight days after it was made but three days after its existence was revealed through an Agence France-Presse report out of Mali. So they then knew we had been alive on Day 52, but again the RCMP offered no further update.

I had written a letter to Mary to accompany the second video, but she was not told of its existence for many days and not allowed to see it for two weeks. Even then she was shown only a copy. To this day, the RCMP insists on retaining the original of my letter to my wife "as evidence."

RCMP officials were incapable of seeing our situation outside the narrow and highly distorted prism of a Canadian criminal investigation; beyond, that is, the compilation of a case file, the amassing of forensic evidence. For "the Force" it was exclusively about bringing Mokhtar Belmokhtar and his accomplices to court in Mali or even in Canada, securing a conviction, and putting him and the members of his *katiba* in jail. The RCMP officers were neither capable of understanding nor much interested in the broader geopolitical complexities and implications of the fraught and dangerous situation in which we found ourselves, even though many of those complexities were quite capable of ending our lives.

The first Canadians I spoke to following our release were RCMP officers, and they interviewed me endlessly: on the plane from Gao to Bamako, in the Radisson Hotel in Bamako, between tests at the hospital in Germany, and as soon as I set foot back in Ottawa. They were not interested in learning how to defeat Al Qaeda, how to protect Canadians working in that part of the world from experiencing what we had just been through, or how to rescue the two remaining captives. Their exclusive interest was forensic—whom had I brushed up against and when during my captivity so they could search for and catalogue the relevant DNA on the sleeve of my tattered shirt in order to build a case for the criminal prosecution of our AQIM kidnappers. I believe that, instead, we ought to have been using most of that energy, those resources, and every available moment to work with others simply to destroy the threat that AQIM represents.

Our misadventure took place dramatically far beyond the RCMP's known world and bore little resemblance to a kidnapping in Canada. Nevertheless, the RCMP jealously defended its turf as "the Canadian government's hostage negotiator," insisting that this authority applied to Tombouctou as fully as it did to Regina and that its expertise was equally applicable to either, when so manifestly it was not. Its officers consistently asserted that theirs was "the lead department" (and while some have denied this was the case, there were certainly no other evident contenders), but never understood the extent to which West Africa was not western Canada.

All this said, a number of individual RCMP officers worked selflessly and tirelessly and to the very best of their abilities, risking their health and abandoning their families, to secure our freedom, and I owe them a debt of gratitude.

By now it will be all too evident that I believe the RCMP did not manage our kidnapping intelligently, expeditiously, or effectively, and certainly not sensitively. I do not think those police officers are equipped to handle cases of such complexity—cases that go far beyond the purview of international police liaison, the RCMP's classic international remit. The RCMP is a huge bureaucracy and bound to have its weaknesses, but our case revealed that the most egregious ones were at the top. In addition, the way our kidnapping was managed exposed fundamental failures of policy and procedure and highlighted significant jurisdictional anomalies.

On 23 February, in a briefing at Foreign Affairs during which Mary asked for confirmation of the accuracy of media reports that suggested AQIM had made ransom demands, a senior RCMP officer interrupted, pointing his finger across the table to where she sat, and gratuitously snapped, "As long as I am in charge of this investigation not one cent will be paid for the release of these high muckety-mucks." Her confidence in the RCMP, or at least its senior management, was finally and irrevocably shattered.

The issue that still causes me visceral anger is the lack of trust, courtesy—even respect—on the part of some of those charged with dealing with our families. This attitude, in our family's view, too often threatens, however unreasonably, to overshadow the hard, innovative work done by so many others to win our release. This particular high muckety-muck has nothing but scorn for a senior RCMP officer who would seek to bully Al Qaeda kidnap victims' families already distraught and vulnerable enough, and nothing but contempt for those who would stand aside and allow this to happen.

This book is not the place to engage more broadly the current and recurring woes of the RCMP. Suffice it to say that any suggestion it is an organization suffering a deep leadership crisis and in need of radical repair, and a fundamental re-examination of its mandate, would meet with my hearty agreement. The thought that these posturing naïfs are the locus of knowledge and expertise regarding international kidnappings and are responsible within the Canadian government for managing and negotiating complex international hostage crises, to say nothing of playing an essential part in countering terrorist threats to Canada, simply chills the soul. They are not, in my view, up to such tasks, and the sooner the government comes to understand this stark reality the better it will be for all Canadians.

The significant exceptions to the above assessment were the warm, sympathetic, and stalwart family liaison officers, or FLOs, whom I will always admire for the way they cared for Mary and our girls. Tony and Mike's regular duties consisted of considerably more hands-on police work. Mary and the girls reported that they were open minded and had strong, proud family, professional, and civic values—in addition to being downright decent guys. They will forever remain a welcome extension of the Fowler clan.

Most personally disappointing, however, is that those few in DFAIT, my old department, charged with the management of our case in Ottawa allowed themselves to be browbeaten and marginalized to the point that the Department of Foreign Affairs and International Trade was often incapable of bringing to bear its now too often vestigial understanding of how things really work in far-flung parts of the world. While this is deplorable, nobody who follows the fortunes of that once proud department could pretend to be surprised. That DFAIT allowed our families to be treated with such disdain by the RCMP is, however, nothing short of disgraceful.

The vast bulk of our colleagues in the cowed and bankrupt Foreign Affairs department strove mightily, against the aforementioned odds, to bring us home, and they have my deep respect and gratitude. Similarly, in other departments and agencies of government, legions of people worked tirelessly and effectively on our behalf and were prepared to assume significant personal risks to get the job done.

I should stress that my criticisms should not be read to include Mr. Harper's government. I have been and remain a vocal critic of his foreign policy, but I am assured the Prime Minister set the tone for the response to our kidnapping from the outset, making clear that no effort should be spared to get us home. Had that not been the case, such an outcome could never have been achieved.

On Sunday, 26 April, while Louis and I were undergoing medical tests in Germany, AQIM issued the following communiqué: "With this statement, we declare to the public opinion that with praise to Allah alone, four prisoners among our mujahedeen were released in exchange for the release of the hostages of the organization, namely: the Canadians (Robert Fowler and Louis Guay), the German (Marianne Petzold), and the Swiss (Gabriella Burco Greiner). On the other hand, we declare that the organization still holds the British tourist (Edwen [sic] Dyer) and the Swiss tourist (Werner Greiner) until the achievement of our legitimate demands."

A few days later I learned of Abou Zeid's demand for the release of Abou Qatada (allegedly the head of Al Qaeda operations in Europe) from a UK prison in return for Edwin Dyer's life. I knew then—was certain—that Mr. Dyer would be killed and offered that view, unbidden, to DFAIT along with my prognosis that after an unbearably horrible number of weeks or, less likely, months, Werner Greiner would be released, were he to survive the aftermath of such torment and summer in the Sahara.

However much I had expected that AQIM would kill someone, I was devastated by Dyer's beheading, on 31 May 2009, principally, of course, because so very often I had envisaged that Louis or I, or both of us, would suffer just such an end. And how easily it might have been one of us. Greiner then had to spend a further six weeks as Abou Zeid's prisoner before being released on 12 July 2009.

The next Westerner to be executed by AQIM was Michel Germaneau, a year after Dyer's murder. An Agence France-Presse report out of Mali noted, "The Frenchman was decapitated before the eyes of the head of the radical AQIM group that was holding him, Abdelhamid Abou Zeid, who last year executed a British hostage, Edwin Dyer. . . . AQIM has announced that it executed Germaneau, a seventy-eight-year-old aid worker, on Saturday [24 July 2010], in revenge for a joint raid last Thursday by Mauritanian and French troops, in which six fundamentalists were killed. Germaneau was seized in Niger on April 19."

French hostage Pierre Camatte was released on 23 February 2010, three days after four members of AQIM were freed from Malian jails and after vigorous intercession by both French Foreign Minister Bernard Kouchner and President Nicolas Sarkozy. Camatte had been taken by the Abou Zeid *katiba* at the end of

November 2009 from his hotel in Ménaka, in the far eastern part of Mali. According to the 30 March 2010 edition of *Jeune Afrique,* he knew the date of his release because he kept a scrap of cloth in his pocket, which, at the moment of his liberation, contained eighty-nine tiny knots.

There is a vigorous debate—only some of it public—about whether governments should even negotiate, let alone make any kind of deal, with hostage takers or, more specifically, pay ransoms or exchange prisoners to free their citizens. This dilemma is particularly acute when it involves those who have been sent into harm's way by those same governments or international organizations acting on behalf of their member states. The attitudes of governments, organizations, companies, NGOs, and families across the world toward such hostage crises cover the full spectrum of opinion and practice on this thorny question, and a great deal of hot air is expended seeking to justify one stance or another.

There tends also to be a significant difference between what governments do and what they say, and this seems to me quite reasonable. There are good arguments on most sides and a wealth of unhappy experience to buttress just about every position. Every time a "principled position" is invoked, there are exceptions. Many countries adopt what are more or less admittedly pragmatic approaches while others proclaim immutable doctrine, but I know for certain that everybody has blinked at one time or another.

I am also well aware that there is no way I can be objective about such issues. I've tried, but it's just not possible.

In Ottawa, British High Commissioner Anthony Cary formally protested the way Canada managed Louis' and my release (and then called the *Globe and Mail* to say that he had done so, as reported by Geoffrey York on 10 October 2009). According to York, "Sources

say that the British government complained to Canada about its
willingness to let Mali negotiate with the kidnappers, arguing that
Ottawa had 'betrayed international convention.' 'The job of releasing Mr. Dyer was made more difficult,' said a source. 'There was
considerable anger.'"

I cannot but speculate on what Mr. Cary's DFAIT interlocutors
might have said in response. From my perspective, he should have
been told to get stuffed: that Canada neither needed nor appreciated such cravenly self-serving and condescending preaching from
the Brits. And I certainly hope they demanded an explanation of
how my release made freeing Edwin Dyer "more difficult," but I
guess everybody understood full well that what Cary really meant
was that my beheading would have made Mr. Dyer's beheading
easier for the British government to explain.

Further, as the High Commissioner was acting on instructions,
I would like to think he might have been asked to convey to Her
Britannic Majesty's government the view from Canada that they
were a gang of egregious—not to say perfidious—hypocrites.

Perhaps, though, it did not happen that way. Perhaps we said we
were sorry, for that is our default position on most issues. Equally
likely, whichever hand-wringing officials at Foreign Affairs received
Cary's démarche had probably not bothered to do their homework.
Had they done so, they might have discovered that while the Brits
work hard to maintain the façade of a steely-eyed "never make
concessions—never pay" policy, if it's important enough, they find
a way to get the matter sorted.

In that regard, I wonder whether DFAIT called in High
Commissioner Cary in the early moments of 2010 to discuss the
release of Peter Moore, the British IT expert who spent thirty-one
months in captivity after being kidnapped in Baghdad. Moore was
released on 30 December 2009 after being tortured, beaten, and
subjected to mock executions. I am glad that Peter Moore is home
and safe with his family in Britain.

On 2 January 2010, John Burns of the New York Times wrote,

"Britain's Foreign Office has denied it engaged in a deal, saying Britain holds to a policy of not negotiating with hostage-takers and not offering any 'substantive concessions' to them. But within hours of Mr. Moore's release, the leader of the group accused in his kidnapping as well as the deaths of at least five American soldiers was transferred from American custody to Iraqi hands" and subsequently freed.

More recent is the case of Raymond Davis, an American held in a Pakistani jail for seven weeks after he shot two men dead in the streets of Lahore on 29 January 2011. Davis was suddenly released after somebody allegedly paid US$2.34 million to members of the two men's families. Secretary of State Hillary Clinton insisted that the United States did not pay, but somebody did.

Then there was the release on 21 September 2011 of Josh Fattal and Shane Bauer, who had been jailed in Iran for espionage since their arrest in July 2009 on the border with Iraq. Upon their liberation, President Obama said, "We are deeply grateful to His Majesty Sultan Qaboos bin Said of Oman, Iraqi President Jalal Talabani, the Swiss government, and to all our partners and allies around the world who have worked steadfastly over the past two years to secure the release of Shane and Josh." On 23 September *USA Today* reported that according to the lawyer for the two men, Masoud Shafiei, "Oman paid the $1 million bail." How happy I am that they are home, and, yes, how generous of the Sultan.

My point here is not to question or challenge policy—anyone's—but rather to highlight the fact that a degree of flexibility and innovation, not to mention humility, is inevitably part of any successful outcome. When, instead, doctrinaire and vainglorious posturing replace effective diplomacy, people get dead. I am also, of course, suggesting that henceforth, Canadians take no hypocritical crap from our close friends.

❖

Despite the profound commitment of so many, it seems to me that few of the lessons that should have been learned (principally by senior officials in the Ottawa bureaucracy) about the command and control of such a complicated case have even been acknowledged. On our return to Canada, Louis and I were asked by the RCMP and by DFAIT to participate in "lessons learned" exercises, and, of course, we were happy to agree to do so. As far as we are aware, though, neither organization has held such exercises. Neither Louis, who continued to work for DFAIT for more than two years after our release, nor I was ever even debriefed by DFAIT following our return from Al Qaeda captivity. I have, however, been extensively and, in most cases, expertly debriefed by other agencies, domestic and foreign—including the United Nations and even the New York Police Department—but not by Canada's Department of Foreign Affairs. As I am convinced that similar cases will inevitably occur, I hope this account might encourage better management at home and abroad, as well as the selection and training of appropriate individuals in order that they may be qualified to handle such cases before they happen.

In the fall and winter of 2009, over a period of a few months, AQIM took three Spaniards, two Italians, and two Frenchmen in separate kidnappings and then murdered the seventy-eight-year-old Michel Germaneau after he had spent three months as their captive. On 16 September 2010 they took seven people—five French, one Togolese, and one Malagasy—releasing the French woman and the two Africans five months later. In early January 2011, they took two young Frenchmen from a restaurant in downtown Niamey and headed north. They were intercepted, first by Nigerien forces and then by very fast-acting French Special Forces, but tragically both hostages were killed in the ensuing battles. Also in January 2011, they took an Italian woman from southern Algeria.

Our release was in so many respects "a near run thing," as the subsequent deaths of Edwin Dyer, Michel Germaneau, Antoine de Leocour, and Vincent Delory have brought home so clearly. If we are alive today, and even relatively sane, it is because some remarkably fine and skilled people were able to navigate impossibly complex national and international shoals to make the scenarios I doubted were practicable, as I lay there in the sand, achievable. I owe those brave, tireless, and creative few, and all who helped them, an enormous debt of gratitude.

For years Canada has been in the forefront of efforts to bring a measure of stability to the troubled Sahel region. We were leaders in the initial "coalition of the willing" seeking to restore order in Somalia. Despite the appalling torture-murder incident involving our troops that so marred that deployment, Canadian soldiers had considerable success in bringing an all too temporary respite to the violence that had plagued the region in central Somalia they were charged with protecting. Our diplomats, aid workers, and soldiers also struggled, along with many others, to bring an end to the murderous civil war between the Arab north and the African south of Sudan and then to monitor the ensuing peace agreement.

A number of us—notably Allan Rock, then representing Canada at the United Nations—made a serious, if not yet successful, stab at stopping the predations of Joseph Kony's Lord's Resistance Army, which has laid waste to northern Uganda for a generation and more recently to the northern Congo, and seen the abduction, rape, and murder of over thirty thousand children over the last two decades.

Canadians helped bring order to the prevailing chaos in the region through peacekeeping along the Ethiopia–Eritrea ceasefire line and by supporting Lloyd Axworthy's UN Good Offices Mission between those warring cousins. We have been deeply engaged in the search for a durable peace in Darfur, in western Sudan, and across the fragile border in eastern Chad. Canadians have been prominent in their steadfast support of multilateral efforts to ease the suffering of the seven million Darfuris through assistance to

African Union and UN peacekeepers and effective international agencies like the World Food Programme, UNICEF, and the UN High Commission for Refugees, and stalwart NGOs like Oxfam, CARE, and Médecins Sans Frontières.

I became involved in these efforts through my appointment in the spring of 2005 by Prime Minister Paul Martin as the leader of his Special Advisory Team on Sudan (in company with Senators Roméo Dallaire and Mobina Jaffer), as we channelled nearly $200 million in equipment, training, and support to the African Union's peacekeeping mission as it deployed to Darfur.

Canada's enormous development efforts undertaken across the Sahel over many years, but particularly in Senegal, Mali, Ghana, and Ethiopia, have been a key part of this same attempt to stabilize and support the region. But all this work would be for naught were a Somalia-like contagion to sweep across the Sahel, which is AQIM's avowed objective. It behooves Canada to stay the course and continue to bend every effort to help our friends in this fragile part of the world to resist such an appalling eventuality.

This is by no means the stuff of exaggerated threat analysis, nor is it about the puffing of military budgets. Rather, such unrest is an evidently present danger, as recent attacks in Nigeria so eloquently attest. Early in 2011, AQIM issued a statement offering support, weapons, and training to Boko Haram, a violent *jihadi* sect operating across northern Nigeria. The sect also has acknowledged links to the Somali terrorist group al-Shabab. In June 2011, Boko Haram (which might be translated as "Western education is dangerous") attacked police headquarters in Abuja, the Nigerian capital, killing seven people, and on 26 August a Boko Haram suicide bomber destroyed UN headquarters in Nigeria, killing twenty-three and wounding more than eighty.

Following the bombing of UN headquarters in Baghdad in 2003 and the attack on UN facilities in Algiers in 2007, this most recent assault on the United Nations underlines the extent to which the hatred of the UN by the *jihadis* is profound and implacable.

Further, the expansion of violent Islamic extremism into Africa's most populous and influential country has sombre implications for the stability of the entire West African region. It also puts paid to any suggestion that in the wake of the elimination of Bin Laden, Al Qaeda is dying and its affiliates are withering away.

It is virtually certain that a goodly portion of the enormous quantity of arms—some quite sophisticated, like state-of-the-art, shoulder-fired anti-air missiles (SA-24s)—looted from Gaddafi's arsenals in Libya will have found their way to *jihadi* movements throughout Africa and perhaps beyond. This will only embolden AQIM and enlarge the *jihadi* threat to the broadest definition of regional stability.

Inevitably, and always surprisingly, I am asked whether I came to "like" any of our captors. Usually this is at least in part a query about whether we were to any extent afflicted with the much-documented Stockholm syndrome, whereby captives come to empathize with their captors. I'm afraid, though, that the answer is neither nuanced nor complicated. The gulf between who and what they are—between their beliefs, methods, and purposes and mine—was simply too wide to allow for any possibility of friendship or empathy. After seven years as a hostage of Islamic *jihad* in Lebanon, Terry Anderson nailed it just right when he replied to the same line of questioning by saying that the minds of his captors were alien to him.

We spent the lion's share of our time in captivity with Omar One. He had an intriguing background and was an entertaining storyteller, but how could that trump the fact that he had constantly threatened our lives and caused us and our families to suffer such extreme anxiety? How could we be friendly with a rabid zealot who almost frothed at the mouth in one discussion about the United Nations, as he spoke longingly of donning the "martyr's vest" and joining a meeting of international delegates discussing woman's rights and equality between the sexes? One who was sufficiently unhinged to espouse a version of the infamous "blood libel," an anti-Semitic calumny that dates back to the first century?

Omar's version launched from the unfortunate contemporary fiasco that resulted in the government of Chad taking legal proceedings against six members of the French NGO L'Arche de Zoé in 2007 for abducting over a hundred children. With flagrant disregard for just about everything, the NGO had taken children from the war-torn areas of eastern Chad and Darfur, supposedly but not necessarily orphans, and sought to dispatch them to "good homes" in France. This, sadly, is more or less fact. According to Omar, however, their real purpose was to import young Muslim children from Darfur and Chad to be sacrificed in secret Jewish blood ceremonies.

He told us—and there is no question in my mind but that this lycée-educated, well-travelled, multilingual individual believed every word—that these children were placed in transparent drums on a stage before rapt audiences of Jews across Europe. Spikes would then be introduced into the barrels until they reached the children, and as the poor wretches writhed in an effort to escape, more spikes would be added. As the barrels slowly filled with blood it would be siphoned off by ingenious plumbing to a bakery below the stage, where it would be added to matzo cakes to be consumed by the audience during dark religious rites. How could there be any kind of bond with people who thought like that?

On occasion I am asked how the experience has changed my outlook on life. The answer is, superficially, hardly at all. More profoundly, perhaps a little more so, although that is not terribly evident in my day-to-day behaviour. In the wretched months described in this book I didn't really believe that I would be given a chance to answer this question, but I convinced myself that if I did, everything would be different. But it wasn't and isn't. I'm fortunate to be among those who have suffered such experiences without becoming afflicted with post-traumatic stress disorder—at least, not so far—but I regret that I've seen most of my good intentions dissipate over the months following my release. I'm ashamed to find myself muttering about the driving habits of the guy in front of me, or how long it takes to get served at the post office, but those reactions are more rote than real.

Nevertheless, as perhaps has become all too evident, I no longer have any time for political correctness and circumlocution. I am appalled by the extent to which our contemporary lives are attention disordered, informed by valueless priorities, and affected by posturing, visionless politicians, by shallow media, and by our pervasive ignorance of history and the world around us. So, yes, I've become a grumpy old man.

I now find it more difficult to share the pet peeves of friends and members of my family. But nothing is more important to me than those people. My friend Allan Gotlieb talks of QTR (quality time remaining), and the nurturing of mine has become a lot more important than ever it was. Now it is mostly about spending it well with my family and those close friends. I doubt that, absent this searing experience, I would have understood this to the extent I do now. I know with surprising confidence that every day is a gift and should be honoured as such and fearlessly, triumphantly celebrated.

APPENDIX A

A CONCISE HISTORY OF AL QAEDA IN THE ISLAMIC MAGHREB

The following encapsulated history of AQIM is gleaned largely from diverse Internet sites.

In the late 1980s the Algerians decided to give multiparty democracy a try, and a number of religious parties prepared to contest the election called for the end of 1991. Vice-President Ali Belhadj of the Front Islamique du Salut (FIS, or Islamic Salvation Front), the most important Islamic party, was a young preacher, born in Tunisia of Algerian parents. Belhadj had already spent some time in jail for threatening the security of the state through his preaching. He offered telling views on democracy in the long run-up to the elections, which not incidentally had been urged upon Algeria's traditional military-backed governments—dominated by the Front de Libération Nationale (FLN, or National Liberation Front)—by a number of Western countries, Canada among them. In February 1989 Belhadj stated, in words that could have sprung directly from the lips of my zealot kidnappers, "There is no democracy because the only source of power is Allah through the Qur'an, and not the people. If the people vote against the law of God, this is nothing other than blasphemy. In this case, it is necessary to kill the non-believers for the good reason that they wish to substitute their authority for that of God."

On 26 December 1991 the FIS easily won the first round of parliamentary elections, attracting 48 percent of the overall popular vote and capturing 188 of the 232 seats decided. When an FIS government seemed inevitable, the army moved quickly to intervene. It was well understood that FIS leaders did not think any more of democracy than did the FLN, even if they could make it work for their purposes, and many observers believed that an FIS government would, as U.S. Assistant Secretary of State Edward Djerejian put it at the time, insist on "one man, one vote, one time." Some observers of the 2011 Arab Spring harbour similar fears.

On 11 January 1992 the army cancelled the election, forcing President Chadli Bendjedid to resign, and brought in the exiled independence fighter Mohammed Boudiaf to serve as a new puppet president. In response, FIS supporters got the gun, beginning a struggle between moderate pragmatists and militant Islamic fundamentalists (Salafists) that continues to the present and has claimed between 150,000 and 200,000 Algerian lives over the past twenty years.

The Groupe Islamique Armée (GIA, or Armed Islamic Group) was founded in 1992 from a collection of Salafist groups (movements that struggled to return to the fundamentals of Islam, based on the original Islamic texts and scriptures). Many leading members of the FIS were "Afghan-Arabs"; that is, they were *mujahideen* returning from the successful struggle against Soviet occupation of Afghanistan. Inexorably, the political FIS evolved into a more militant and focused GIA. Initially, GIA guerrillas targeted the army and police as supporters of the government, but later they embarked on a series of massacres, killing tens of thousands of Muslim Algerian civilians and conducting a massive purge of journalists and "intellectuals," including many schoolteachers who were deemed to be poisoning young minds against the true practice of the faith. The GIA, however, was wracked with internal dissension and retribution, and its popularity declined as extreme violence became its signature theme. Indeed, the GIA set the scene for many subsequent Al Qaeda horrors.

In December 1994, seven years before 9/11, the GIA hijacked an Air France jetliner in a failed bid to crash it into the streets of Paris. The hijackers ordered the pilots to fly from Algiers to Marseilles, where the aircraft was to be fully fuelled. French military commandos stormed the plane without warning in Marseilles, freeing all 171 passengers and killing the four hijackers.

In 1998 the Groupe Salafiste pour la Prédication et le Combat (GSPC, or Salafist Group for Call and Combat) was formed by splintering from the GIA, in the belief that its brutal tactics were hurting the Islamist cause. The GSPC gained support from the Algerian population by vowing to continue fighting the government while avoiding the indiscriminate killing of civilians.

In 2000 the GSPC made a murderous attack on an Algerian base, killing over forty paratroopers, and over the next two years authorities in Europe foiled GSPC attacks in Frankfurt and against the American Embassy in Rome. Dutch authorities thwarted a planned bombing of the American Embassy in Paris by the GSPC in September 2001. Following the 11 September 2001 terrorist attacks against the United States, the GSPC issued a public statement supporting Osama Bin Laden's *jihad* against America.

Attracting a great deal of media attention, particularly in Europe, the GSPC began a trend of which I was to become part when, in May 2003, its members kidnapped thirty-two European tourists, most of them German, Austrian, or Swiss, killing one. Mokhtar Belmokhtar, the "emir" of the group that took Louis and me, is thought to have been involved in this operation. Algerian troops subsequently rescued seventeen of the hostages and the remainder were released a few months later when, allegedly, a ransom of 5 million Euros was paid.

The next couple of years were punctuated by frequent murderous operations against Algerian security personnel and facilities. By

2000 the GSPC had consolidated its operations and taken over the GIA's assets in Europe as well as its funding network.

In September 2006 the GSPC joined forces with Al Qaeda, whose then second-in-command (now commander), Ayman Al Zawahiri, welcomed a "blessed union" between the groups, declaring France an enemy and indicating that the newly formed group would fight against French and American interests. In January 2007 the GSPC announced that it had changed its name to Al Qaeda in the Islamic Maghreb (AQIM) to reflect its alliance with Al Qaeda, from which it receives material and financial support.

Two buildings were attacked in April 2007, one of them the UN headquarters in Algiers, where thirty-seven were killed and two hundred wounded. In September 2007 an AQIM suicide bomber attempted to assassinate Algeria's President Abdelaziz Bouteflika, and although the president was not harmed, 107 Algerians were wounded and twenty-two were killed. At the end of December 2007, four French tourists were murdered as they picnicked on the side of a road near Aleg, a small town 150 miles east of Mauritania's capital, Nouakchott. (The incident acted as a springboard for a novel by Jean-Christophe Rufin entitled *Katiba,* with a protagonist named Kader Bel Kader rather than, say, Mokhtar Belmokhtar.)

The death toll continued to mount in 2008. Back-to-back attacks on 19 and 20 August killed dozens of people. The first was a suicide car bombing at a police college in Issers, east of Algiers, killing forty-eight people. A day later, two more car bombs struck in Bouira, southeast of Algiers. The second explosion in Bouira killed twelve Algerian employees of the Canadian engineering firm SNC-Lavalin, although my abductors insisted that the victims were all Canadians.

A year later, in October 2009, six private security guards working for SNC-Lavalin were killed during an ambush in the Kabylie region, east of Algiers, and an Algerian employee of SNC-Lavalin was kidnapped in January 2010. According to the U.S.-based security-monitoring group Site, AQIM was responsible for thirty-two attacks on Algerian security forces between 7 July and 29 August 2011, killing and injuring more than two hundred.

AQIM aims to weaken and ultimately overthrow the Algerian government, which it seeks to replace with Islamic rule based on a "pure" interpretation of the Qur'an.

In May 2011, AQIM allegedly kidnapped a British and an Italian engineer in Birnin Kebbi, a city in the far northwestern part of Nigeria, located just across the border from Niger and only a couple of hundred kilometres from Niamey. Press reports alleged connivance between AQIM and Boko Haram, a violent terrorist sect of Islamic extremists operating across the northern half of Nigeria. While AQIM appears not to have claimed responsibility for this abduction, further indication that AQIM is expanding its reach into Nigeria—an allegation that Nigerian government representatives maintain is true—would have deeply unsettling implications. Over the past ten years, extreme violence between the Christian and Islamic communities in Nigeria has become endemic and has seen many thousands of people killed—just the sort of situation AQIM would be eager to exploit. Boko Haram's June 2011 attack on police headquarters in Abuja, the Nigerian capital, and its destruction of UN headquarters in Nigeria two months later—an assault that caused appalling casualties—offer chilling insight into the impact of AQIM's expanding reach.

Originally, AQIM's objectives seemed limited to the overthrow of Algeria's secular military government and the re-establishment of the Islamic caliphate, a theocracy based on *Shari'a* law that for twelve centuries spanned much of the Muslim world. Counter-terrorism experts believe, however, that the group's folding into the global Al Qaeda structure may indicate a shift to take up the banner of global *jihad* and collude on future attacks in North and West Africa and western Europe.

According to Blake Mobley and Eric Rosenbach of the Center for Policing Terrorism at the Manhattan Institute, AQIM's organizational methods "are not well understood, but they seem to structure themselves in Algeria according to seven defined and homogenous territorial blocks (with an emir at the top), an overarching 'media' unit, 'production' unit, and council of notables, which may function as an executive board. GSPC operations in Europe seem to be arranged into small cells scattered among major European cities, much like Al Qaeda's structure."

While Mobley and Rosenbach insist that they are only speculating, everything I saw fits such a structure. In fact, I think that the meeting described in Chapter 3 of this book with representatives of what Louis and I assumed to be some kind of board of directors could well have been with members of such an overseeing body as a council of notables.

AQIM engages in bombings, assassinations, kidnappings, and paramilitary operations. Since the 1990s the group has focused most of its attacks on Algerian security personnel and facilities and foreign workers to achieve its primary goal of overthrowing the Algerian government and ridding at least that "Muslim land" of the presence of infidels. Following its formal alliance with Al Qaeda, AQIM expanded its aims and declared its intention to attack Western targets more generally. AQIM employs conventional terrorist tactics for the most part, such as guerrilla-style ambushes and mortar, rocket, and IED attacks. The group added suicide bombings to its repertoire in April 2007. AQIM operates primarily in northern coastal areas of Algeria and in parts of the desert regions of southern Algeria and northern Mali, Mauritania, and Niger. Its principal sources of funding are extortion, kidnapping, donations, and the trafficking of narcotics, people, and weapons.

The Algerian government has accused Iran and Sudan of financing AQIM, but whatever the merits of those accusations, the group seems to receive funding from sizable, sympathetic diasporas in Western countries and from the Persian Gulf region and, more recently, from drug trafficking through an allegedly budding association with FARC in Colombia. Al Qaeda–Central also provides materiel, media, and financial support to AQIM. In addition, AQIM has many members abroad, the majority located in western Europe, who provide direct financial and logistical support, much of it raised through illegal activities. It would be foolhardy to presume that AQIM is not also well established in North America, within the North African diaspora communities.

The Algerian government alleges that its counter-terrorism efforts have reduced the group's ranks to fewer than a thousand, a number, incidentally, that our captors also used to describe their current strength. This is just about the only thing of which I am aware on which the Algerian government and AQIM agree.

APPENDIX B

MANAGING THE AQIM THREAT

In the context of misconceptions and myth busting, since our kidnapping and release there has been a lot of frankly ill-informed commentary on whether or not the countries of the Sahel are doing enough to counter, and defeat, the AQIM threat.

Olivier Guitta, a security and geopolitical consultant based in Europe, wrote in a special to *GlobalPost* on 20 February 2010, "Mali is very much at risk of losing its image of neutrality. Years of hard work and good governance could go up in smoke unless the current regime implements a true, cohesive counterterrorism policy." How, though, does Mr. Guitta believe that Mali, which ranked 178 out of the 182 countries rated by the United Nations Development Programme in its 2009 *Human Development Report*, is going to accomplish this miracle?

Mali is close to a hundred times the size of the Six Counties that constitute Northern Ireland. At the height of "The Troubles," in the early 1970s, close to 45,000 soldiers and police were engaged in the struggle to defeat the Irish Republican Army, a force five or six times the size of Mali's armed forces. The British army was, and remains, one of the most effective armed forces in the world, but nobody has offered such an assessment of the Malian forces. The British were well equipped in their fight against the IRA, employing state-of-the-art surveillance gear on the ground and in the air, and they had extensive experience in counter-insurgency and anti-terrorist operations. Mali's military equipment could not be more rudimentary.

At the peak of its operations, the IRA might have been able to field as many as eight hundred fighters, with many others in support; three to four hundred on active service was their steady state, again with perhaps three times that number offering various kinds of assistance. As noted previously, AQIM might now have as many as a thousand men under arms, but no more than two to three hundred are likely to be operating in the vicinity of northern Mali. The British forces never defeated the IRA in the field, a field a lot more benign than the Sahara desert. How could anybody reasonably expect the Malians to do better against AQIM? But all too often one sees and hears such suggestions.

Today Algeria boasts a regular armed force (Armée Nationale Populaire, or ANP) of 140,000, which includes a relatively sophisticated air force, a reserve force of 100,000, the Gendarmerie Nationale with 60,000, and the Sûreté Nationale with 30,000. In nearly twenty years, Algeria has failed to eradicate the Salafist threat (FIS, GIA, GSPC, and AQIM) despite using tactics that, recalling Dean Acheson's memorable application of Wordsworth to his impression of Canada, would have caused the "stern daughter of the voice of God" to quiver with indignation—had we paid much attention.

In October 2010, on the ninth anniversary of "the American invasion," there were 120,000 troops from forty-seven coalition countries in Afghanistan, as the Taliban claimed it controlled 75 percent of the country. According to the UN special representative's quarterly report to the Security Council at the end of September 2010, violence was 69 percent higher for the three months ending on 14 September than it had been for the same period the previous year, the deterioration of security being most evident in the increase in roadside bomb explosions, which rose 82 percent over the same period in 2009.

If the Brits could not defeat the IRA in tiny Northern Ireland over decades of struggle, a forty-seven-nation NATO-led (i.e., American) venture has not been able to defeat the Taliban in ten years, and 110,000 Soviets met with similar success over the previous decade, our expectations of what the impoverished nations of West Africa might achieve ought to be modest indeed.

I also contend, however, that the fight against AQIM in the Sahara, in addition to being more relevant to Western interests, is likely to be more easily prosecuted and with significantly less "collateral damage" to the inhabitants of the region than any other counterinsurgency operation I can think of. This is, first, because there are almost no permanent settlements within this vast region and, second, because there are very few innocent civilians transiting it and they could, at least for a time, be discouraged from traversing a war zone. Clearly, classic and extravagant Algerian prickliness remains an issue but surely that could be managed with a little focused diplomacy.

The impoverished nations of the Sahel—under siege from a radically changing climate as the Sahara marches relentlessly southward, chronic food insufficiencies, an exponentially increasing population, and an expanding Islamic fundamentalist insurgency seeking to establish self-sustaining safe havens—desperately need help. They cannot possibly defeat this threat on their own. The consequences of not helping and allowing AQIM to expand and prosper would be felt throughout western Europe and well beyond.

According to a 20 November 2010 report in the Algerian daily *Ennahar*, Mali's President Touré, commenting on the worsening plight of the seven employees of the giant French nuclear company, Areva, who were kidnapped from their beds in Arlit in northern Niger two months earlier, said he considered AQIM "an increasing danger," adding that he believed "an invisible and highly mobile enemy that crosses borders and benefits from collusion may be more dangerous than people think. But," he insisted, "the threat is not only military, it is also ideological. And there, nobody knows the limits."

Could anybody claim that whatever we are doing in Afghanistan and others are doing in Yemen is more relevant, more important, or more pressing in terms of the preservation of our Western values and the lives and livelihoods of our citizens (to say nothing of the impact on the friendships and alliances we have nurtured throughout western and northern Africa for fifty years) than allowing AQIM—the largest of the Al Qaeda franchises—to root itself deeply into a seven-thousand-kilometre wide, thousand-kilometre deep corridor across the widest part of Africa between the Atlantic and Indian oceans?

The United States and others have for some time been discreetly providing much-needed training and equipment to Mali's armed forces under the Pan-Sahel Initiative. Recently, Algeria has spear-headed efforts to improve coordination among that country, Mali, Mauritania, and Niger in efforts to fight AQIM by establishing a uni-fied command centre in the southern Algerian town of Tamanrasset, something they had all been talking about for years. In addition, the four countries agreed to establish the Sahel–Saharan Intelligence Cen-tre, or CRS (Centre de Renseignement sur le Sahel) in Algiers, made up of senior officers from the member countries. It is currently headed by Major-General Attafi, the head of Algeria's counter-espionage directorate and Algeria's counter-terrorism coordinator.

Following the kidnapping of the Areva seven in September 2010, the chiefs of staff of these countries met in Tamanrasset to discuss counter-terrorist operations. According to the website Magharebia, after the meeting the venerable Algerian General Ahmed Gaid Salah said, "We must shoulder our responsibilities and respect our commitment and the initiation of the actual work on the ground." He then pointed out that Algeria had organized the meeting in order to "explore areas of co-operation" and to upgrade them "to a more mature level, as well as to clarify all the circumstances that still exist, such as paving the way for effective action, and thus achieve the objectives underlined in the strategy to combat terrorism and organized crime." I doubt that leaves Al Qaeda in the Islamic Maghreb quaking in their boots.

ACKNOWLEDGEMENTS

This book is what it is because my editor at HarperCollins Canada, Jim Gifford, was able to conceive what it ought to be and then guide me toward that vision; because my meticulous copy editor, Camilla Blakeley, and rigorous proofreader, Sarah Wight, worked so assiduously with this neophyte author to provide clarity and consistency and focus to the manuscript; and because Noelle Zitzer, HarperCollins' managing editor, had the compassion and foresight to bring it all together. I thank them for their patience and understanding and consummate professionalism.

Canada's über-literary agent, Michael Levine of Westwood Creative Artists, has been an enthusiastic supporter and promoter of this project. He shepherded me through the maze and revealed the mysteries of the publishing business with flair and forcefulness. I am grateful for his wise counsel and amazing Rolodex.

Jennifer Pagliaro, a student at Carleton University's School of Journalism, provided invaluable and generous assistance in producing the maps and plan of Camp Canada at the beginning of the book.

Ken and Odile Calder, my sister Robin Fowler-Anderson, Andrew Cohen, Charlotte Gray, Julie Beatty, Paul Durand, and all four of our daughters devoted huge amounts of time and energy to help me make this book as good as it could be and I am deeply grateful for their invaluable input. All the errors and omissions are very much my own.

Patrick Wilson and Melanie Provost of the University of Ottawa's Graduate School of Public and International Affairs kindly helped me with my initial research.

While she could not have done it alone, I know in my heart that my wife, Mary, brought me home figuratively and literally. Her love sustained me, and her strength and resolve pulled me through. Not only did she keep the home fires burning and the family strong and united but she went to extraordinary lengths to ensure that everything that could be done was being and would be done to win our freedom. In addition, she suffered the ravages of the two-year gestation of this book and assisted with the preparation of the manuscript in innumerable ways, offering sage advice while challenging everything. I am ever in her debt.

Our girls, Linton, Ruth, Antonia, and Justine, their partners, Rob, Joseph, Wayne, and Angus, and our grandchildren, Grier, Alice, Henry (and now George), proffered unstinting encouragement to Mary and each other through the dark months, and in every possible way did me proud by their love, strength, and resolve. Tony Gollob and Mike Flannery of the RCMP could not have provided more sympathetic and sensitive support to our family.

An enormous effort was mounted by our colleagues and our government to bring us home. There are, however, a handful of individuals whose insight, imagination, diplomatic skills and perseverance made the difference between an enormous effort and a successful one. Janet Graham, then the director general for Africa at DFAIT, extended heart and soul to Mary and Mai up to the point—a few weeks before our release—when she was suddenly posted to Addis Ababa, from where, terminally ill, she returned to Ottawa only a few months later. Her family saw too little of her during our kidnapping and lost her to cancer only a few months after our release. Isabelle Roy, the director of the West and Central African Division at DFAIT, strove mightily to cause African realities to be brought to bear as strategies were developed and deployed.

Ambassador Marc Lortie, Canada's representative in France, and his wife, Patricia, extended every courtesy to Mary and cemented and sustained the active and touchingly engaged assistance of the French government in the search for effective solutions. Another friend and colleague of long standing, Jacques Bilodeau, was torn out of retirement to undertake repeated rounds of the face-to-face diplomacy that was crucial to our survival, engaging so rapidly as to leave his family and seventy-five invitees to the Bilodeau Réveillon de Nöel without a host.

In Ottawa, Anne Marie Doyle, Charles and Sandra Bassett, and my sister Robin, who showed up when needed from Vancouver, were there for Mary day and night. David Angell had the unenviable task of informing my family, through our youngest daughter, Justine, of my disappearance and kept in close touch with Mary, offering her constant support. So too did a couple of great pals from my days in the Defence department, now retired, Larry Murray and Keith Coulter. Paul Hunter and Jill and Don Sinclair were the best friends and neighbours anybody could hope for.

Kofi Annan extended his shoulder to Mary and offered to engage directly with a view to bringing our nightmare in the Sahara to the earliest possible conclusion, as did Brian Mulroney, Jean Chrétien, and Paul Martin.

Our friends throughout the UN system—including a number of my former colleagues who represented their countries at the United Nations—provided Mary with encouragement and with as much hope as they could muster. My old friend Haile Menkerios recruited me for my ill-fated assignment, and offered Mary unstinting personal support and empathy, as did Niger Desk Officer Gumisai Mutume, who called a couple of times a week to make sure Mary was all right. Jean-Jacques Graisse and Isabelle Lierman guided Mary through the toughest times with fast friendship and vital knowledge.

Two of my oldest friends, Ivor and Elizabeth Roberts, tendered a steady stream of sage and measured advice from Oxford. My pal

Ted Johnson supported Mary from Day 1 until the moment of our release, providing carefully modulated legal and communications advice and unflagging friendship, as did his wife, Sharon. From New York, Oscar and Didi Schafer extended generous and unstinting help to Mary in my absence and, following my release, safe havens in many lovely places in which to write. Perrin and Julie Beatty, Philippe and Chantal Lette, Valerie Amos, and Iqbal Riza, as always, were steadfast friends.

There are so many others in Canada and abroad in far-flung places throughout the world (not necessarily the most obvious) who, for all sorts of reasons, might not wish to be named in such a list of Fowler family personal heroes. I am deeply indebted to them and often to their families for their selfless and tireless endeavours on our behalf.

Bob Rae, then the Opposition foreign affairs critic, kept in close touch with Mary throughout our ordeal. He was discreet, sympathetic, wise, and ever accessible.

Prime Minister Harper and Governor General Michaëlle Jean took the time to maintain contact with Mary and Mai, offering them encouragement and every assistance. And so too did an absolutely startling array of the friends with whom we have been blessed, friends of our children, friends of their children and legions of friends we didn't know we had.

I began my account by stressing the extent to which Louis Guay made this misadventure bearable, indeed, that I doubted I would have had a chance to write it had it not been for him. I must end it the same way. While he bears no responsibility for its creation or its content, this book is very much his as well as mine—a testament to our shared ordeal and enduring friendship.

SELECTED BIBLIOGRAPHY

I owe a debt to each of the following resources and acknowledge their contribution to this book.

Anderson, Terry. *Den of Lions: Memoirs of Seven Years*. New York: Crown, 1993.

Botha, Anneli. *Terrorism in the Maghreb: The Transnationalisation of Domestic Terrorism*. Institute for Security Studies Monograph Series no. 144. Pretoria/Tshwane: Institute for Strategic Studies, 1 June 2008. www.iss.co.za/pgcontent.php?UID=2198

Brahimi, Lakhdar et al. "Towards a Culture of Security and Account-ability." Report of the Independent Panel on Safety and Security of United Nations Personnel and Premises. New York: United Nations, 9 June 2008. www.un.org/News/dh/infocus/terrorism/PanelOnSafetyReport.pdf

Carew, Tom. *Jihad! The Secret War in Afghanistan*. Edinburgh: Mainstream Publishing, 2000.

Coll, Steve. *The Bin Ladens: An Arabian Family in the American Century*. New York: Penguin, 2008.

————. *Ghost Wars: The Secret History of the CIA, Afghanistan, and Bin Laden, from the Soviet Invasion to September 10, 2001.* New York: Penguin Books, 2005.

Cook, Michael. *The Koran: A Very Short Introduction.* Oxford: Oxford University Press, 2000.

Darwish, Nonie. *Cruel and Unusual Punishment: The Terrifying Global Implications of Islamic Law.* Nashville: Thomas Nelson, 2008.

Esposito, John L. *Unholy War: Terror in the Name of Islam.* New York: Oxford University Press, 2002.

Filkins, Dexter. *The Forever War.* New York: Alfred A. Knopf, 2008.

Foner, Eric. *The Fiery Trial: Abraham Lincoln and American Slavery.* New York: W. W. Norton, 2010.

Fury, Dalton. *Kill Bin Laden: A Delta Force Commander's Account of the Hunt for the World's Most Wanted Man.* New York: St. Martin's Press, 2008.

Gonsalves, Marc, Keith Stansell, and Tom Howes, with Gary Brozek. *Out of Captivity: Surviving 1,967 Days in the Colombian Jungle.* Toronto: HarperCollins Canada, 2008.

Hamid, Mohsin. *The Reluctant Fundamentalist.* New York: Harcourt, 2007.

Hirtenstein, Stephen, and Martin Notcutt. *Divine Sayings: 101 Hadith Qudsi—The Mishkat al-Anwar of Ibn 'Arabi,* 2nd ed. Arabic text and English translation. Oxford: Anqa Publishing, 2010.

Huntington, Samuel P. "The Clash of Civilizations?" *Foreign Affairs* (Summer 1993). www.foreignaffairs.com/articles/48950/samuel -p-huntington/the-clash-of-civilizations

Ibrahim, Raymond. *The Al Qaeda Reader.* New York: Doubleday, 2007.

Kagan, Robert. *The Return of History and the End of Dreams.* New York: Alfred A. Knopf, 2008.

Kohlmann, Evan F. *Two Decades of Jihad in Algeria: The GIA, the GSPC, and Al-Qaida.* Part 1, *The Afghan Theater.* NEFA Foundation, May 2007. www.nefafoundation.org/index.cfm

Lewis, Bernard. "Terrorism: How the West Can Win." In *Islamic Terrorism?* ed. Benjamin Netanyahu. New York: Farrar Straus Giroux, 1987.

MacEoin, Denis. "Why Do Muslims Execute Innocent People?" *Middle East Quarterly* 13, no. 4 (2006): 15–25.

Mayer, Jane. *The Dark Side: The Inside Story of How the War on Terror Turned into a War on American Ideals.* New York, Anchor, 2009.

McCants, William. "Training for the Lone Jihadi." 19 August 2008. www.jihadica.com/training-for-the-lone-jihadi

McCarthy, Andrew C. *Willful Blindness: Memoir of the Jihad.* New York and London: Encounter Books, 2008.

Mills, Sgt. Dan. *Sniper One: On Scope and under Siege with a Sniper Team in Iraq.* New York: St. Martin's Press, 2007.

Naji, Abu Bakir. *The Management of Savagery: The Most Critical Stage through Which the Umma Will Pass.* Translated by William McCants. John M. Olin Institute for Strategic Studies at Harvard University, Cambridge, MA, 23 May 2006. www.wcfia.harvard .edu/olin/publications/miscpubs.htm

Pelton, Robert Young. *Licenced to Kill: Hired Guns in the War on Terror.* New York: Crown Publishers, 2006.

Phares, Walid. *Future Jihad: Terrorist Strategies against America.* New York: Palgrave MacMillan, 2005.

Richardson, Louise. *What Terrorists Want: Understanding the Enemy, Containing the Threat.* New York: Random House, 2006.

Rohde, David, and Kristen Mulvihill. *A Rope and a Prayer: A Kidnapping from Two Sides.* New York: Viking, 2010.

Ruthven, Malise. *Fundamentalism: A Very Short Introduction.* Oxford University Press, 2007.

Schanzer, David, Charles Kurzman, and Ebrahim Moosa. *Anti-Terror Lessonsof Muslim-Americans.* National Institute of Justice, U.S. Department of Justice, 6 January 2010. www.sanford.duke .edu/news/Schanzer_Kurzman_Moosa_Anti-Terror_Lessons.pdf

Scheuer, Michael. *Imperial Hubris: Why the West Is Losing the War on Terror.* Dulles, VA: Brassey's, 2004.

Spencer, Robert. *The Politically Incorrect Guide to Islam (and the Crusades).* Washington, DC: Regency Publishing, 2005.

———. *Stealth Jihad: How Radical Islam Is Subverting America without Guns or Bombs.* Washington, DC: Regency Publishing, 2008.

Waite, Terry. *Taken on Trust: An Autobiography.* Toronto: Doubleday, 1993.

Wright, Lawrence. *The Looming Tower: Al-Qaeda and the Road to 9/11.* New York: Alfred A. Knopf, 2006.

Zakaria, Fareed. *The Post-American World.* New York: W. W. Norton, 2008.

WEBSITES

Africa News
www.africanews.com

Afrik.News
www.afrik-news.com

American Enterprise Institute, Center for Defense Studies
www.defensestudies.org

Bullfax
www.bullfax.com

Consultancy Africa Intelligence
www.consultancyafrica.com

Council on Foreign Relations
www.cfr.org

Counterterrorism Blog
www.counterterrorismblog.org

Defence Viewpoints from UK Defence Forum
www.defenceviewpoints.co.uk

Ennahar Online
www.ennaharonline.com

European Interagency Security Forum
www.eisf.eu

Family Security Matters
www.familysecuritymatters.org

Flashpoint Partners
www.flashpoint-intel.com

Geostrategy-Direct
http://geostrategy-direct.com

IBN Live
www.ibnlive.in.com

IntelCenter
www.intelcenter.com

Jamestown Foundation
www.jamestown.org

Jihadica
www.jihadica.com

Magharebia
www.magharebia.com

Menas Associates
www.menas.co.uk

Middle East and Central Asia Security Report (MECASR)
http://mecasr.blogspot.com

Middle East Observatory
www.meobservatory.com

Middle East Studies Online Journal
www.middle-east-studies.net

Morung Express
www.morungexpress.com

Nine Eleven Finding Answers (NEFA) Foundation
www.nefafoundation.org

Norwegian Defence Research Establishment (FFI)
www.jihadismstudies.net

Perspectives on Terrorism
http://terrorismanalysts.com

Public Safety Canada, Currently Listed Entities
www.publicsafety.gc.ca/prg/ns/le/cle-eng.aspx

Sahel Blog
http://sahelblog.wordpress.com

SITE Intelligence Group
www.siteintelgroup.com

Temoust
www.temoust.org

This Is Africa
www.thisisafricaonline.com

UK Home Office, Counter-terrorism
www.homeoffice.gov.uk/counter-terrorism/

United Nations. List established and maintained by the
Committee pursuant to resolutions 1267 (1999) and 1989 (2011)
with respect to individuals, groups, undertakings and entities
associated with Al-Qaida
www.un.org/sc/committees/1267/aq_sanctions_list.shtml

U.S. Department of State. Foreign Terrorist Organizations
www.state.gov/s/ct/rls/other/des/123085.htm

PHOTO CREDITS

The photographs reproduced in the insert pages all appear courtesy of the author, except for those noted below:

Kofi Annan and Robert Fowler at the UN Security Council: Courtesy of the United Nations

Omar One: AQIM video

Mokhtar Belmokhtar: Courtesy of the Government of Mali

Al Jabbar: AQIM video

Imam Abdallah: AQIM video

Abou Isaac: AQIM video

Moussa: AQIM video

Harissa: AQIM video

Day 52 proof-of-life video: Courtesy of *The Globe and Mail*

Louis Guay and Robert Fowler wearing "serviettes": AQIM

Mujahid making phone call: AQIM video

Robert Fowler's SMS message: Courtesy of the CBC

Edwin Dyer: AQIM video

Michel Germaneau: Courtesy Enminal/Mairie de Marcoussis

Mustapha Chaffi: Courtesy of the Burkinabé Presidency

Baba Ould Cheik: Courtesy of *The Globe and Mail*

Liberation screenshot: AQIM video

Amadou Toumani Touré et al: AP Photo/Harouna Traore

Robert Fowler and Blaise Compaoré: Courtesy of the Burkinabé Presidency

Mary Fowler receiving Robert's call: Courtesy of Charles Bassett

Robert Fowler's "before" photo: Courtesy of the RCMP

Mary and Mai at Ramstein Air Base: Courtesy of Colonel Tony Battista

A walk in Trier: Courtesy of Colonel Tony Battista

Robert and Louis's farewell: Foreign Affairs and International Trade Canada, 2010. Reproduced with the permission of Her Majesty the Queen in Right of Canada, represented by the Minister of Foreign Affairs, 2010

The Fowlers with UN Secretary-General Ban Ki-moon: Courtesy of the United Nations